Madam Kitty

A true story
by Peter Norden

Translated by J. Maxwell Brownjohn

Abelard-Schuman
London

© by Südwest Verlag München
© This translation by Abelard-Schuman Ltd., 1973
First published in Great Britain in 1973
ISBN 200 71956 4

Printed in Great Britain

Abelard-Schuman Limited
158 Buckingham Palace Road, London, SW1
24 Market Square, Aylesbury, Buckinghamshire

Contents

Chapter 1

Berlin, March 1939. Sunlight flooded the Tiergarten and Zoo, the Linden and Kurfürstendamm. The day was cold but radiantly fine.

SS-Obersturmführer Walter Schellenberg drove to Heydrich's headquarters in Prinz Albrechtstrasse. He was currently working on a plan to combine the Gestapo and Security Service in a single department. Heydrich had entrusted him with the project and he was proud to be carrying it out. It was also his birthday, another fact which helped to boost his morale.

He reached Prinz Albrechtstrasse and took the steps two at a time. There was good news waiting for him, he could sense it.

'Heil Hitler, Gruppenführer!' Schellenberg saluted stiffly and waited for Heydrich's signal to approach.

Reinhard Heydrich rose from behind his desk and advanced to meet him. 'Come in, Schellenberg,' he said cordially, indicating a group of arm-chairs. 'Take a seat.'

Schellenberg waited until his chief was comfortably installed and then joined him, sitting as erect as the soft upholstery allowed. He gave Heydrich an inquiring glance.

Heydrich seemed to have forgotten his visitor. He stared past him through the lofty windows and continued to do so for nearly a minute. Then he surfaced with a sudden start. 'Our plans for the SD—how are they going?'

Schellenberg knew Heydrich too well not to guess that this was merely a prelude to something else. He was about to submit his report when Heydrich silenced him with a gesture. 'No,' he said, smiling, 'leave that for the moment. How's your wife?'

Schellenberg was prepared for most eventualities, but the Gruppenführer's ostensible concern for his wife's health wasn't one of them. He gave a little bow and said crisply: 'Fine, thank you.'

Heydrich turned to look straight at him. His next question came with the speed and impact of a bullet. 'Are you faithful to her?' He regarded his subordinate intently. Schellenberg's mind whirled. What did it mean? Heydrich must be hatching something, but what? The man was inscrutable. Anything was grist to his mill—he might even have been keeping him, Schellenberg, under surveillance.

Cautiously, Schellenberg played the ball back. 'I am, Gruppenführer,' he replied with all the firmness he could muster.

Again Heydrich's mouth twisted in the thin smile whose significance was so hard to gauge. 'I see,' he said tersely, then : 'Pity.' The single word was a categorical statement.

Heydrich jumped up, lithe and agile as a cat, and strode to his desk. Schellenberg rose deferentially and followed him. He had seldom felt so at sea or so incapable of guessing what Heydrich was after.

The Gruppenführer sat down in his characteristically abrupt fashion. Without giving Schellenberg another glance, he scribbled a brief note and inserted it in a folder, which he closed again. The words TOP SECRET were stamped in red on the cover. Schellenberg stared at the man who ruled his destiny and claimed his unswerving loyalty. Being privy to so many of the SD's plans, he could afford to risk an implied question. 'Gruppenführer,' he said, 'what you asked me just now—I don't quite understand. . . .'

'Sit down,' Heydrich said. 'Cigarette?' He proffered a silver case.

Schellenberg helped himself and lit up.

'It's time we improved our sources of information,' Heydrich began, 'above all, information about our own senior officials and their foreign visitors. Getting it through the usual channels presents problems, and much of what we receive from Military Intelligence is unreliable, if not downright inaccurate. I've dreamed up a way of changing things and I thought you might handle the project. On the face of it, you're the ideal candidate.'

Schellenberg stiffened. Heydrich had come to the point at last. 'What does my wife have to do with it,' he asked, permitting himself a faint smile, '—or my marital fidelity?'

'A great deal,' Heydrich said curtly. 'My plan is to pick a good site and open a—' he paused '—an establishment, here in Berlin. Pretty girls and hard liquor are great aids to relaxation, my friend. It takes a congenial atmosphere to thaw a man out and loosen his tongue. The younger and prettier the girl he's with, and the more he hopes to get out of her, the readier he is to unload.'

Heydrich lit a cigarette.

'If we employ girls we can trust, I think we'll get a better insight into the true character and actual views of men under surveillance than we have done by other means in the past. I expect such an establishment to yield material of vital importance to our own intelligence service.'

Schellenberg, who had been following intently, drew a deep breath. 'An excellent plan, Gruppenführer.' A host of possibilities raced through his mind.

Heydrich was staring past him again. 'I discussed the matter with Reichsführer Himmler and he approves. I wanted to give you the assignment because you're already working on the SD reorganisation scheme, and this falls more or less into the same category. On the other hand, do an over-faithful husband and a potentially jealous wife constitute too high a risk factor?' His eyes swivelled towards Schellenberg.

'I wouldn't be expected to play the pimp, would I?'

Heydrich laughed. 'No, you're not quite the type. On the other hand, you'd have to keep a close check on the place. That would take time—time you couldn't account for.'

'My wife isn't the jealous kind, Gruppenführer.' Schellenberg looked Heydrich full in the eye. 'Please let me handle it. I've already formed an idea of the project. We'll fix ourselves the finest brothel bar none and get our information where it's most readily available.'

Heydrich raised his eyebrows. 'And where's that?'

'In bed, Gruppenführer.'

'You said it, Schellenberg, I didn't.' Heydrich seemed almost resentful that his original scheme hadn't gone quite so far. He rose abruptly. 'Submit your recommendations in due course. Heil Hitler!'

The audience was at an end.

Her name was Kitty Schmidt, her age indeterminate. Neither old nor young, she was generally thought to be pushing forty. In fact, she was considerably older. Kitty had been born in a working-class quarter of Berlin in 1882. By the time the New Year's bells rang in the twentieth century, she knew for a certainty that the limitations of her native suburb were not for her. She wanted a place in the sun, a personal slice of happiness and material prosperity.

Having nothing else to offer, she offered herself—which was plenty. Many things about Kitty Schmidt were debatable, but not her physical charms.

So she laid aside the curling-tongs she had wielded as a hairdresser's assistant and became a hairdresser's patron instead, reclining in comfort as deft fingers piled her hair fashionably high, manicured her nails and massaged her face. She soon became acquainted with the beds of sundry amiable gentlemen, with discreet little hotels and love-nests. Sometimes she operated from an apartment of her own, sometimes only an hotel room, but always with a healthy grasp of life's realities and receptive to what was on offer. Her preference was for gifts of minimum size and maximum value because she never knew when she would have to move on.

She almost loved her first man, even though he was thirty years older, but he deserted her without compunction. This was hard on his successors because it destroyed her capacity for unreserved affection.

Not that she was ungrateful. On the contrary, Kitty was adaptable, tractable and yielding—or outwardly so. She knew her trade, seldom suffered from fits of temperament and was an artist in her own special field.

The word spread. Kitty had less and less time between affairs. Being increasingly in demand, she was able to raise her prices and reduce the extent of her services.

For the first time in her life, she had leisure to devote herself to the things she had heard so much about in conversation—things which were the real object of her endeavours. From now on she was often seen at the Scala and Metropol, took coffee at Kranzler's, dined at Horcher's and attended the opera with friends.

This enhanced her reputation still further. She even indulged in the luxury of a husband but soon sent him packing when she realised that his sole aim was to relieve her of her hard-earned money. The only memento of this marriage was a daughter whom she loved extravagantly but seldom produced in public, perhaps from a reluctance to draw attention to her age.

Kitty's heyday was World War I and the ensuing era of the racketeer and profiteer. During this period she amassed money —lots of it. And, being a realist, she invested it in the only business she knew something about. In 1922 she set up her first brothel at 78 Budapesterstrasse, Berlin. It did a brisk trade from opening day onwards.

In 1932 Kitty had her first face-lift and was so delighted with the result that—now fifty years old—she passed herself off as twenty-five without inviting ridicule.

Kitty won the admiration of all who had known her from way back. They were impressed not only by her dazzling personal appearance but by the resilience with which she survived her 'spot of bother'. This occurred early in 1930, when the authorities closed her establishment in Budapesterstrasse because she had served liquor without a licence. They also imposed a fine of RM5000.

She paid up without a murmur, applied for a licence in the regulation manner, and was granted one in March 1930. Then she opened a new brothel, this time in the Kurfürstendamm.

For Kitty, this was the culmination of her career to date. She had early enlisted the financial advice of her best clients and deposited her capital safely in London, so she lost no money during the German inflation or the critical period of mass unemployment.

Her new house was staffed by as many as twenty girls, all of whom she selected personally in full and detailed knowledge of her clients' requirements. The members of her domestic staff, likewise trained by her, were renowned for their tact and discretion. For all that, many of her clients complained that the Kurfürstendamm establishment occupied too conspicuous a site. With a heavy heart, Kitty decided to move once more. She found suitable premises just round the corner at 11 Giesebrechtstrasse, an old house spacious enough to accommodate the 'Pension Schmidt' with ease.

Her decision soon paid off. There were many 'salons' in Berlin at this period but Kitty Schmidt's was unquestionably the most successful.

Kitty celebrated the Nazi accession on 30 January 1933 with Jews and Brownshirts alike. To Kitty, all men were members of the same breed, and she had never taken an interest in politics.

The importance of politics abruptly dawned on her one day when a trio of regular customers named Herz, Levy and Cohn informed her that they were not only leaving Berlin but quitting Germany altogether. Kitty realised that Hitler had something against the Jews but could not fathom what this had to do with her old friends Herz, Levy and Cohn. The news that they planned to settle in grey and foggy London gave her food for thought. In 1934, now that her ties with the British capital were human as well as financial, she decided to take her first trip abroad.

Herz, Levy and Cohn welcomed her to London with a dinner at the Dorchester, where she was staying. Her friends saw to it that she was treated like royalty, and the following day the four of them held a long and momentous conference.

Its outcome was that, at regular intervals in the years that followed, Kitty transferred large sums to her London account. To do this she needed a permit which was renewed without demur until 1936.

In January 1937 the German authorities became obstructive for the first time, so she promptly changed her tactics. Still at regular intervals, she sent trusted members of her staff to London via Paris. These young ladies conveyed sums of money to the British capital sewn into specially designed corsets. It has since transpired that these sums totalled several million marks. In July 1938 Kitty again tried to transfer funds to London through legal channels, but she had so much trouble with the tax and customs authorities that she reverted to illegal means.

She was twice denounced for currency smuggling but managed to extricate herself by tapping her personal connections among the new German élite. Even so, she began to wonder if the game was worth the candle.

Trade still flourished, true, but there was her daughter's future to be considered. Also, many of her erstwhile regulars had ceased to patronise the establishment or slunk furtively into her private den after dark. On such occasions she heard harrowing things which made her realise with astonishment that she was not just cold and calculating—that the heart which beat inside her could feel compassion for others—and she was shrewd enough to grasp that this might signal the end of her business career.

By March 1939, Kitty Schmidt had decided to quit Germany

for good. She was fifty-seven years old, though no outsider would have put her past forty. Kitty had husbanded her 'capital' well.

On 4 April 1939 Kitty received a visit from Detective Superintendent Erich Kuhn. Kuhn was a member of the brothel surveillance squad—CID Dept M2, Berlin—and it was one of his duties to grace the 'salon' with his presence from time to time.

He pressed the bell marked 'Pension Schmidt' and heard the familiar buzz. The door was opened a few moments later by a maid in a black dress and white apron.

The girl looked at him inquiringly. Kuhn did not recognise her and assumed that she must be new.

'Is Madame at home?' he asked.

She nodded and opened the door wider. 'Who shall I say?' she asked politely.

Kuhn produced his warrant card. 'Kuhn, CID,' he replied.

Her eyes widened. 'Just a minute,' she said, and scuttled through a small door to his left. Kuhn knew the door. It was Kitty's 'bolt-hole', as she called it. Another, larger, door led to the reception rooms—drawing-room and parlour—where patrons of the establishment were normally greeted by Kitty in person.

Erich Kuhn had little time to inspect the rather ornate hall with its abundance of moulding, brocade and faience mirrors. He heard the girl's agitated voice followed by the deeper tones of Madame, then the small door opened again. Kitty was wearing her most affable smile. She came to meet him with her hand outstretched. 'My dear Superintendent . . .' she said, and a stranger would have thought she was welcoming an old and valued friend.

The girl in the black dress stood there with her mouth hanging open, but her expression changed to one of awed respect when Kitty took Kuhn's arm and drew him into what was commonly referred to as her 'snuggery'.

'Elvira!' she called, and, when the girl followed them timidly inside : 'Take the Superintendent's coat.' She turned to the policeman. 'Coffee, brandy? A glass of champagne, perhaps?' Kuhn nodded. 'Do sit down,' she went on, then turning back to Elvira : 'Bring us a bottle of No 1.' No 1 was the best champagne in the house.

Kitty felt quite unperturbed by the Superintendent's visit. They were old acquaintances and had often chatted together about current affairs, the state of business and people in general—in fact it could have been said that they were on cordial terms. Kitty had never attempted to bribe Kuhn and was far too wary to tolerate his becoming a patron of her establishment. On the other hand, she never failed to treat the Superintendent as a distinguished visitor and make herself pleasant.

Meanwhile, Elvira had returned with a laden tray. Deftly, she opened the bottle and filled their glasses.

'Your health, Superintendent,' Kitty raised her glass.

Kuhn followed suit, then glanced at the girl. Kitty understood. 'Out!' she said imperiously, and Elvira vanished.

'Can she hear us?' asked Kuhn.

Kitty stared at him in surprise. She rose without speaking and closed a thickly padded inner door. 'Not now,' she said, smiling. 'Why, state secrets?' It was meant in jest, but Kitty scented instinctively that today's visit was more than a routine tour of inspection.

'Something like that,' Kuhn replied. They swapped small talk for a while before he got down to business. 'I've been detailed to discuss a problem with you, Frau Schmidt,' he began, 'a problem connected with the surveillance of certain persons. After a good deal of thought, we hit on the idea of enlisting your services?'

'Really?' Kitty raised her eyebrows. 'How can I help?'

'It's quite simple.' Kuhn's manner became official as he outlined the plan devised by Berlin's police chief, Arthur Nebe. Nebe's intention was to dilute Kitty's regular girls with female undercover agents who would be specially trained for the assignment. After that, selected senior members of the Party, armed forces and diplomatic corps would be channelled into the Pension Schmidt and pumped during tête-à-têtes with the undercover girls, who would duly transmit their information to the CID. Kuhn stressed that the scheme would benefit Kitty herself as well as the Security Services. Not only would it substantially increase her turnover, but the authorities were prepared to ignore her professional activities altogether instead of merely winking at them.

Kitty was an expert listener and an old hand. She sat there serenely as Kuhn said his piece. Sometimes she gave a faint smile, sometimes a nod of approval. All she said when Kuhn had finished was: 'Smart idea.'

The Superintendent took this as an affirmative. 'So you'll co-operate, Frau Schmidt?' he asked, to make doubly certain.

Kitty stared into space for a moment. 'Give me a week to think it over,' she said. 'Perhaps I'll come up with a few refinements of my own.'

'Very well,' said Kuhn, 'I'll pass that on. See you in a week's time.'

They rose. Kitty walked Kuhn to the front door, as cordial to the bearer of strange tidings as she had been when she greeted him.

If Detective Superintendent Kuhn had known what steps Kitty took as soon as the door closed behind him, he would have arrested her on the spot.

Her first move was to telephone her bank and fix an appointment. Then she rang a good friend, an Italian named Guido Brisalla, and asked him to come over at once. Brisalla, a tropical fruit importer, ran a thriving business in Alexanderplatz. From Alexanderplatz to Giesebrechtstrasse was a good half-hour, but Kitty did not remain idle. In quick succession, she telephoned Lufthansa and German State Railways to inquire the departure times of the next planes and trains to London. Then she scribbled a few lines on a slip of paper and summoned Elvira.

'How's business?' she asked.

'Quiet,' the girl replied. 'Margret and Inge are entertaining in the parlour—two bottles so far—and I've just taken coffee and brandy to No 7 for the Rhineland girl and her gentleman friend. The rest are out back. . . .'

'Good,' said Kitty. 'Tell Elke to take over the front door. I want you to run an errand for me.'

'Right away, Kitty.' Elvira excused herself for two minutes. She warned Elke, put a coat on and returned to the snuggery. 'Where to?' she asked.

Kitty pressed the slip of paper into her hand, together with a fifty-mark note. 'Go to the post office in Lietzenburgerstrasse and send this telegram. And make sure you write the sender's name and address just the way I've put it. I'm doing it as a favour to a customer.'

Elvira nodded and set off. She didn't look at the piece of paper until she reached Lietzenburgerstrasse. The message puzzled her a little. It read : 'Rosa died today. Await your decision whether to attend funeral. In sorrow, Karl.' The sender's name and address were given as 'Karl Georg Schuster, 14 Promenadenweg, Leipzig', and the telegram was addressed to Sam Lewis, Esq, 14 Grandpont St, London SW. Elvira had already forgotten the details by the time she left the post office.

Meanwhile, Kitty had received a visit from Guido Brisalla. The thickly padded inner door was again closed.

'What's the matter, light of my eyes?' Brisalla demanded with typical Latin exuberance. He swept her up in his strong arms and swung her round. Then, noticing the look on her face, he gently released her. 'Forgive me,' he said.

Kitty did not waste words. 'The police were here,' she said, and there was contempt in her voice. 'They want to rope me in but I won't play.'

Brisalla listened intently as she told him about Kuhn's visit. Then he said : 'So Rosa's dead?'

Kitty nodded. A sudden pang of regret smote her. She had decided months ago to leave Berlin and everything dear to her —turn her back on the city where she had lived for so long. The decision and all its implications had been carefully weighed, her plans for departure laid with the utmost secrecy, but it was doubtful if she had ever seriously considered the prospect of leaving. Now, after the Superintendent's visit and request, Kitty sensed that she must move fast or suffer the consequences.

She knew very well that her periodic transfers of funds to London could not have passed unnoticed, so she had to take it for granted that difficulties would be raised if she applied for an exit visa in the normal way. Brisalla had therefore volunteered to convey her daughter and valuables via Italy to London, where Samuel Levy—now known as Sam Lewis—would handle the problems of immigration and accommodation. The whole plan was known by the codeword 'Rosa's death'.

Guido Brisalla swung into action. 'When do we start?'

'Kuhn wants a final decision this time next week. Everything must be wrapped up by then.'

'*Va bene*,' said Brisalla. 'You can count on me.'

Kitty had no doubts on that score. 'Will you drive me to the bank?' she asked.

The Italian gave a sweeping bow. 'Behold your new chauffeur.'

'In that case, let's go.' Kitty swiftly but expertly checked her appearance in the mirror and allowed Brisalla to help her into her light mink. She called Elke, told her that she would be back in an hour's time, and left the house with Brisalla. Just outside the door they bumped into Elvira.

'Did you do as I asked?'

The girl nodded and handed over the change from Kitty's fifty-mark note.

'Where's the piece of paper?'

'I threw it away.'

'Idiot,' said Kitty, and made a mental note to frame her instructions more precisely in future.

SS-Obersturmführer Walter Schellenberg was sitting in his office at 10 Meineckestrasse when an SD plainclothesman asked to see him. A telegram form fluttered across his desk.

'Lietzenburger post office,' the man explained. 'Message from a Herr Schuster to a Mr Lewis in London : "Rosa died today. Await your decision whether to attend funeral. In sorrow, Karl." '

Schellenberg shrugged. 'Well?'

'Lewis must be Levy,' the man went on, '—a Jew.' He grimaced at the word as if he had bitten into a lemon. 'Then there's the sender's address—Leipzig, not Berlin. Our post office informant smelt a rat. No Jew would come to Germany—not of his own free will.'

'You may be right,' Schellenberg said after a moment's thought. 'There's something fishy about it. Get Leipzig to check if we've got anything on this Karl Georg Schuster and report back to me.'

'What about the telegram?' asked the man. 'Shall we release it?'

Schellenberg re-read the message and gave it back. 'Yes, but make a copy for our files. Who handed it in?'

'A girl, apparently. The counter clerk hadn't seen her before.'

'Try and trace her,' said Schellenberg, and returned to his papers. He only half-heard the man's parting 'Heil Hitler, Obersturmführer!' 'Heil Hitler,' he murmured, casually raising his right arm in the prescribed manner.

Detective Superintendent Kuhn set to work on his report immediately. It was addressed to CID Communications Centre, the original source of his instructions. He described his preliminary interview with Frau Schmidt and noted that—in his opinion—she had not seemed averse to accepting the proposed assignment.

The file was marked 'Confidential' but had no priority rating, so he sent it to CID Communications Centre by normal service post in the hope that he would receive further instructions in good time.

On 11 April 1939, when he had heard no more and the entry 'Pension Schmidt' turned up in his desk diary, Kuhn telephoned CID Communications Centre and raised the subject of his assignment. He was informed that the whole scheme would take longer than expected and told to possess his soul in patience.

Kuhn picked up the phone again and dialled 32 10 32, Kitty Schmidt's number.

She answered with surprising speed. 'Superintendent?'

'I'm sorry, Frau Schmidt, we're not ready for you yet. I've spoken to my superiors. They may be big wheels but they don't turn in a hurry.' He chuckled. 'You understand?'

'Perfectly,' said Kitty, and if the Superintendent had been able to see her at that moment he could not have missed the glee on her face. Determined to burn her boats, she went a stage further. 'When can I expect to hear from you?'

'I honestly don't know,' Kuhn told her. 'It may take weeks to come down the pipeline, but as far as your place is concerned I'll keep both eyes shut from now on. Just as long as we understand each other, Frau Schmidt—not a word to anyone, right?'

'That goes without saying,' Kitty replied, and hung up. She had to sit down for a moment because her legs were trembling. She felt simultaneously relieved and drained of energy. Then she proceeded to make a series of blunders—blunders she was soon to regret bitterly. First she drafted another telegram to Sam Lewis in London. The text read 'Rosa is better' and the sender's name was again Karl Georg Schuster of Leipzig. Elvira took it to the post office in Lieztenburgerstrasse as before. Chance had it that the clerk on duty was the one who had served her a week earlier, and he was still glowing from the SD man's tribute to his powers of observation.

So, when Elvira presented her new telegram, he excused himself on some pretext and rang the SD from the postmaster's office. The SD promised to send a man within minutes and told him to delay his customer accordingly.

The clerk returned to his counter and engaged Elvira in conversation.

'Your sister, is it?' he inquired sympathetically.

'No,' Elvira told him. 'The telegram's from my mistress—she's sending it for a customer. It's nothing to do with me. How much?' She was eager to pay.

Laboriously, the clerk totted up the number of words. Then he said : 'There's a new rate for telegrams to England. Hang on, I won't be a minute.' He started to rummage among his books.

'Get a move on,' Elvira grumbled. 'I haven't got all day. She'll bawl me out for taking so long.'

'Can't help that,' the clerk said huffily, '—and keep a civil tongue in your head.' He pored over his tables with extra deliberation until he saw a man sidle up to the counter.

'What about a bit of service?' demanded the newcomer. It was the prearranged signal.

'All right, all right,' said the clerk. With magical speed he found the missing tariff and gave Elvira her change.

'Thanks,' said Elvira. 'Can I have my piece of paper back?' She had not forgotten Kitty's reprimand.

The clerk shot an inquiring glance at the stranger, who nodded. 'There you are.'

Elvira hurried out and made straight for Giesebrechtstrasse. She had taken no notice of the stranger and was unaware of being followed. Her suspicions were not aroused even when he travelled up in the lift with her. On the contrary. 'Coming to Kitty's place?' she asked him amiably, and the SD man was so intrigued by her invitation that he said yes.

It didn't take him long to grasp the nature of his destination. Kitty led him into the parlour and introduced a number of girls who happened to be on the premises. None of them seemed to meet the new customer's requirements, so she showed him her albums, in which a bewildering profusion of blondes, brunettes and redheads displayed what they had to offer. The man proved hard to please. When he raised the question of price, Kitty was so anxious to be rid of him that she doubled the normal rate.

Her hopes were well founded. The man left without even ordering a drink.

That afternoon, the new telegram arrived on Obersturm-führer Schellenberg's desk. He read it and ordered it to be sent.

'Any news from Leipzig?' he asked.

'No sir,' said the SD plainclothesman. 'It's the same old story.'

19

The same old story was a persistent conflict of authority between CID and SD, a battle which some veteran CID officers carried to such lengths that they more or less openly sabotaged the SD's operations by working to rule.

'In that case,' said Schellenberg, 'call in the Gestapo and have the Schmidt woman unobtrusively watched.'

'Yessir,' replied the SD man, clicking his heels.

From that day until Kitty concluded her pact with the devil, unseen observers noted every step she took.

CID Communications Centre had duly passed Superintendent Kuhn's report to CID chief Arthur Nebe.

Nebe added the report to others of a like nature, most of them concerning establishments which helped to give Berlin the sophisticated allure of a cosmopolitan city. They included, among others, the gaming club run by Maria and Karen von Osterroth at 16 Helmstedterstrasse, where men-about-town and diplomats played for high stakes in the company of beautiful women, likewise a brothel in the diplomatic quarter which later functioned, albeit inadequately, as a Gestapo intelligence centre. Nebe's dossier also listed 3 Steinplatz, the residence of Freddy Horstmann, former German ambassador in Brussels, a rendezvous where diplomats and heads of mission often gathered to attend all-night parties and while away the small hours by swapping political indiscretions.

Arthur Nebe had noted all this and more in a constant endeavour to open up new channels of information for his own benefit and that of the police. He laid his plans independent of Heydrich and Schellenberg, and may even be assumed to have hit on the Salon Kitty idea well in advance of the SD.

It was not, however, until June 1939 that Superintendent Kuhn received orders to conduct further negotiations with Kitty Schmidt and obtain her definite assent.

Accordingly, Kuhn retraced his steps to the Pension Schmidt. He was cordially received, as before. Elvira, who opened the door, ushered him straight into Madame's snuggery with none of her former diffidence. Kitty again sent for a bottle of champagne, although—or perhaps because—she sensed that the critical moment had come.

She had not wasted the intervening weeks. Almost all her liquid reserves had been gradually withdrawn from the bank and remitted by Guido Brisalla to his firm in Genoa. From there, by devious routes, the money went to Switzerland, whence it found its way into Kitty's London account. She had a well-padded cash reserve in the house which would have enabled her to leave Berlin by any means of transport, however expensive. She had also provided for her daughter, made a will, applied for exit visas and obtained a passport in another name. All in all, Kitty had been busy. Thus armed, she did not find it difficult to answer the Superintendent's question when it came.

'My dear Herr Kuhn, we've known each other for a long time. You must be as familiar with the nature of my business as I am. I'm always ready to oblige the police, but this scheme is out of the question. I'm a complete ignoramus in such matters. Our job is to brighten the lives of lonely men, not spy on them. Customers patronise us because we're discreet, not because we broadcast their little secrets to all and sundry.'

Superintendent Kuhn could hardly believe his ears. 'You mean. . . .'

Kitty cut him short. 'I mean I won't play,' she said firmly.

'You'll regret this, Frau Schmidt.' Kuhn felt suddenly exasperated. He had been visualising himself as the head of a new department. Unscheduled promotion wouldn't have been beyond the bounds of possibility—anything was possible under the present régime—and now this had to happen. 'Have you thought what it'll mean if I report your refusal? They'll close you down.'

Kitty shrugged. 'I can't help that.'

Kuhn deliberated for a moment. Somehow, the woman impressed him. 'You've got guts, I'll say that much.'

'I'm not a girl any longer,' said Kitty.

They chatted for a while, carefully skirting the subject. Then they went their separate ways, Kitty to seek the company of her girls and Kuhn to his office. He put off writing his report until next day. His thoughts returned repeatedly to Kitty Schmidt that evening. He contemplated discussing the problem with his wife but decided that it would be tactless.

Superintendent Kuhn spent a sleepless night.

'However dark the night or day, Schuster's lamps will light your way' read the silver lettering on the display window of Schuster

Electricals, 14 Promenadenweg, Leipzig. Karl Georg Schuster had composed the jingle himself and was as proud of it as he had been that day, three years before, when he first saw it adorning the window of his new shop.

It was three years, too, since he married Rosa, whose contribution to the business had been a handsome dowry. True, she had earned the money in a somewhat unconventional way, but Karl Schuster was a broadminded man. He held devoutly to the belief that money was money, whatever its source. Rosa and he had resolved to become solid citizens, and that was that.

Thereafter, Schuster stationed himself behind his counter punctually at eight every morning. He sold bulbs and lamps, plugs, sockets and flex, and—occasionally—one of those newfangled electric irons. Contentment descended on him when he shut up shop at 7 p.m. and checked the till. There were even times when he felt something akin to a renewed spirit of enterprise and dreamed of augmenting his income by branching out into the repairs and installation business.

Trade flourished and the shop was seldom empty, so he failed to notice the two men in long leather coats who waited patiently for their turn at the counter.

One of them said : 'Are you Karl Georg Schuster?' He spoke so quietly that none of the other customers could have overheard.

Schuster examined the questioner more closely. Being no innocent, he identified him at once. 'Police?' he inquired curtly. The men nodded.

'Rosa!' Schuster called over his shoulder. A young woman poked her head round the door. 'What's up?'

'Take over for a minute,' Schuster told her, and beckoned to the two men to follow him.

The woman took his place at the counter. Schuster led the policemen into the back room, where he turned to face them with a puzzled expression. Frantically, he dredged his memory for a possible reason why they should have honoured him with their presence. Nothing occurred to him.

'Well?' he said, and the single word conveyed all the caution of a man who was no stranger to the police.

'Are you married, Herr Schuster?' asked one of the men.

'Yes, that's my wife out front. You just saw her.'

'Is her name Rosa?'

'I shouted it loud enough.' Schuster thought hard. Had Rosa been up to something? Hardly—she seldom left the shop and was happy with her new way of life. He dismissed the suspicion.

'Has she been ill?'

Schuster had expected anything but that. 'How do you mean?' he asked warily. Perhaps it was a hang-over from the old days after all.

'I mean, has she been ill recently, seriously ill—on the danger list, so to speak?'

Schuster laughed. Now he knew they were off the track. 'Does she look sick?' he demanded.

'No,' conceded the first policeman. He extracted a folder from his briefcase, thumbed through it quickly, and then adopted an official tone. 'You are Karl Georg Schuster, resident at 14 Promenadenweg, Leipzig, correct?'

'Of course I am, but. . . .'

'Who is Sam Lewis?' snapped the policeman.

'I don't know anyone called Sam Lewis,' Schuster replied, truthfully.

The policeman showed him a copy of the first telegram. 'Did you send that?'

Schuster glanced at it. 'No, I don't know anyone called Lewis and I never sent him any telegram. . . .'

'When were you last in Berlin?'

'Two or three years back—I don't recall exactly. Yes, hang on, I went up there for the Olympics in 'thirty-six.'

'And you haven't been there since?' There was an ominous pause. 'Think carefully, Herr Schuster. You won't get anywhere by lying to us.'

'Why should I lie to you? I've no cause to. I spend every day in the shop, and Sundays I lie in. That's my life. I keep my nose clean these days, believe me!'

The two policemen, who had been watching him closely, realised that he was telling the truth. They asked a few more questions and took their leave—politely, by Gestapo standards. 'If you've been lying, Schuster, you won't know what hit you.'

The door had hardly closed behind them when Schuster summoned his wife. 'Shut up shop and come in here,' he roared.

Never taking his eyes off her face, he told her about the telegrams. She fidgeted and looked uneasy.

'Well,' he said harshly, 'what's it all about?'

'It's Kitty,' Rosa said. She told him all she knew, which wasn't much. As a former employee, she had felt under an obligation to Kitty. Kitty had contacted her a year earlier and confided that she might one day have to leave the country in a hurry. Would Rosa allow her to use 14 Promenadenweg as an accommodation address when she came to notify her friends in London? That was all. Rosa had no misgivings.

The past that had not reared its head for three years reared it now. Karl Georg Schuster stood up and clouted his wife as hard as he could. 'Stupid bitch!' he shouted. 'You whore, you imbecile! Know what you've gone and done? Sent us to a concentration camp, that's what!' He continued to belabour her.

Rosa endured it patiently, just as she had endured her clients' whims in the old days. Tears poured down her cheeks. Knowing Karl, she realised that his fit of anger would subside. He stopped hitting her as abruptly as he had begun, then slumped heavily into a chair and propped his head on his hands. He always did that when he was thinking hard. Is wasn't long before he made his mind up. 'Better tip her the wink,' he said quietly. 'Give her a quick buzz.'

Rosa dried her tears and dialled the exchange. 'Berlin 32 10 32,' she said in a faint voice.

While she was waiting, Karl poured two beers and put them on the table. 'You're an angel,' she said tenderly.

'Don't talk soft.' He turned away, looking embarrassed. He couldn't leave Rosa in the lurch, not now.

The phone rang. Rosa was brief. 'Kitty,' she said, 'the police were here. They had copies of your telegrams. You'd better get out fast.'

Kitty knew what to do.

Guido Brisalla, who arrived within half an hour of the call from Leipzig, found her rummaging in a cupboard. She produced a bundle of notes and counted out twenty thousand marks on the desk.

'When's your next trip to Italy?' she asked.

'I'm scheduled to leave on Tuesday. Will that be too late?'

Kitty deliberated for a moment. 'What do you think they'll do?'

'Make every effort to find out who Sam Lewis is. And when they discover he's the same person as Samuel Levy it won't be long before they get wise to the way you've been salting money away for years. And then. . . . ' He didn't specify what would happen then, but the words hung unspoken in the room.

'So it's now or never,' Kitty said quietly.

Brisalla nodded. 'You can't afford to wait any longer. I know it's hard on you, but you're in danger here. You've got to get away while you can.'

Kitty sank into the big arm-chair where she had spent so many hours. Sadness welled up inside her, compounded with rage—rage at Erich Kuhn, whom she thought of as the sole author of her misfortunes. 'That swine . . .' she said, and bit her handkerchief to stifle an outburst of sobbing. She ordered a coffee and schnapps for herself and a large brandy for Brisalla. 'Charge it to me,' she told Elvira.

'One drink, no more,' Brisalla said warningly. 'You need your wits about you.'

'What's the difference? But of course, Guido, you're right.' Kitty felt unsure of herself. Now that the moment had come, her clarity of thought deserted her. 'What do I do now?'

'How much cash do you have there?' Brisalla asked.

'Enough. Twenty thousand or so.'

'What about foreign exchange?'

'A thousand pounds in my corset.' She could hardly restrain a chuckle.

'In that case you'd better travel to Hanover this evening. I have a friend there—you can stay with him, but only for one night. I'll phone him and get him to drive you to Oldenburg. From there you can take the train to Amsterdam. Once you're over the frontier you'll be safe. Is your visa in order?'

'Yes,' Kitty replied in a flat voice, grateful to Brisalla for taking the initiative. She found her passport and handed it to him.

Brisalla examined it. The visa was in order and valid for another three weeks. With a bit of luck, she'd make it. He guessed that she must be under surveillance but did not add to her worries by mentioning the subject. He pocketed the banknotes without a word. 'I'll take you to the station,' he said before leaving. 'And don't send any more telegrams. You see how careful you have to be?'

'Do you think they're tapping my phone?' she asked.

'Don't touch the thing, just in case,' he advised. 'I'll pick you up at nine. The train leaves at ten-thirty. We'll go and have a farewell drink somewhere first. And remember, don't bring more than an overnight case.'

Kitty threw up the window when he had gone. It was mild outside, a typical early summer's day in Berlin. She stared down into the courtyard as if she were seeing it for the first time.

Elvira came in. 'What's the matter, Kitty?' she asked. 'Didn't you hear the phone?'

Kitty swung round. 'No, who is it?'

'He didn't give his name.'

'Well find out,' snapped Kitty.

Elvira returned almost at once. 'He says his name's Boris.'

Boris Finkelstein—yet another cross to bear. . . . He had been living in concealment with non-Jewish friends for the past two years. Kitty took the receiver. 'Rosa's dead,' she said flatly, and hung up. Boris knew what that meant. His last hope of escape had gone.

Guido Brisalla was punctual. The daylight had faded into dusk. It was a fine evening.

They climbed into Brisalla's car and Elvira put the overnight case on the back seat. 'I'll be home the day after tomorrow,' Kitty told her. 'Look after the place and don't do anything silly, understand?' The old Kitty revived for a moment, lucid and business-like, attentive to every detail.

'Ah, Berlin,' she sighed when they were installed on the terrace of the Berliner Kindl, drinking beer and watching the bustle of activity in the Kurfürstendamm.

Brisalla said : 'You ought to eat something.'

Kitty shook her head. 'I couldn't,' she said, and quietly started to weep.

Brisalla stole a glance at the neighbouring tables but failed to spot anyone taking a suspicious interest in them.

'Stop it,' he told her good naturedly, after a while. 'That won't help.' He beckoned the waiter and paid him.

They drove to the station in silence. Brisalla carried her bag to a first-class compartment. 'Try and get some sleep,' he said, adding, when he was outside on the platform : 'You'll be met by Norbert Giesecke. Rest up at his place and move on tomorrow.'

The train gave a jerk. Brisalla called 'Addio, Kitty!' and waved his handkerchief. It suddenly dawned on him that he might never see her again. He turned and walked quickly to the exit. It was shortly after 10.30 p.m. on 28 June 1939.

Barely an hour earlier, Schellenberg had received a phone call at his home. It was the SD plainclothesman.

'The Schmidt woman is doing a midnight flit, Obersturm-führer.'

'Where to?'

'No idea. Shall we stick with her?'

'By all means. If you need help, ring me. Detain her if necessary, understand?'

'Certainly, Obersturmführer.'

'Very well. Heil Hitler!'

'Heil Hitler, Obersturmführer!' There was a click and the line went dead.

The express drew into Hanover's main line station at 2 a.m. The holiday season had not yet begun. Few passengers alighted and there were even fewer people on the platform. Kitty took stock of her surroundings but could not see anyone waiting for her, so she picked up her case and headed for the barrier.

Once outside, she was accosted by an elderly man in a green Bavarian overcoat and a felt hat.

'Frau Schmidt?'

Kitty recoiled a step. 'Yes,' she whispered, fearful that he might be from the police.

'My name is Giesecke,' he said quietly, taking her bag. 'Please come with me.' He walked on ahead and Kitty followed him with relief.

His car was parked outside. Politely, he held the door for her and got in behind the wheel. 'I feel it would be better if we drove straight to Oldenburg. I don't think you ought to waste any time. Guido has told me all I need to know.'

'I'm awfully tired,' Kitty said, wondering at herself. She was usually wide awake at this hour, but somehow, as her excitement began to subside, the craving for sleep had become hard to resist.

'Make yourself comfortable,' said Giesecke. 'There's a rug on the seat behind you. I think we'd be well advised to drive through the night.'

They set off, unaware of the taxi that was trailing them at a discreet distance.

By dawn they were in Gütersloh, and two hours later in Münster. Giesecke had a shave in a barber's shop while Kitty blearily drank some coffee. Then, at Giesecke's insistence, they continued their journey. They reached Oldenburg just before midday and drove straight to the station. Giesecke got out and studied the time-table.

'The next train to Enschede leaves in two hours. You can get a connection there to Amsterdam. I hope you get across safely. . . .' There was concern in his voice.

All at once, the spirit of adventure awoke in Kitty. She stared at the stranger who had driven her so far. He was no youngster, and the sleepless night showed in his face. 'You must be tired,' she said. 'Drop me here and drive to the nearest hotel. Catch up on your sleep.'

She felt a sudden glow of happiness. Men usually wanted something out of her. This was the first total stranger who had given her something for nothing. 'Why are you doing all this?' she asked.

The man shook his head uncomprehendingly. 'All what?'

'You drive me all this way, Herr Giesecke, you sacrifice your night's sleep—you even risk your neck. Why?'

Giesecke stared at her for a moment, weary and pensive. Then he said : 'I'd like nothing better than to come with you.'

'Why don't you?'

'I'm too old and too much of a coward.' Giesecke took her bag and deposited it on the pavement. 'Lots of luck, Frau Schmidt,' he said, squeezing her hand, then turned away, stiff-faced, and climbed back into the car. He gave a little wave as he drove off. The watching SD man made a careful note of his licence number before advancing on Kitty and raising his hat.

'Allow me.' He reached for her bag.

Kitty scrutinised the bland face. 'That's very nice of you. I was just going to the first-class waiting-room.'

As they passed the ticket office, she bought a single to Enschede with the SD man at her elbow. The remaining sequence of events might have been lifted from a second-rate thriller. The agent escorted her to the waiting-room and courteously took his leave.

One glance at his credentials and the railway police put a call through to Berlin. Schellenberg decreed that Kitty should be allowed through German customs and detained by the frontier police as soon as her passport was rubber-stamped—'the finest piece of evidence we could possibly have', as he put it.

Everything went according to plan. Kitty Schmidt was arrested at the Dutch border on 29 June 1939, after completing all her exit formalities. Her corset yielded an illegal cache of foreign currency and her handbag a forged passport. She was escorted back to Berlin by the nice young man who had been kind enough to carry her bag at Oldenburg.

'Why are you doing all this?' she asked him, too, when she had recovered from the initial shock. Unlike Giesecke, the young man did not hesitate.

'Orders, Frau Schmidt.'

Chapter 2

If Kitty had been exhausted by her journey back to Berlin in a wooden-seated third-class compartment worse discomforts awaited her there. She was locked up in one of the Prinz Albrechtstrasse dungeons. Her cell had a heavy door with an inset grille and no windows, and the only illumination came from a dim bulb which burned between 6 a.m. and 6 p.m.

They stripped her of everything, her jewellery, her luggage, her mink coat. She was so cold, in spite of the time of year, that she was happy to crawl beneath the rough blanket that covered her straw mattress. Sometimes she dozed off for minutes—or was it hours?—and wild dreams raced through her head. Then, bathed in sweat, she would wake up and scream until one of the SS guards came.

The result was invariable. She was hurled back on her palliasse, sworn at, threatened, and told to shut up.

Kitty found herself in an alien world which she had always suspected to be a figment of the Jewish imagination and dismissed as exaggerated. It was too late to meditate on that. She thought her last hour had come. Two or three times she was summoned for interrogation. These ordeals took place in equally chill and impersonal rooms. Harsh lights shone on her sagging face, questions assailed her buzzing ears. She answered truthfully but said nothing of her friends or the size of her deposit account in England. Questioned about Sam Lewis, she said: 'He's an old English friend of mine—we've known each other for twenty years.'

That earned her a slap in the face, not that she minded.

She was beaten again when she asked if someone would telephone Walch, her lawyer.

The rest of the time they left her in peace. She was given mugs of watery coffee and a little bread, the odd bowl of soup and on one occasion some thick stew. At first she thought she wouldn't be able to swallow a morsel, but her revulsion waned and she later realised to her astonishment that she was actually eager for meal-times to come round.

Incarceration, uncertainty and perpetual gloom preyed on her nerves. She was permitted to wash once a day, but there was no mirror to reflect the steady deterioration in her personal appearance.

One day the door of her cell was thrown open. She rose, expecting to be led off for interrogation, but another woman was thrust inside. Then the heavy barred door swung to with a crash.

Kitty stared at the newcomer, filled with curiosity and delight at being alone no longer. She tried to engage her in conversation, but the woman only sobbed inconsolably. Kitty led her to the palliasse and drew the blanket over her, stroking her handsome black hair with a gentle and sympathetic touch.

It seemed hours before the woman calmed down, but when next Kitty spoke to her she found she had fallen asleep.

Outside, the corridors rang with the footsteps of the SS guards who manned the Prinz Albrechtstrasse cellars. Sometimes screams or muffled sobbing could be heard, but Kitty felt so old an inmate that the noises began to seem commonplace.

Then the key turned in the lock again and an SS man entered. 'Schmidt!' he bellowed.

'Here,' said Kitty, noticing that her new cell-mate had stirred.

'Come with me,' said the guard.

Kitty felt the woman grope for her hand. 'I'll be back soon,' she whispered, but the guard was shouting again.

'Shut up and make it snappy!'

He took a step into the cell and stuck both thumbs in his belt, with its awesome-looking holster. 'Come on, move!'

Kitty rose and followed him. It quickly dawned on her that she was being taken somewhere different. Then the guard flung open a door and she had to shield her eyes from a blaze of sunlight.

Parked in the courtyard was a police van with an SS number-plate. Two young men in black uniforms chivvied her into the mobile cell. One of them drew his pistol and sat down beside her. 'One false move and I'll use it,' was all he said.

Kitty experienced a combination of fear and hope. The vehicle got under way, throwing her off balance as it turned a sharp corner. She couldn't see where they were going, but she could hear the screech of tram wheels, the tooting of buses and the muffled roar of big-city traffic.

The trip did not last long. She was prodded out of the van into a typical Berlin courtyard, then thrust into a room with heavily barred windows and left to her own devices.

A guard allowed her to open one of the windows, and she stared up at the little patch of blue sky. Occasional puffs of fair-weather cloud flitted across it. Kitty sniffed the summer air and awaited her fate. She guessed that it was about to be decided, here and now, and felt a yearning for life and all that freedom meant to her.

Over an hour passed before they came to fetch her. The SS man thrust a comb into her hand and escorted her to the wash-room. 'Tidy yourself up a bit,' he told her brusquely.

Kitty flinched when she caught sight of herself in the mirror. She had aged ten years. Her face looked shrunken without powder and rouge, and there were deep crow's-feet round her eyes and the corners of her mouth. Laboriously, she combed her knotted hair into some semblance of order.

And that was how she met Walter Schellenberg for the first time.

He was seated behind his massive desk, staring at her with veiled curiosity. Behind him hung photographs of Hitler and Himmler, also a calendar. The date-frame said 14 July.

'Sit down, Frau Schmidt.' Schellenberg's tone was off-hand, indifferent. He began to leaf through a bulky file, leisurely but intently.

Kitty examined the young man with a keen eye. So he was the one who would decide her fate. She sensed at once that he wielded authority. He had an intelligent face and his suit had come from a first-class tailor. The only incongruous feature was the Party badge in his buttonhole. A carnation would have suited him better, Kitty reflected. Pleasurably, she inhaled his discreet Eau de Cologne and the scent of his cigarette.

At last he spoke. 'You run a brothel in Giesebrechtstrasse?'

'A private hotel, Herr . . . ?' Kitty had no idea how to address him.

'Schellenberg, Obersturmführer Schellenberg—and don't beat about the bush. You'd like to get out of here, right? Then don't lie to me. You want something from me, I may conceivably want something from you. Wasting time won't benefit either of us. The quicker we come to terms the better for you. Understand?'

Kitty had listened to the man with mounting attention, surprised by his clear, succinct and not unfriendly manner of speaking. She merely said : 'Yes, Obersturmführer,' and waited.

'How many girls work at your establishment?'

'The number varies. I always keep four or five on the premises —for emergencies, so to speak. Otherwise, I show clients my photograph albums and they wait for the girls to join them. It doesn't take long by cab.'

'Do you serve drinks?'

'I have a licence. . . .'

'Yes, yes, I'm aware of that. Go on. What happens then?'

'Well, they generally have a drink in the parlour or one of the bedrooms. And then—well, the usual. . . .'

'How long do the gentlemen stay?' Schellenberg uttered the word 'gentlemen' with studied contempt.

'There's no universal rule. Some stay half an hour, others the whole night. After all, we're registered as a private hotel.'

Schellenberg cut her short. 'You don't have to camouflage your activities, not in my presence. Go on. Do you employ any ordinary staff?'

'Yes, a housekeeper and two maidservants. Every guest gets clean towels and bed-linen. It's all very comfortable—surely you've inspected the place?'

He shook his head. 'Not yet, but it's a dubious privilege I may not be able to dodge.' He changed the subject. 'Tell me, why were you making for Holland?'

'I was on my way to England.'

Schellenberg stared at her with a hint of surprise, knowing it to be the truth. Meditatively, he gnawed the knuckle of his right forefinger.

'What made you run for it?'

'You should know, Obersturmführer.'

Schellenberg's surprise deepened. 'What gives you that idea?'

'Surely it was you who sent Superintendent Kuhn to see me?'

'Who's Superintendent Kuhn?'

'He works for the vice squad, Obersturmführer. I was asked to turn my place into a nest of spies, but I refused. Then I got frightened and ran. And now I'm here. . . .'

Schellenberg silenced her with a gesture and picked up the phone. 'Tell Decker I want him,' he said into the mouthpiece, then turned to Kitty.

'All right. Talk, and take your time.'

She told him the whole story from the beginning. How Kuhn had visited her and broached the subject, how she had made preparations to leave at that early stage but postponed her departure when Kuhn phoned to inform her that there was no urgency after all. Then his second visit and her flat refusal of the CID's request. Finally she had lost her head and bolted.

An NCO appeared in the doorway. 'You sent for me, Obersturmführer?'

'Yes, Decker. Take this woman next door and give her some cigarettes, then come back here. I want you to do something for me, quickly.' Schellenberg reached for the phone again.

'Get me Police Headquarters,' he said, and, when the bell rang, 'Nebe?'

It was Arthur Nebe, chief of the Criminal Police. The conversation lasted half an hour, with Oberscharführer Decker listening in. When Schellenberg put down the phone he knew what he wanted to know. 'All right, Decker,' he said, 'you've got the picture. Drive over to Nebe and fetch me those files—and send in the Schmidt woman before you go.'

Kitty had scarcely sat down when Schellenberg resumed his interrogation.

'What are they like, your girls? Dumb, smart? Well, speak up.'

'They aren't dumb,' Kitty told him, 'but they're a mixed bunch. A few of them are country girls who want to earn a dowry. Others are grass widows with time on their hands and others do it simply because they can't get satisfaction any other way. The one thing they all have in common is this : they're fond of money and they're nice to my clients—as nice as I pay them to be.'

'What do they earn?'

'It depends on demand. At least a thousand marks a month, anyway, though some earn more—much more. As I say, there's no general rule.'

'What about you, Frau Schmidt?'

'I take fifty per cent, but I have a lot of overheads. Maintenance, decoration, linen, wages. . . .'

'Save it,' Schellenberg told her curtly. 'You've helped Jews to leave the country by illicit means. That's a punishable offence and you know it. If I chose to, I could bury you in a concentration camp for life. You've illegally procured foreign exchange. That's a punishable offence too—it renders you liable to a minimum of two years' imprisonment. You've also smuggled money out of Germany. . . .' He shrugged as if to convey that he couldn't even guess at the extent of the penalty for this crime. 'Finally, you tried to sneak out of the country on a forged passport. What have you got to say for yourself, Frau Schmidt?'

'What can I say? It sounds terrible the way you put it, Obersturmführer, but it wasn't intended that way. I didn't mean to do anything bad. . . .'

Schellenberg jumped to his feet. 'Oh no, you didn't mean to do anything bad!' he shouted, and began to pace the office like a caged panther. 'You people always have second thoughts when you're sitting there on that chair, when it's too late or we've nabbed you in the nick of time. You're in big trouble, Frau Schmidt!' Schellenberg slowly recovered his composure and sat down. He was accustomed to thinking swiftly and with precision. The woman was intimidated now. He had no doubt that she would co-operate. His plans were cut and dried. He didn't know when he would put them into effect, but it couldn't be long now. He must speak to Heydrich as soon as possible, agree on a definite schedule before the civil police went off at half-cock. Well, he'd know more when Arthur Nebe's files arrived.

He studied Kitty Schmidt thoughtfully. She was of an age when women cling to life, and her establishment was renowned throughout Berlin for its elegance and cleanliness. He couldn't conceive why any man should confide in such a pathetic scarecrow of a woman, but she must be discreet or possess other qualities not immediately apparent to him.

'I could finish you with a stroke of the pen,' he said menacingly.

'I know,' Kitty said. Bravely, she added : 'Give me another chance—please!'

'Help yourself to a cigarette and listen carefully,' he told her. 'I may consent to release you if you sign an undertaking never to discuss what has happened. If I hear the slightest whisper, you'll disappear into a concentration camp for good. You understand?'

Kitty nodded. Hope gave her the courage to say : 'I'll do anything you want.'

'Good,' said Schellenberg. 'In that case I shall release you today. You'll get your belongings back—everything except the foreign exchange—and remain in Berlin. You'll report daily at 4 p.m. to my outer office, here at Meineckestrasse. In other respects you'll carry on as before. You'll give information to no one, and that includes Superintendent Kuhn. If people ask questions, refer them to me. Is that clear?'

'Yes, Obersturmführer.' Kitty almost felt drawn to the man who held her life in his hand.

'You'll talk to no one, not even your best friend, understand?'

'Yes.'

'Not even Signor Brisalla.'

Kitty gave a start. 'Guido? What about him?'

'He'll be released too, but I advise you never to see him again. Another thing : I shall require to be consulted in advance about any staff changes at your establishment. Elvira stays, is that clear?'

Elvira? Kitty's mind, barely able to digest the prospect of freedom, whirled again. An informer in the house—Elvira, of all people. . . .

'I said, is that clear?' The reiterated question rang dully in her ears.

Kitty had reached the end of her tether. She would have agreed to anything.

'Quite clear, Obersturmführer.'

Detective Superintendent Kuhn still had no inkling of Kitty's fate. Having duly informed CID Communications Centre, Berlin, that Frau Schmidt had declined to co-operate, he was patiently awaiting further instructions.

From one angle, he was almost glad not to have heard anything. He quite liked Kitty and would have been sorry if unpleasantnesses had stemmed from her refusal to co-operate because he could well imagine the form such unpleasantnesses would take.

He felt a sporadic urge to warn her but stifled it, wavering between duty and inclination.

Arthur Nebe, chief of the Criminal Police, was in much the same state of indecision. Other and more important matters had repeatedly prevented him from pursuing his plan to open up a new intelligence channel, so Operation Surveillance Centre, to quote his own name for the Salon Kitty project, remained in abeyance until Walter Schellenberg's phone call.

Nebe's interest revived at this. He had no qualms about surrendering the Schmidt file to Schellenberg and the Security Service, especially as it contained nothing of importance apart from Superintendent Kuhn's rather meagre notes.

Meanwhile, Oberscharführer Rolf Decker had been active on quite another front. It was he who had received the tip-off about Elvira from Lietzenburgerstrasse post office and shadowed her to the Pension Schmidt. It was he, too, who had approached Elvira afterwards and assured her that he had only followed her inside because she attracted him—that it had never occurred to him to enter the Pension Schmidt for any other reason.

Decker also suggested that they might meet again soon. Elvira took a fancy to the big blond SS man, so the reunion was not long in coming. What made things easier was that Kitty did not return forty-eight hours later. Instead, someone telephoned to say that she might be away for several days longer. Infatuated with her new boy-friend, Elvira succumbed to the magic of the warm summer nights and confided almost all she knew about Kitty and her activities. Then, when Decker started talking about the future —their future together, Elvira took it to mean—her last inhibitions crumbled and she told him everything he wanted to know.

Within a few days, the Pension Schmidt lapsed into a routine which Kitty would never have tolerated. Parties became noisier and more frequent—so much so that they drew vehement complaints from a next-door neighbour at 12 Giesebrechtstrasse, a certain Dr Ernst Kaltenbrunner.

Such was the situation on the evening of 14 July 1939, when Kitty, mentally and physically exhausted, returned to her domain.

During the next few weeks she left the house only once a day to make her obligatory report. She always took a taxi and was back within half an hour. The establishment was soon firmly in hand again and doing even better business than before. Kitty went around in a sort of daze for the first week, but then her spirits revived. Strong coffee and plenty of schnapps helped the memory of her ordeal to fade.

Even so, she shunned the company of friends and strangers alike, and her conversations with regular customers were kept to a minimum. She began to take an interest in press reports and news broadcasts, and spent more and more time in her snuggery, sensing that something was afoot in the wider world outside.

Then, with an abruptness which took Kitty completely by surprise, the war came : 1 September 1939, rationing, paeans of victory from Poland. . . .

Kitty did not omit to present herself at Meineckestrasse every day on the stroke of four. She avoided doing anything which might prompt the SD to rearrest her. She also made herself agreeable to Elvira, although the old warmth that had existed between them was gone.

Victory fanfares blared from radios and cinemas. Goebbels's propaganda machine steamrollered the sceptics, and if Kitty still harboured secret ideas of escape they, too, were lost in the universal delirium of victory.

Two men exploited the general mood for their own ends : Reinhard Heydrich and his subordinate Walter Schellenberg.

Schellenberg had quietly completed his plans for a reorganised State Security Service and got Heydrich's agreement. Together, they secured the approval of Heinrich Himmler, Reichsführer-SS and chief of the German police.

On 27 September 1939 Warsaw fell and Poland capitulated. On the same day, the Reich Central Security Office came into being.

Also on the same day, Walter Schellenberg decided to put one of his many schemes into effect. It was a top secret operation code-named 'Salon Kitty'.

Chapter 3

Schellenberg tackled the Salon Kitty project with the precision for which he was renowned. His first step was to appoint Untersturmführer Karl Schwarz executive officer and make him responsible for planning and organisation.

Escorted by Schwarz, he paid a visit to 11 Giesebrechtstrasse during the first week in October.

They rang the bell and were admitted by Elvira. Schellenberg handed the girl his card and told her to inform Frau Schmidt of their arrival.

To Elvira's surprise, Kitty had the visitors shown straight into the main drawing-room—an unusual mark of honour.

Schellenberg examined his surroundings with interest. There was a grand piano by the window, draped in a rich brocade cloth, a large and obviously genuine Persian carpet, and an assortment of sumptuously upholstered sofas and arm-chairs. Other features included heavy velvet curtains, a gramophone on a pedestal, crystal chandeliers and tasselled standard lamps, some good paintings, lots of plush and figurines, and two cabinets crowded with knick-knacks and cut glass. The whole room was clean as a new pin and redolent of solid middle-class comfort.

'Madame will be with you in a minute,' said Elvira, not suspecting who the two men were.

And then Kitty swept in. She had titivated herself for the occasion. Schellenberg hardly recognised her. Was this the haggard, elderly creature who had sat facing him in his office? Wrestling with his incredulity, he now found it easier to accept the reports he had compiled about her. There was little doubt that she would be able to run the establishment without arousing unwelcome suspicion. He was satisfied.

'Frau Schmidt . . .' he began.

'Please sit down, gentlemen,' Kitty interrupted him amiably. 'May I offer you a little refreshment, Obersturmführer?'

'You can dispense with ranks here,' Schellenberg said with a smile, quickly adapting himself to the situation. 'Permit me to introduce Herr Schwarz.'

Kitty eyed Untersturmführer Schwarz keenly as he took her hand.

'We should very much like to inspect your premises,' Schellenberg began. 'Herr Schwarz will be your contact in future. Please follow his instructions to the letter, is that clear?'

There it was again, the peremptory question which had haunted her dreams for weeks.

'Quite clear,' she said, aware of how utterly at their mercy she was but equally conscious of her will to survive.

'Shall we go?' said Schellenberg.

'One moment, gentlemen.' Kitty rang for Elvira. 'How busy are we?' she asked.

'No 7's occupied and so is No 4,' the girl replied briskly. 'Elke's having a nap in No 3 but there's no one else around.'

'Thank you, that's all for the moment.' Kitty tried to detect signs of a secret understanding between Elvira and the two SS men, but they did not seem to know each other.

'May I lead the way?'

Schellenberg nodded.

They passed through tall double doors into a long passage pleasantly illuminated by wall-brackets which shed a soft pink glow. Now it was Schwarz's turn to nod approvingly. 'Very nice,' he said.

Kitty put a finger to her lips. 'Ssh!' she whispered. 'Customers!'

They walked down the thickly carpeted passage to a door at the far end. Kitty ushered them inside. It was a spacious room furnished with a wide French double bed, frivolous little armchairs nesting in deep pile carpets, and a small trolley—'for drinks,' Kitty explained. There were mirrors on the walls, also on the ceiling above the bed. A screen concealed a wash-basin and bidet. It was agreeably warm.

'All my rooms look much the same as this,' Kitty said.

'Delightful,' chuckled Schellenberg, 'really delightful. How about it, Schwarz—shall I leave you behind to sample the service?' It was meant as a joke, and Schwarz's earnest face twitched in a dutiful smile.

Schellenberg dropped into one of the arm-chairs. 'Do you serve coffee?'

'But of course.' Kitty pressed the bell. A spruce little maidservant put her head round the door and stiffened visibly when she saw her employer.

'Coffee for three,' said Kitty.

Coffee was served on the trolley in fine old china cups. Schellenberg remarked on them.

'Meissen,' Kitty said, and he gave another approving nod.

Meanwhile, Schwarz was inspecting the room. He examined the bed-linen and towels, glanced out of the window, peered into the wardrobe and asked, pointing to a small communicating door : 'Where does that lead to?'

'The bathroom.' Kitty rose and opened it. 'There's one bathroom to every two bedrooms. We're well equipped here, as you can see.'

The two men finished their coffee and followed Kitty back to the drawing-room. 'Where's your office?' asked Schellenberg.

Kitty showed them into her snuggery.

'This is it—I don't have a proper office.'

Once again Schwarz peered carefully round the room and out of the window. He pursed his lips every now and then, as though thinking hard.

'Do you have a safe?' he asked at length.

Kitty tilted a picture to reveal the outlines of a wall safe.

'That's all right.' Schwarz sounded almost apologetic. 'I only wanted to know.' Schellenberg walked to the door. 'We'll be in touch,' he said. 'You need only report once a week from now on, but kindly don't leave Berlin.' It was an order.

When they had gone, Kitty found that her hands were trembling.

Schwarz called on Kitty next morning, the morning of 18 October 1939. He had himself shown into her snuggery and came straight to the point.

'Frau Schmidt, please regard anything I discuss with you today or in the future as strictly confidential. I've brought along a document for you to sign.'

He rummaged in his briefcase and produced a sheet of paper, which he placed in front of her.

The document stated that Kitty Schmidt pledged herself to carry out all SD instructions, discuss them with no one and promptly report all relevant information to Untersturmführer Schwarz. Violation of any such directive would be a breach of security punishable by death.

Kitty carefully read the document through. It was clear that her new masters would brook no refusal. She thought with dread of the fortnight's imprisonment which had given her a small foretaste of what she could expect if she violated the agreement, even technically.

'Do you have a pen?' was all she said.

Schwarz unscrewed his fountain pen and handed it over without a word.

Kitty signed. When she looked for a duplicate, she found to her surprise that there wasn't one.

'Don't I get a copy?' she asked.

'No,' Schwarz said curtly. 'If you ever feel the need to re-read what you've signed, report to my office any time. The document will be in my safe. Don't ask anyone else in my department, though—apply to me personally. Is that clear?'

'Yes,' she said. 'What do I do now?'

'Nothing, simply follow our instructions. My first job will be to inspect the whole premises again, very thoroughly. We may have to make some alterations, so I'll bring an architect along. Whatever orders I give, never withhold your approval—the consequences could be extremely unpleasant. Also, whatever work is undertaken, I shall hold you responsible for seeing that no one ever discovers our connection with it. Change the subject or think up a plausible explanation of some kind. Is that clear too?'

'Yes, but . . .'

'No buts. When would be the best time to admit workmen?'

Kitty suppressed a smile. The singular Herr Schwarz did not seem too well briefed on her trade. 'Mornings would be best,' she said. 'Say between nine and midday. The place is almost deserted then, apart from the girls who sleep here.'

'How many do?'

'It all depends—you understand?'

Schwarz did not understand. 'No.'

Whatever they wanted from her, Kitty deduced that its connection with her trade must be secondary or they would have sent a more experienced man—Superintendent Kuhn, for example, or someone from his department. She said : 'Well, my clients occasionally express a wish to stay here overnight.'

'I see,' said Schwarz. 'Could you dissuade them if necessary?'

'Of course. I don't let them stay unless the girl is willing. It's one of my rules never to compel anyone to do anything. All my girls live off the premises. They don't get here before 11 a.m., normally speaking. In any case, there's nothing doing before that.'

'Very good. And now, kindly show me round again.'

It became clear to Untersturmführer Schwarz, as they went from room to room, that a great deal of money had been invested in the place. He also realised that the Salon Kitty venture would swallow a great deal more money if the house was to retain its reputation—and its reputation was just the commodity that he and Schellenberg were anxious to preserve for their own purposes.

Schwarz tapped walls and opened windows, peered down into the rear courtyard, which seemed to claim his particular attention, checked the thickness of partitions and the quality of curtains, listened at closed doors while Kitty talked or sang on the far side at his request. He accompanied Kitty to the cellar, noted the dimensions of every room, and briefed himself on the other occupants of No 11 Giesebrechtstrasse. He inspected the central heating and lighting circuits, got Kitty to draw up an itemised list of disbursements on linen, liquor and staff wages, confiscated her albums containing photographs of pretty girls and demanded the name and address of each. 'Herr Schwarz', as he insisted on being called, put in a hard morning's work. Finally he prepared to leave.

'When do I get my albums back?' asked Kitty. 'It would seem odd if they weren't available. My clients are always asking for them.'

Schwarz took her point. He thought for a moment, then handed the books back. 'You're right—we'll have copies made. Glad to see you're using your head, Frau Schmidt. You'll need to do that more and more as time goes by.'

The SS man departed without accepting a beer or a cup of

coffee. He'd rampaged around all morning, but to Kitty his humourless zeal signified that he was merely an amateur. She noted with satisfaction that even the SS were not omniscient, and that there was still a small sector in which her own talents and experience reigned supreme.

This realisation soothed her considerably. The future was already looking a shade brighter. She would guard her trade secrets as jealously as the gentlemen of the SS or SD guarded theirs. Without being entirely clear in her own mind, she sensed the growth of a partnership based on mutual dependence. How had Schellenberg put it? 'I may conceivably want something from you. . . .' Well, it was obvious that he didn't want to sleep with her.

Superintendent Kuhn had mentioned something about an intelligence centre. The SD must be similarly interested in such a scheme, but how did they propose to tackle it? Kitty couldn't imagine. Her thoughts returned to the idea again and again. Did they plan to train her girls as agents? She had to laugh when she contemplated the possibility. Of the twenty or thirty girls and women who earned their pin-money at the Pension Schmidt, none—in her opinion—had the makings. They were all nice little things with a yen for money or men, or both. But spies?

Kitty resolved to keep her eyes open at all costs and conserve her professional know-how. There were many features which still baffled her, but the future would make everything clear.

She could not know that Untersturmführer Schwarz was thinking along much the same lines. He too found the situation novel and unfamiliar, but he felt confident of his ability to get the hang of it just as he had mastered many other specialised subjects in the past. He had years of intelligence work behind him.

The next meeting between Schellenberg and Schwarz took place on 12 November. On 9 November Schwarz had been detached for duty in Munich to help guard Hitler during his annual address to Party veterans. He went on to spend two days' leave with his sister in Rosenheim. The sister had recently married a Brownshirt who was on the look-out for a new job. He was currently trading in cattle, an occupation which he found unfulfilling at this epic moment in the nation's history. He envisaged something bigger—a post bringing more power, responsibility and money—and had not illogically conjectured that his brother-in-law in the SS might help him on his way. All this was still churning around in Schwarz's head as he submitted his ideas to Schellenberg.

'Fire away,' said Schellenberg, when Schwarz had explained the scheme in outline.

'I propose to turn the basement of 11 Giesebrechtstrasse into a monitoring centre. It has two entrances, one interior and one from the yard,' Schwarz explained. 'Discreet inquiries have elicited that the yard entrance could be sealed off to accommodate the listening-post in secrecy. That would virtually rule out the possibility of detection. Our men would have to be relieved via the inside entrance. Sanitary installations could be built in. . . .'

'Good,' observed Schellenberg. 'What about microphones?'

'That's fixed too. I consulted Party Member Fritsche, and he referred me to the technical division of the State Broadcasting Service, where I was given detailed information about the latest microphones. We'd have to plaster over all the wires and lead them down to the basement inside a single sheath. I suggest running the multi-core cable down the drainpipe so no one will be able to spot anything from outside. We could purchase the necessary equipment from Telefunken. I already obtained some leaflets from them via a third party. Telefunken have been led to believe that the microphones and monitoring gadgets are intended for big Party rallies. They'll supply the most up-to-the-minute rig they can put together.'

Schellenberg nodded approvingly. His judgement hadn't failed him. Schwarz was just the man for the job.

'And the recording devices?' he asked.

'No problem there, sir. All conversations will be recorded on wax discs and the latter stored in cabinets. I thought we might file them under three subheadings—subject matter, person and official capacity. Conversations will be simultaneously monitored through headphones and important extracts relayed to you or me direct. That will enable us to decide promptly on any steps to be taken.'

'Sounds good,' Schellenberg's face creased in a faintly ironical smile. 'How about the ladies?'

Schwarz hesitated. The 'ladies' were his real problem. 'We've checked on all the girls who work at the Salon Kitty. A nice-looking bunch, and I've no doubt they know their job. About a third of them are married and another third controlled by pimps of varying notoriety. The rest are free-lance. Given the right treatment, the first two categories might be pressured into working for us. The question is, would it pay?'

Schellenberg leant forward intently. 'Can you suggest an alternative?'

'I think so, sir.'

'In that case, let's have it.'

'Well, it seems to me that our operatives should be loyal National Socialists with a high intelligence rating and faith in the Führer and his aims. They must also be capable of grasping the essence of the whole operation. What's more, in the event of their entertaining foreign visitors, they must be fluent in the relevant language so as to minimise the risk of misunderstanding. Finally, they must be prepared, in the last resort, to . . .' Schwarz paused, seeking the right word.

'Yield, shall we say?' Schellenberg suggested.

'Precisely, sir. What we're looking for, in other words, is an ideal combination of all our requirements.'

'And where do you propose to find these paragons?' Schellenberg's tone was dry.

'I shall train them,' Schwarz said dispassionately, as if it was the most natural thing in the world. 'I thought of sending a confidential circular to all senior SS and police officers, inviting suitable recommendations. I also thought we might throw our colleagues off the scent by re-locating our establishment in a foreign capital. In my view, we should do our utmost to divert attention from Berlin. They say Prague is a pretty lively city. . . .'

'You seem to have covered everything, Untersturmführer.' Schellenberg gave another approving nod. 'The Prague idea is a good one. Who's going to sign this circular?'

'I thought you might prevail on Gruppenführer Wolff,' Schwarz said coolly.

Schellenberg whistled through his teeth. 'Wolff of *Lebensborn*, you mean?' he asked with a smile.

'Precisely, sir.'

It was a neat plan. Gruppenführer Wolff was chief of Reichsführer Himmler's personal staff, and in that capacity head of the *Lebensborn* ('Fount of Life') organisation, which was dedicated to breeding babies of irreproachably Aryan stock. If Wolff agreed to sponsor the request for suitable girls, no hint of suspicion would attach to the SD and the Central Security Office. Untersturmführer Schwarz had indeed thought of everything.

'I'll speak to Gruppenführer Wolff,' Schellenberg said. 'How is Frau Schmidt behaving herself?'

'I'm not quite sure, yet. I've been keeping up the pressure on her. She knows there's something in the wind, of course, because the police made her a similar proposition once before. Our full intentions are a closed book to her and will remain so. Business is good—possibly too good. We may have to damp it down a little, later on. Our information about Frau Schmidt comes from three sources. First, there's the CID—I've put Superintendent Kuhn on to her. Then there's the maidservant, Elvira—Oberscharführer Decker and she are on intimate terms. Finally, there are the girls who work for her. None of our three sources knows what's going on, but their reports tally. Frau Schmidt hasn't talked to a soul, not so far.'

'Could she be dangerous?' Schellenberg asked.

'Hardly, sir. Even she won't know more than the bare bones.'

'Fine, so that's the set-up. How long will it take you to arrange it all?'

'Two months should be enough.'

Schellenberg deliberated. Two months took them to January, normally the height of Berlin's winter season. The war had changed everything, of course. The male urge to relax for a couple of hours would gain in intensity. Also, the black-out rendered it even easier to slip unobserved into a house of dubious reputation. To all appearances, the timing was perfect.

'One more thing, Schwarz. Have you given any thought to how we approach our potential customers?'

'Yes, sir. I've had informal talks with some of the protocol boys at the Foreign Office. I've also sounded out our colleagues in the Party and checked the reactions of members of the armed forces. If we publicise our brothel properly it'll become the toast of Berlin, and no one will smell a rat because Kitty Schmidt has acquired such a classy reputation in recent years. We must also infiltrate Berlin society with suitable agents who can act as touts if necessary. That way, there won't be any risk of our monitoring centre becoming unproductive.'

'So the women are our only weak spot?'

Schwarz nodded. 'Yes, Obersturmführer.'

'I'll get in touch with Gruppenführer Wolff today. With luck, I should be able to give you the go-ahead in a week's time. Heil Hitler!'

Gruppenführer Wolff listened to Schellenberg's proposition with keen interest. Schellenberg did not enlighten him fully but told him enough to warrant the Gruppenführer's circulation of a memorandum couched in unmistakable terms.

So it came about that on 16 November 1939 thirty senior SS and police officers received a top secret circular for their personal perusal and attention. It opened with numerous references to the privilege of serving Führer and Fatherland, and went on to request the names of women and girls with the following qualifications:

(a) intelligence
(b) an attractive appearance
(c) a knowledge of foreign languages
(d) faith in National Socialism, and
(e) a liking for male company.

The thirty SS and police chiefs digested the contents of this circular with much wagging of heads, destroyed it as instructed, and made inquiries which all produced the same result—their discreet approaches were universally rejected. Before the fourteen-day dead-line arrived, all thirty had sent in a nil return. They were happy to have disposed of a tiresome chore, and happier still when they heard no more about it.

Schellenberg realised that Schwarz had laid an egg.

'Well,' he asked, when his subordinate reported total failure, 'what do we do now?'

Schwarz was—for once—destitute of ideas. Not so Schellenberg. 'I'll have a chat with Arthur Nebe and get him to mobilise the vice squad. They should be able to find us some intelligent amateur tarts we can put pressure on—girls who'll co-operate and keep their mouths shut.'

The conversation with Nebe took place the same afternoon, and the police chief promised his full support.

During the next few weeks, vice squad teams attached to CID

Headquarters and the municipal police forces were instructed to carry out a large number of raids and surveillance operations. Each report was submitted to close study by Schwarz and his assistants. Gradually, the Untersturmführer assembled a dossier which encouraged him to ask Schellenberg's permission to start work on converting the Pension Schmidt.

'How many girls do you have?' Schellenberg asked.

'About fifty worth inviting to a preliminary interview,' Schwarz reported.

'And how many will you need?'

'Eight or ten, I thought.'

'They'd better be good,' Schellenberg said soberly.

'They will be, sir.'

Schwarz meant every word. The Salon Kitty operation had become a point of honour with him. The longer he worked on the project the more certain he felt that it would provide an abundant source of valuable and otherwise inaccessible information.

He had talked to friends and acquaintances, SS men and outsiders, trying to discover what made men frequent brothels. He found out that patrons of such establishments were not socially stratified, that money and personal convictions had little bearing on their visits. However, his most important discovery was that, to many men, the prostitute's anonymity afforded their only chance of discussing personal problems with a patient listener—that discretion was the prostitute's daily bread.

Accordingly, Schwarz decided that even his future agents must be kept ignorant of the full picture. They were not to know that their conversations would be overheard but must submit a written report after every tête-à-tête with a public figure.

The women came from all over Germany, from Austria and the Protectorate of Bohemia and Moravia, from Poland and Danzig. They were between twenty and thirty years of age, good to look at, and endowed with above-average intelligence. Their languages, apart from German, included French, Italian, Spanish, English, Russian and Polish. Many of them were fluent in three or more.

One thing they all had in common : some dark episode in their past life which put them at the SD's mercy. Former drug addicts were represented, as were young women with an abortion behind them. Some candidates were convicted criminals, others professional prostitutes, some sexually abnormal, others over-sexed, but all regarded this peculiar undertaking as a possible means of escape from police pressure.

The preliminary meeting was held in the Stuttgart area, in a small hotel specially rented for the occasion by the SD. Untersturmführer Schwarz had occupied this hotel with his men and extracted a pledge of secrecy from the proprietors, who were loyal Nazis.

What followed was surely one of the strangest selection boards ever held under official auspices.

For hours on end, Schwarz and his men questioned the candidates on every conceivable subject, aided in their task by the finest experts the SS could produce—psychologists, psychiatrists, doctors, interpreters and university lecturers. The interviews continued for a week, by the end of which time the original fifty girls had been whittled down to twenty who measured up to Schwarz's standards.

The rejects were sent home and kept under constant police surveillance from then on. The twenty successful candidates fulfilled all the SD requirements. They were single and self-supporting, had few or no family ties, and had never—despite the odd blemish on their private lives—shown themselves hostile to National Socialism. Last but not least, they were exceptionally intelligent and spoke at least one foreign language.

All these qualifications were important, but almost more important was that of immediate availability.

Schwarz treated the remaining girls with studied courtesy, trying to form a human picture of his future agents. He impressed on them that they had a vital task to perform and made them swear that they would never discuss their activities or divulge information to an outsider. Their response to the news that they would be working for the SS and SD was universally favourable.

For another three days Schwarz gave lectures and tested the girls' reactions. He spoke of the enemy without and within, of the need for espionage and counter-espionage, of the sacrifices which everyone had to make in the cause of final victory. He also made it clear that their duties would frequently require them to have sexual intercourse with complete strangers. Unless he was much mistaken, the eyes of his aspiring Mata Haris shone with more than usual enthusiasm and curiosity when he broached this subject.

Untersturmführer Schwarz was pleased with himself and the world in general.

Chapter 4

New Year's Day 1940 dawned, and with it a growing conviction among the inhabitants of the Third Reich that they were part of a national success story. Goebbels saturated Germany and the occupied territories with propaganda, and the lightning victory in Poland provided specious justification for further military adventures. Hitler described in his New Year's proclamation to the Party and armed forces how Central Europe had been 'pacified', welcomed the 'homecoming' of Bohemia, Moravia and Memel, and hailed the restoration of the old German national boundaries secured by the war in Poland and the German-Soviet treaty of non-aggression and consultation.

The task of addressing the German people he delegated to his prime minister, Field Marshal Hermann Goering, who said, *inter alia* :

> . . . the concentrated strength of the Reich now turns against our enemies in the West, who forced this war upon us by their brutal determination to destroy us.
>
> The German nation enters the new year confident, hopeful and assured of victory. Problems of the utmost magnitude confront us. With unshakable faith in our own strength, we shall solve them and overcome all resistance. Fresh sacrifices are inevitable. We shall not evade them, for without sacrifice there can be no victory. We shall deploy the imperishable forces that flow from the depths of the German heart, every fibre of which clings lovingly to its homeland. . . .

Spencer Brown turned off the radio. 'Hollywood ballyhoo churned out by a handful of megalomaniacs,' he observed to the three men who were sharing a decanter of port with him. They were all British agents with admirable qualifications for service in Germany. They spoke perfect German and were familiar with the German way of life, partly because they had lived or studied in Germany for years and partly because they had received further instruction at a special Secret Service training centre. Before long, they were due to be sneaked into Germany to take up their duties on behalf of the British intelligence network.

'The Nazis are flying high,' drawled Roger Wilson, the youngest of the party.

'Oh yes, full of optimism and drunk with victory. Their war-machine is going flat out, and we're on the menu for 1940. It's ten to one they'll attack France the first opportunity they get.'

'How do you rate their chances?' asked Charles Richardson, an ex-Foreign Office man.

'Hard to say.' Brown pulled thoughtfully at his cigarette. 'I have a nasty feeling the French will crack.'

An uneasy silence fell. The four men sipped their port and stared into the open fire.

'Be that as it may,' Brown continued after a pause, 'HM Government needs better sources of information if it's going to guard against unwelcome surprises—and that's where we come in. You two will have to try and reach Germany via our embassy in Switzerland. Roger and I will do our best to get into the country from the Balkan end.

'We've given more thought to the best place for making contact in an emergency.

'A German Jewish refugee named Sam Lewis has been supplying us with some hot tips lately. According to him, the house of Freddy Horstmann—he was Hitler's ambassador in Brussels—has become a rendezvous for opponents of the régime. We're still double-checking because our contact with the circle was suddenly broken six months ago.

'Horstmann left the German foreign service on account of his wife, who's Jewish, but the diplomatic corps hasn't dropped him. He throws masses of parties attended by a wide variety of people.

'You can take it for granted that Horstmann is being watched. On the other hand, it's unlikely that the authorities associate him with espionage.

'If you use his place as a rendezvous, make sure your credentials are above suspicion. In any event, Horstmann is worth bearing in mind.'

'Tell us about this Kitty Schmidt woman,' said Richardson.

'Kitty Schmidt could provide us with a good rendezvous too,' Brown said. 'She runs a brothel in Berlin's West End. She helped Jewish refugees to get their money out of Germany over a period of several years. Then she got cold feet and tried to skip the country herself, but they nabbed her. Latest reports indicate that her establishment is doing better than ever. As you know, brothels make pretty good RVs—especially when they're exclusive and patronised by the top brass.'

Richardson shrugged. 'Seems to me her place would make a better RV than Horstmann's.'

'Both have their points,' Brown replied. 'At Horstmann's you'll meet people who oppose the Nazi régime and may be willing to supply information. The brothel may give us a chance to meet and swap information unobtrusively. Anyway, here's to the success of our mission and your continuing good health.' Brown's tone was almost flippant, but the look in his eye belied it.

The others raised their glasses and drained them.

Kitty's brothel was running like a well-oiled machine. The Christmas holiday brought a lull, of course, because many of her clients were at home with their families and in no position to think up suitable pretexts for a visit to the Pension Schmidt, but as soon as 1940 came in the age-old itch returned and business boomed.

Personal recommendations played their part. War-weary officers came knocking at the door of the Pension Schmidt in growing numbers, more than offsetting the absence of regular customers who had been drafted into the armed forces and posted elsewhere.

Morale seemed generally high. The men chucked their money around and consumed drink at a rate which quickly depleted Kitty's reserves. On her next weekly visit to Meineckestrasse she asked to see Untersturmführer Schwarz in person.

'Heil Hitler,' she said cheerfully, when she was ushered into the presence of her Svengali. 'I've got a problem.'

'What sort of problem?' Schwarz asked curtly.

'I need more wines and spirits. My stocks are at rock bottom and there's virtually nothing for sale. I don't want to use the black market for fear of drawing attention to myself, but the youngsters soak it up as if there won't be any left tomorrow—especially if they're home from the front.'

Schwarz thought for a moment. His plans couldn't and mustn't be allowed to fail for such a trivial reason. 'All right, I'll give you the name of a firm which will keep you supplied in future. Order what you need. Make sure you always have plenty of everything in stock and don't be mean with it. People are welcome to spread the word that you're always good for a drink—it'll boost the attractions of your establishment, won't it?'

'It can't fail to, Untersturmführer, but I'm not sure if we'll be able to cope with the rush. In my view, it's the quality of customers that matters, not the quantity. However, that's only a personal opinion.'

'In that case, raise your drinks prices high enough to scare away any undesirables.'

'As you wish.' Kitty screwed up her courage to make another request. 'Another thing, Untersturmführer. I report here every week on the dot. I'm not saying I'm a public figure, but lots of my clients know me personally. They may get the wrong idea if they see me traipsing in and out of here at regular intervals.'

'Well,' Schwarz said brusquely, 'what do you want?'

'I'd like your permission not to report in future.' Kitty paused for effect and added : 'In your interests as well as mine.'

It irritated Schwarz that her argument was a good one. He had been dealing with the Schmidt woman for nearly four months now, but would he ever really know her? He had tried to persuade himself that she was a worthless old madame, but her circle of friends and clients simply didn't warrant such a conclusion. There was her memory, too. She always seemed to know in advance what was necessary and what had to be done. He often found himself issuing instructions which matched her suggestions of a few days earlier.

'You'll be hearing from us,' he said, more curtly than he intended.

Kitty wondered if she had done the right thing, but four days later her routine visits to Meineckestrasse were discontinued.

The structural alterations posed greater problems than Schellenberg and Schwarz had foreseen.

A report from an SS-enlisted architect stated that the premises could not be successfully converted while they were in use. The

55

few quiet hours of the day offered no guaranteee of absolute secrecy.

'What now?' Schwarz asked his superior.

'There's only one way,' Schellenberg decided. 'We must close the place temporarily. Frau Schmidt and her employees will be sent on holiday and told to stay out of Berlin until we recall them. How long will the alterations take?'

'We should be able to complete them in ten days, Obersturmführer.'

'Very well, make an immediate start and don't waste a moment. I shall hold you responsible for ensuring that the work is carried out unobtrusively and in the strictest secrecy. The redecoration must be perfect—so perfect that nobody will spot the difference.'

'Certainly, Obersturmführer!' Schwarz raised his hand in salute and marched out of the office.

And so began the installation of one of the Central Security Office's major intelligence centres.

Walls were drilled and grooved to accommodate microphones and their leads, all of which ran to a provisional listening-post in the cellar.

Before the holes were finally grouted and sealed, a dress rehearsal took place. It went without a hitch. The walls were primed and hung with hessian, which was lightly skimmed with plaster.

Schwarz and his assistants even managed to obtain new wallpaper which matched the old. Technical experiments were then conducted to test the acoustics. They, too, went off to Schwarz's entire satisfaction.

The microphones were inset so high up the walls that a normal man could not reach them with his outstretched hand. Schwarz was keen to prevent suspicious eyes from spotting his secret too easily.

The listening-post was a masterpiece of ingenuity. As originally planned, the various leads were combined into a multi-core cable which ran along the guttering and down the drainpipe. Passing under the floor joists, they led from the reception rooms and bedrooms, via the corridor, to the separate cellar entrance belonging to Kitty's establishment. From there they ran straight into the cellar, newly subdivided by a solid brick wall. The major structural work did not attract attention because it was restricted to the nether regions of 11 Giesebrechtstrasse.

The listening-post itself contained five monitoring desks equipped with two turntables each. This made it possible, when necessary, to record conversations from ten rooms at the same time. Embedded in the walls of the drawing-room and parlour were two sets of eight microphones, each connected to a single pick-up. The seven bedrooms, Kitty's snuggery and the kitchen contained four microphones each, so only the bathrooms and WCs were without means of surveillance.

Schwarz was delighted with the result of his endeavours and proudly arranged a demonstration for Schellenberg's benefit. The Obersturmführer, too, was surprised by the excellent quality of the test recordings, which finally convinced him of the brothel's potential value as a source of information. Only one thing worried him.

'What about security?' he asked. 'Can you guarantee it?'

'I'd vouch for all the men who worked on the job,' Schwarz reported. 'I've used most of them for years. They're all SS men, and sworn to secrecy.'

'What about Frau Schmidt?'

'She doesn't even know the place has been spring-cleaned.'

'And the neighbours? You don't think anyone's spotted anything?'

'Nothing that matters, Obersturmführer. Officially, we've been carrying out emergency repairs in the cellar. Only a handful of people know, and the one comment we received so far was "About time too", or words to that effect. What's more, we've given the local inhabitants an air-raid shelter they can be proud of—right next door to the monitoring centre.'

'You seem to be enjoying yourself, Schwarz.'

Schellenberg's tone was faintly sarcastic, but his subordinate was far too preoccupied with his own achievements to detect the subtle dig. 'I am indeed, sir,' he said staunchly.

Schellenberg became serious again. 'How are the girls shaping?'

'Extremely well, sir.' Schwarz produced a photograph from his pocket. It showed twenty SS women auxiliaries lined up on parade.

'Who are they?' Schellenberg inquired.

'Our team. I had them inducted into the SS and made them

57

swear the usual oath of allegiance to the Führer. They're now members of the Waffen-SS seconded for duty with the SD. We're giving them basic military training as well as special tuition. From all I hear, they're keen as mustard!'

'Just occasionally, Schwarz,' said Schellenberg, 'your ideas are even brighter than mine.'

Schwarz turned up, unannounced as usual, at Kitty's holiday quarters outside Berlin.

'The accountant's here,' Elvira reported laconically.

Kitty knew that Schwarz meant business. She had developed an almost infallible capacity for scenting situations in advance.

The SS man gave her little time to indulge in presentiment. 'Come with me,' he said, as though commanding an SS company. 'You can have five minutes to pack.'

'May I ask where we're going?'

'Back to your place,' he replied sharply.

Kitty fetched her things and accompanied him to the car, filled with curiosity. They drove to 11 Giesebrechtstrasse, where a miraculous change had been wrought. The same rooms, the same wall-paper, the same curtains and carpets, but everything looked a little newer, smarter—more respectable, even.

Schwarz savoured Kitty's surprise without showing it. 'Renovations,' he said. 'You're going to foot the bill.'

'Me?' Kitty ventured to object. 'It must have cost a mint of money.'

'You can afford it, on your income.'

Kitty pondered for a few moments. She liked the new look, somehow, but couldn't refrain from asking : 'Why renovate the place? We were doing all right before.'

Schwarz shot her a brief, suspicious glance. She was always trying to pump him. 'In future,' he said, conscious that he must give her a plausible explanation, 'you'll be getting customers who may be even more finicky than your previous regulars.'

'How shall I recognise these new customers of mine?' she asked at length.

'If someone tells you he comes from Rothenburg, he'll be there on my recommendation.' Schwarz snapped his fingers at a non-descript man in plain clothes who had been trailing them with a bulky briefcase. 'Hand it over!' he barked.

'Yessir,' said the man, clicking his heels.

'Cut that out!' Schwarz told him sharply. He opened the briefcase and produced two large photograph albums, which he placed on the kitchen table.

They were albums of the kind Kitty used. The photographs they contained were of young women—blondes, brunettes and redheads—in suggestive poses which displayed their physical charms to full advantage. Each page carried a neatly typed list of personal particulars. It was all very efficiently done.

Kitty's jaw dropped. 'But I don't know these girls,' she said.

'You'll meet them in due course. Whenever someone uses the codeword Rothenburg, make sure you show him these albums, understand?'

'Yes,' she replied, marvelling at the precision with which he had arranged everything.

'When these girls are on the premises, book any expenses to us. When their gentlemen friends pay, take the money and remit it to me. We'll work out a way of compensating you—once you've paid off the cost of doing your place up.' Schwarz paused. 'All right, I'll say it again. Codeword Rothenburg means that you're only to show girls from these two albums. You know what'll happen if I find you've disobeyed my instructions.'

Kitty could guess. 'When will the first Rothenburger turn up?' she asked.

'Sometime soon—I don't know. Make sure your staff are on their toes, and keep your mouth shut. One slip and you've had it.' He turned abruptly on his heel, beckoned to his subordinate, and added as he was leaving: 'All right, don't let me hear any complaints.'

As soon as Kitty heard the door shut she returned to the kitchen and skimmed through the albums again. They were pretty girls. Although she knew almost every 'reputable' prostitute in Berlin, she recognised none of them.

It was as clear as daylight. The girls were SD agents whose job was to pump clients and report their findings to Schwarz and his men.

'Balls!' she said, loudly and with uncharacteristic vulgarity.

Unbeknown to her, Untersturmführer Schwarz was still in the building. He had gone downstairs to the cellar and disappeared through a door bearing the ominous inscription 'Danger—High

Tension Cables—Keep Out!' After negotiating two bomb-shelters, he emerged into a brightly lit chamber equipped with turntables.

'How was it?' he asked.

An NCO jumped up, grinning broadly. 'Loud and clear, sir. Would you like a sample?'

He put a record on and they listened to the dialogue between Kitty and Schwarz.

'Fine,' said Schwarz, 'that's enough. The reproduction is excellent. I'd like all the preliminaries recorded. Have the disks delivered to my office by 18.30 hours, right?'

'Certainly, sir!' The NCO clicked his heels and gave the Nazi salute.

There was virtually nothing to prevent the refurbished Salon Kitty from opening its doors to the public. The SD's Intelligence Service had embarked on one of its most audacious and elaborate ventures. The next few weeks would show whether the idea was workable.

Left alone with her thoughts, Kitty rang for Elvira and, in defiance of Schwarz's order to restrict her contacts with staff to a minimum, engaged the girl in conversation.

'Come in and talk to me, Elvira,' she said, trying to penetrate her new-found reserve. 'What's happening out front?'

'Nothing much,' the girl said diffidently. 'Only one customer so far.'

'Be an angel and make me some coffee—and bring a cup for yourself.'

Elvira disappeared. She was back with the coffee in five minutes, also a glass of schnapps which she placed beside Kitty's cup, unasked.

'What's that for?' demanded Kitty.

'You always need a schnapps when you've been with Herr Schwarz. Is he from the tax office?'

'Something like that,' sighed Kitty. 'Tell me a bit about yourself. We hardly exchange a word these days.'

'There's nothing much to tell. I do my work, then I go home —one day's much the same as another.'

'Don't you have a boy-friend?'

Elvira went pink. So that was the way the wind blew. . . . To judge from her behaviour, Elvira had never been an SD informer —Kitty was positive. But the boy-friend?

'Is he nice?' she asked casually.

Elvira's eyes shone. 'I'm not supposed to tell you anything, Rolf says, because you run a place like this. But he's smashing—all tall and blond, a proper SS man.' The words came out with a rush. 'I'm not sure yet, but I think he wants to marry me. . . .'

So she hadn't been mistaken. There was a man behind it, an SS man. That was how they'd got hold of Elvira. Kitty resolved to be even more careful in future. The business about the tax office was good. Schwarz really looked the part, and Elvira would be bound to pass it on to her SS boy-friend.

'Off to the kitchen with you, now,' she said at length. 'I have to fill out my tax return.'

Elvira went, only to return a moment later. 'Superintendent Kuhn to see you,' she announced gravely.

'Show him in,' Kitty said. It was a day of surprises, but the schnapps had put backbone into her. She greeted the policeman with her usual warmth.

'My dear Herr Kuhn . . .' Kitty's manner was regal. She turned to Elvira. 'A bottle of No 1,' then, to Kuhn : 'You will join me, won't you?'

'Delighted,' said Kuhn. 'I'm glad to find you in such good form, Frau Schmidt. By the way, where do you manage to get the champagne from these days?'

'Are you asking as a man or a policeman?' Kitty retorted. She laughed, filled with sudden bravado. Having plumbed Elvira's little secret, she might be able to get the measure of Kuhn as well. On the other hand, the superintendent might be a trap laid by Schwarz. What was it Schellenberg had told her? Not a word to anyone, be he friend, customer or policeman. Very well, if that was the game, she'd play it by the book.

Kuhn laughed back. 'You never see me as anything but a policeman. How's business? It's been ages since I called.'

He wondered whether to tell her about his adverse report on her attitude, but a pang of conscience dissuaded him.

'I still have some old stocks left, but I'll have to look around for another source of supply if the war goes on much longer,' Kitty said, in answer to his question about champagne.

Kuhn changed the subject. 'As a matter of interest, Frau

Schmidt, I'm not responsible for you any longer. All. . . .' He began to stammer. He had meant to say 'brothels' but could not bring himself to utter the word in Kitty's presence.

'All what?' she asked.

'Well, all checks are now being made by the SD, direct. I thought you might appreciate a little advance warning.'

Good old Kuhn. Kitty's knowledge of human nature told her that this was no trap. The man seemed sad, somehow, that he had been taken out of service and deprived of his pet preserve. Kitty saw that it would be unwise to tackle him on the subject of the SD. She longed to draw him out but was scared of making a blunder.

They sat there sipping their champagne in silence for a while, two ageing people who had been robbed of their professional enjoyment. Kuhn seemed to feel the loss even more than she did.

'You'll still drop in on me sometimes, won't you?' asked Kitty.

'It'll be a pleasure,' Kuhn assured her. Again he stopped short, as if even that remark was out of place. Then he stood up. 'I have to go now. All the best, Kitty, and many thanks for the bubbly.'

'You're welcome,' said Kitty, and escorted him to the door. She had no time to dwell on the events of the day because trade was picking up. It was all she could do to prevent clients from bumping into each other—something which few of them wanted to do in an establishment such as hers—but her ingenious 'one-way traffic' system proved equal to the occasion.

The Wholesale Drinks Corporation of Berlin normally dealt in lemonade and mineral waters only. From February 1940 onwards, it also supplied the Pension Schmidt with alcoholic beverages of high quality: French champagnes and cognacs, Scotch whisky and Polish vodka, château-bottled red and white wines, and a profusion of hard liquor.

Kitty had no idea that nearly seventy per cent of the Third Reich's entire soft drinks industry were controlled by the SS, but she was indifferent to her source of supply as long as it delivered the goods.

It sometimes puzzled her that she hadn't seen Untersturm-führer Schwarz for so long. On the other hand, she was delighted not to be presented with demands which might involve her in clashes with authority.

Her chief emotion was disappointment rather than surprise when, at the end of February 1940, Schwarz turned up with the abruptness which he no doubt cultivated on principle. Elvira ushered him in.

Schwarz strode into Kitty's snuggery and closed the padded inner door behind him.

'Well, Frau Schmidt,' he said without preamble, 'only another four weeks.'

Kitty felt her jaw drop stupidly. She realised that a new phase in her life was beginning and dreaded the unknown—the forbidden subject. She detested being in the dark about anything, but she was chary of asking questions. The memory of her fortnight's incarceration still hung over her like a chill cloud.

'May I ask what happens in another few weeks?'

'Four weeks, I said.' Schwarz could see she was dying to pump him and derived a sadistic pleasure from the fact that she didn't dare. 'Another four weeks and we're in business.'

Chapter 5

The Ordensburg at Sonthofen was normally reserved for officer cadets of the SS, but in spring 1940 it also housed a squad of young SS women auxiliaries who were being trained for a special assignment.

Their training programme was a tough and comprehensive one. It was not displayed on any notice-board and kept them well segregated from the officer cadet school, so the girls in mouse-grey uniforms attracted little attention.

Because they never left the school precincts, few people came into contact with them or had the chance to. They were driven to the rifle range in a closed bus, unlike the cadets, who marched there, and all their public appearances were similarly camouflaged and motorised.

Of no interest to the local inhabitants, they ceased to be a topic of conversation soon after their arrival. They simply didn't exist, which suited Untersturmführer Schwarz admirably.

Had anyone stolen a glance at their training schedule, he would have treated the young ladies with respect. It covered marksmanship, unarmed combat, first aid, foreign languages, lectures on venereal diseases and contraception, hairdressing, cosmetics, the art of conversation, political indoctrination, social etiquette, wartime economics and National Socialist policy, uniforms and decorations worn by the armed forces of all friendly powers, also unusual subjects such as the encoding and decoding of messages, intelligence techniques in general, domestic science and gastronomy.

Schwarz was well pleased when he inspected his creations in March 1940 and got them to demonstrate their skills. They were adept in striking up a conversation with members of the opposite sex in the shortest possible time, and even Schwarz caught himself falling for their wiles. He knew now that his bomb was well and truly primed. The time had come to detonate it.

Meanwhile, the new Salon Kitty was running in smoothly. Most of Kitty's regulars welcomed the renovation of 11 Giesebrechtstrasse.

No 'Rothenburgers' had turned up yet. Untersturmführer Schwarz had managed to shroud his project in such secrecy that, apart from a few insiders and the monitoring teams, no one had any inkling of the establishment's future function, and even initiates were only briefed on isolated features of the scheme. Workmen had been repeatedly switched and SS squads relieved and posted far from Berlin.

The SS technicians who manned the monitoring desks grew bored. A few weeks of duty turned them into acoustic voyeurs who could capture even the most softly whispered endearments on wax.

Early in April 1940, Schwarz—now a rare visitor to the upper reaches of No 11 Giesebrechtstrasse—dispatched his first guinea-pig to test the system's efficiency.

The guinea-pig was a young Obersturmführer in the Waffen-SS who had distinguished himself in Poland and was spending some home leave in Berlin. Schwarz had met him at a social function and tipped him off about the Salon Kitty. His name was Wolfgang Reichert. He came from Swabia, and was unmarried. 'Just say Rothenburg,' Schwarz told him, 'and you'll get the best girls on Kitty's books. You ought to sample them—they're really hot stuff.'

Wolfgang Reichert, thirsting after exploits of a non-military kind, took his advice.

The young officer presented himself just before 5 p.m. on 8 April 1940. Elvira opened the door to him in the customary way and ushered him into the small parlour. Business was slack at this hour.

'Is this your first visit?' she asked.

'Yes,' he replied, blushing a little. Eventually, he came out with the codeword.

Elvira cocked her head and smiled. Kitty had drilled her carefully. 'Rothenburg?' she repeated.

Reichert nodded. 'That's right.'

'One moment, please.' Elvira scuttled off to Kitty's snuggery. 'Rothenburg,' she whispered, as if imparting a state secret. She couldn't know that she was doing just that.

Kitty sank back in her arm-chair. The moment had come. All that surprised her was her total lack of surprise. Quite calmly, she went to fetch the two special albums from her desk. With a final reassuring glance at herself in the mirror, she made her way to the parlour.

'My dear boy,' she said affably, as she entered the room, 'let's go next door, shall we?' Seeing disappointment on the young man's face, she went on quickly : 'Don't worry, I only want to show you something.'

She took his arm and shepherded him into the drawing-room. 'Would you care for a drink? A café cognac, perhaps, or a glass of champagne?'

Reichert was still recovering from his initial misconception. 'Just a beer, thank you,' he stammered. The situation was new to him.

'Why not sit down?' Kitty suggested amiably. She wondered what Schwarz hoped to extract from the young man. He didn't look like a repository of dark secrets.

The young SS officer sat down, still diffidently, and Kitty put her albums on the table in front of him.

'The loveliest girls in Berlin work for me,' she said with some pride, opening the first album. Reichert hardly dared to look.

'Choose yourself a nice girl—take your time.' Kitty rose and rang for Elvira.

'A beer for our guest,' she said, no less amiably, when Elvira's head appeared round the door.

'Right away, madam,' trilled Elvira. She raced to the kitchen and back with weasel-like rapidity. Kitty had barely resumed her seat.

'That's what I call service,' said Reichert, who was slowly thawing out.

'We aim to please,' Kitty replied lightly. She turned to face him. 'Well, have you found something that appeals to you?'

The young Obersturmführer hummed and hawed, evidently finding it hard to commit himself. 'I was told by this friend of mine,' he said tentatively, 'that you had something to suit everyone. . . .'

Kitty rose to the occasion with ease. She donned her celebrated smile—half teasing, half reassuring—and leafed slowly through the two albums. 'Here, take a look,' she said at length. 'How about Ingelore? She ought to suit you—an adorable little blonde. Or what about . . .'

She never finished. Reichert was only too delighted to be spared the torment of further indecision. 'Yes, yes,' he cut in hastily, running a finger round the collar of his uniform tunic, which seemed to have become too tight for him, 'Ingelore sounds fine.'

'There you are, then,' chuckled Kitty. She picked up the phone and carefully dialled a number. Not having met any of her 'new girls', she was interested to see if there would be a reply.

'Yes?' said a female voice.

'Ingelore?' asked Kitty, and, when she received an affirmative answer, went on quickly : 'Kitty here. You're wanted. . . .'

'Very well,' said the stranger. 'I'll be with you in ten minutes.' There was a click and the line went dead.

'Another beer?' Kitty asked.

Wolfgang Reichert merely nodded. Schwarz was right—it really did seem to be a well-run establishment. Secretly, he made a mental inventory of his ready cash. He couldn't afford to overreach himself.

'Excuse me a minute.' Kitty got up and left the parlour. She went to her snuggery and rang for Elvira.

'There's a new girl coming,' she said. 'Show her in here for a moment before she goes on duty.'

Elvira tittered. 'Certainly, Kitty. Shall I take the young man another drink?'

Kitty ordered another beer and sat down in her arm-chair. She felt pleased with herself for the first time in ages. Schwarz, the secret service perfectionist, the sinister intruder into her thoughts and every-day life, had made a blunder. She resolved to nurse it until the time came to take advantage of it. She caught herself rubbing her hands with glee.

Then the door-bell rang and Elvira showed the new girl in.

'Where's the client?' was her sole greeting. Kitty scrutinised her. She was a pretty blonde with regular features and her hair done up in the Olympic roll which was currently in fashion.

'So you're Ingelore,' Kitty said conversationally.

'That's right,' the girl replied. She didn't seem disposed to chat. 'Where's the client?' she repeated.

Kitty remembered Schwarz and his orders. The Rothenburg girls were to be taken straight to their clients. She couldn't afford to make any mistakes at this stage, so she smiled at the newcomer and said: 'Come with me.'

She led the way into the drawing-room. The young Obersturmführer jumped up politely and clicked his heels. Ingelore's personal appearance had the desired effect.

For the first time, a friendly smile illuminated the girl's face. 'Good afternoon,' she said demurely, and waited for Kitty to introduce her.

'Allow me to present Fräulein Ingelore,' said Kitty.

'My pleasure,' said Reichert.

'Sit down, the pair of you—make yourselves comfortable.' Kitty waited long enough to see that Ingelore reacted promptly, then headed for the door. 'I'll send Elvira,' she added as she left the room.

Outside in the passage, she almost collided with Elvira.

'She's an amateur,' Elvira whispered.

Kitty rounded on her. 'If I catch you eavesdropping just once more, I'll fire you without a reference, understand?'

Elvira shuffled her feet and nodded.

'Stop pouting! Get in there and ask what they want to drink.'

Kitty would have liked nothing better than to eavesdrop herself, but she suppressed the urge rather than court trouble. She returned to the snuggery and dialled Schwarz's number. 'The first Rothenburger is here,' she reported, almost in military style. 'Shall I take any money from him?'

It was no news to Schwarz. The listening-post had already notified him and he was on the point of leaving to attend the opening performance in person. 'Yes,' he said tersely. 'Charge him fifty marks. No harm in letting him know you're expensive.' He didn't wait for a reply, simply rang off.

Schwarz drove to Giesebrechtstrasse in an inconspicuous Opel P4. He gained access to the air-raid shelter and listening-post via the rear courtyard.

The duty NCO jumped to his feet and saluted, but Schwarz gave him a genial wave. 'How's it going?' he asked eagerly.

'Our bird is hot stuff, but her boy-friend doesn't seem very quick off the mark. He sounds shy. He's been talking about the weather, his parents, going on leave—things like that.'

'Are they in the bedroom yet?'

'No, sir. They've been sitting in the parlour for half an hour, drinking champagne.'

'Good. Record every word just the same,' Schwarz commanded. 'The main thing is to test the system in action.' He pulled up a chair and sat down.

In fact, Schwarz's timing was perfect. Ingelore had finally prevailed on Wolfgang Reichert to accompany her to one of the bedrooms.

They would now see if the system worked. Would the agent manage to draw out the young SS officer in the way the Security Service hoped? Would Reichert divulge any military secrets, however unimportant? Would Heydrich's plan, refined by Walter Schellenberg and carefully implemented by Schwarz himself, come to fruition?

There was a deafening crackle in the headphones.

'What's that?' demanded Schwarz.

The NCO adjusted his ear-pieces. 'It always happens when doors are opened or shut, drinks deposited on trays, beds turned down—that sort of thing.'

'Can't you do something about it?'

'Not at the moment, sir.' The NCO gave an apologetic shrug. 'The microphones are adjusted so as to pick up every whisper. Incidental noises are unavoidable, I'm afraid.'

Schwarz realised that the man was right. Something else occurred to him at the same time. Once the Salon Kitty was in full operation, his men would be subjected to considerable mental stress. That meant shorter spells of duty, which in turn meant the employment of more men and a correspondingly greater risk of security leaks. He made a note to discuss the problem with Schellenberg.

For the moment, however, his attention was claimed by what was happening overhead.

Ingelore had ordered another bottle of champagne.

'Go easy,' said the young SS officer, 'I'm not too flush.'

The girl laughed. It was a nice, reassuring laugh. 'Silly boy,' she said. 'I like you. This bottle is on me.'

Reichert tried to protest, evidently because he found it hard to reconcile such a suggestion with his code of honour, but the girl silenced his misgivings with a kiss.

There ensued the usual conversation—the series of questions which every other customer put. Why did she do it when she could earn a 'respectable' living? He, Wolfgang Reichert, would help her to escape—help her to rediscover her lost innocence.

Schwarz's girl agents were trained to parry such questions. Ingelore launched into what Schwarz had christened 'mental massage'. She talked of the man who had got her pregnant and walked out, of her sick mother and drink-sodden father, of high rents and crippling debts.

It was an old but effective tale of woe, and one whose chief merit was to conjure up such a host of responsibilities that the customer, however sympathetic, swiftly reverted to the real object of his visit.

'Tell me about yourself for a change,' said Ingelore, embracing him tenderly. 'Have you seen any fighting yet?'

That was an effective gambit too. The young warrior could hardly resist this metaphorical tug at his sword-knot.

Schwarz was curious to see what would happen. He knew Reichert's background and had studied his personal file. How far would he go?

Wolfgang Reichert reacted normally. He expatiated on his parental home, his school days, his ambition to become an officer. He reminisced about the Hitler Youth, in which he had attained senior rank. Finally, he spoke of Führer and Fatherland. Somewhat nebulously, somewhat confusedly, he trotted out slogans which had been concocted by the Propaganda Ministry. He was obviously repeating them parrot-fashion, but he was talking. He became more relaxed, more responsive.

A satisfied smile settled on Schwarz's face. Even if nothing more emerged, this would be enough in itself to demonsrate that the method was well chosen.

'Ah, the Führer,' sighed Ingelore. 'What a wonderful man!'

SS-Obersturmführer Reichert was faithful to the Party line. Schwarz half-decided to make a transcript of what followed and forward copies to the Propaganda Ministry. It was a hymn of praise to Hitler couched in the simple language of a young officer.

'You put it so marvellously,' Ingelore said in an admiring tone, then cut the torrent short. 'Will you be staying long in Berlin?'

70

'No,' Reichert replied, lowering his voice. 'As a matter of fact, my leave ends tonight. I'm off to Flensburg.'

'Flensburg?' Ingelore sounded surprised that a battle-tried veteran like Reichert should be posted to a dreamy back-water like Flensburg.

The young officer's voice sank to a whisper. 'It's starting again soon—in the north.'

'You really think so?' Ingelore was whispering too. She was genuinely excited, convinced that she stood on the threshold of her first great success—that the young man was about to entrust her with top secret information. She could hardly wait to draft a long report on the subject, unaware that the SD were listening to every word. Her orders were to note clients' remarks in writing at the end of each assignment. 'Are we going to invade Sweden?' she asked.

'No, not Sweden,' he whispered back. 'I don't know for certain myself, yet, but it's my guess we'll occupy Denmark. I shouldn't really be saying all this—promise you won't tell anyone. . . .'

Ingelore sealed his lips with another kiss. She nestled against him. He felt the warmth of her body and inhaled her perfume. Assuaging his conscience with the thought that all would be common knowledge tomorrow or the day after, he abandoned himself to the pleasures of the moment.

Down in the cellar, the duty NCO had sprung to his feet. 'But that's terrible, sir!'

'Take it easy,' Schwarz commanded. 'I hold you personally responsible for ensuring that nothing of what you and your men overhear in the course of your duties leaves this room—not the smallest detail, is that clear? Any infringement is punishable by death. Have you impressed that on your men?'

'Yessir,' said the NCO.

'I'll take both the records with me,' decreed Schwarz.

SS technicians had recorded the entire conversation on wax disks. They packed them carefully in a cardboard box.

The couple upstairs had found their voices again. 'You were wonderful . . .' breathed Reichert.

'Will you write to me sometimes?' asked Ingelore.

'Of course. Where do you live?'

Ingelore jotted down an address. It belonged to a trustworthy person whose house Schwarz had designated as an accommodation address for all his agents. The girls ostensibly lived there as tenants, and Schwarz would be notified at once if a client presented himself at the door. He had forgotten nothing.

Satisfied, he took his disks and departed. He was aware, as he drove back to Meineckestrasse, that the SD's Intelligence Service had acquired an effective new weapon. His task now was to keep that weapon serviceable for as long as he could. Security was the chief problem.

Next day, as SD agent Ingelore was drafting her report, she heard the following radio announcement:

> Radio Berlin calling. Today, 9 April 1940, the High Command of the Armed Forces issued this communiqué: In order to counter current British violations of Danish and Norwegian neutrality, the German armed forces have undertaken the military protection of those countries. To this end, strong German formations of all arms this morning entered or landed in both countries.

All German radio stations proceeded to broadcast the text of the government's memorandum to Norway and Denmark. It began as follows:

> Contrary to the sincere desire of the German people and its government to live in peace and amity with the British and French peoples, and despite the absence of any reasonable grounds for mutual conflict, ruling circles in London and Paris declared war on the German people. . . .

Ingelore had listened to the announcer in breathless silence. She completed her report at top speed, checked through it carefully, and left her flat. She then took a taxi to the accommodation address and asked the housekeeper to notify Untersturmführer Schwarz.

Schwarz arrived about half an hour later, wearing plain clothes. He seemed to be in a bad mood.

But not for long, Ingelore told herself. Eagerly, she described the course of her first Rothenburg assignment and handed Schwarz her written report.

Schwarz flicked through the pages. Without removing his overcoat, he dropped into an arm-chair.

'When did you work on this SS officer?' he demanded curtly.

'Yesterday afternoon between 17.00 and 19.00 hours, Untersturmführer.'

'And when did the subject of Denmark crop up?'

'About 18.00 hours,' Ingelore replied truthfully.

'And what time is it now?' Schwarz's tone had acquired an edge.

The girl looked at her watch. '14.00 hours.' It dawned on her that she had been slow. 'I wanted to make my report as full as possible,' she said apologetically.

'So you sat on top secret information for almost twenty-four hours!' Schwarz jumped up and started to pace the room with a face like thunder. 'Do you realise what that means? Haven't you grasped what you're employed to do? Your job is to detect leaks in our security. Well, that was a leak, and you kept it to yourself for twenty-four hours.' He didn't shout. Every word was uttered in a normal tone which made it sound even worse. Schwarz hissed through his teeth like an angry snake. 'I shall have to consider whether to relieve you of your duties. I can't tolerate slackness and irresponsibility of this sort.'

Ingelore, who had been expecting a pat on the back, cringed. She realised what dismissal would mean. She knew that she was privy to confidential information, and she knew what the SS did with agents who fell into disfavour—it had been dinned into her often enough during her course of instruction. She was fighting for survival and she knew it.

'Untersturmführer,' she said staunchly, 'it won't happen again. I'll work round the clock in future. I'm sorry I didn't realise how urgent the matter was. It'll never happen again, believe me.'

Schwarz gave her a sidelong look and came to an abrupt halt. 'You'll be hearing from me,' he said, and turned on his heel. His car was waiting outside with an NCO at the wheel.

'Well, sir?' the man inquired, grinning. 'How did it go?'

'She trembled like a leaf, but her report seems accurate enough. She'll never put another foot wrong.' Schwarz was content with his mission and his tactics.

Schwarz was more than usually active during the next few days. Via agents and informers, diplomats and senior Party officials, War Office personnel and frequenters of salons such as those of the Osterroths and Freddy Horstmann, he circulated the magic word 'Rothenburg'.

Simultaneously, after consultation with Schellenberg, he busied himself with the extension of the monitoring service because he guessed that the whole venture would stand or fall by the efficiency with which listening-watch was maintained. He seldom contacted Kitty Schmidt throughout this period.

Kitty herself noted with covert satisfaction that a growing number of those who visited her establishment belonged to the upper crust, though she made herself equally agreeable to everyone. Thanks to her well-stocked and widely assorted cellar, the parties on her premises became increasingly gay and protracted.

Where Elvira had once greeted generals or senior diplomats with the awestruck deference due to a rare specimen, she now took them in her stride. The Salon Kitty was accustomed to receiving visitations from on high. Famous actors came too, which helped to relax the atmosphere and inject a certain sophistication.

One problem which arose after a few days was that of payment for services rendered. Kitty found it genuinely hard to differentiate between normal and 'Rothenburg' clients in this respect. Having no wish to court trouble, she decided to contact Schwarz by phone. To her surprise, he promptly agreed to meet her on Sunday, 14 April. She was told that she would be fetched by car and must be ready to leave by 2 p.m.

Kitty made herself so smart for the occasion that a stranger might have deducted twenty years from her real age. The car turned up punctually—it was an elegant Mercedes—and a driver in plain clothes conducted her downstairs.

'Allow me,' he said politely, opening the door for her.

Kitty had long ceased to be surprised at any of Schwarz's manoeuvres. The car drove down the Kurfürstendamm, turned into Grunewald and drew up at an underground station.

'Please wait here,' said the driver, and got out.

A few moments later he returned with Schwarz, who climbed in swiftly and unobtrusively. The car moved off again, small curtains in the rear masking its occupants from the gaze of outsiders.

Schwarz opened the conversation at once. 'All right, what's the trouble?' Kitty explained her problem while he listened attentively.

'This is turning into an expensive business,' he mused.

'The gentlemen who patronise us these days can well afford to pay normal prices,' Kitty said. 'Why rob them of the pleasure?'

'Very well,' Schwarz replied, 'I agree. Adjust your prices so the standard doesn't drop. You're probably right—some people may be put off your establishment if it's too cheap. Make a careful note of your takings, though—I'm a stickler for accuracy. What about the girls? How are they doing?'

Kitty could truthfully submit a glowing report. The Rothenburg girls behaved with far more decorum than the other members of her stable. Her only complaint was that they occupied the rooms for such long periods. It was bad for business, and she said so.

'Don't worry,' Schwarz told her. 'Just tot up their hours and submit an account.'

This was just what Kitty had been hoping to hear. She now knew where she stood and where her business interests lay. She felt almost grateful to SS-Untersturmführer Schwarz. Never before had such prominent figures frequented her premises, never before had the atmosphere seemed so sophisticated and refined, never before had her clients put away so much food and drink. If she hadn't known that it was all an iniquitous scheme on the part of the Security Service, things would have been positively ideal.

Schwarz ventured a compliment. 'You're looking radiant today, Frau Schmidt.'

'Thank you, Untersturmführer,' said Kitty. 'I ought to be getting back now. Do you mind if I take a taxi?'

Schwarz assented. They dropped her at the next cab rank and quickly drove on.

But Kitty didn't take a taxi after all. Spring was in the air and the sun shone serenely, inviting her to do what she had not done for many years. She walked home, at peace with herself and the world.

Chapter 6

Next day, 15 April 1940, the Salon Kitty started to make history.

The two clients who arrived just before 3 p.m. were Bernardo Attolico, the Italian ambassador, and Consul-General Wüster, head of the Southern Department of the German Foreign Office and one of the Ribbentrop's senior advisors. Kitty had previously received an urgent call from Schwarz, asking her to give them preferential treatment.

Kitty saw to it that Elvira put on a freshly starched cap and apron. Then she ran through her albums to see which girls she might recommend on the basis of her few days' experience. To her surprise, she found that two-thirds of Schwarz's girls spoke Italian. That, too, was noted in his albums with Prussian precision.

In response to the codeword 'Rothenburg', Elvira conducted the new arrivals straight into the drawing-room, where Kitty welcomed them with a bottle of vintage champagne.

She proceeded to submit her special selection, but the two men seemed more interested in having a quiet chat. 'We'll revert to that later,' said the ambassador. 'Can we talk here undisturbed, Signora?'

Kitty reassured him with alacrity, flattered that her establishment should have become a venue for diplomatic discussions.

She gave strict instructions that the two gentlemen were not to be disturbed. 'If you want anything, just ring.' She indicated the bell-push and took her leave.

Attolico looked round. 'Charming, quite charming,' he observed. 'An excellent suggestion of yours, my dear Wüster.'

'The Führer has set the première of Mussolini's *Cavour* for 9 May,' Wüster began. 'He wants to give his friend the Duce a treat—after all, 9 May is your Empire Day. The performance will be held at the State Theatre. Gustaf Gründgens is directing, so I think we can look forward to a really memorable production.'

'A magnificent achievement on your part, Wüster,' declared Attolico. 'The play would never have been staged at all without your wire-pulling behind the scenes.'

Wüster thanked him modestly. 'Don't forget Werner von der Schulenburg. He only started on the German version a month ago. Two weeks' work, and he had the play far enough advanced to submit it to the Duce. Fortunately, Mussolini only took three days to sanction its presentation in Germany under his name. Rehearsals have been going full speed ahead since then.'

The Italian ambassador nodded and took a sip of champagne.

'My only remaining problem,' Wüster went on, 'is the organisation of the première itself. That's what I wanted to discuss with you, Your Excellency.'

Attolico glanced at his companion and took another sip of champagne. Settling himself comfortably in Kitty's opulent armchair, he began to speak in a low voice.

'I'd like nothing better than to help you, my dear Wüster. We've always seen eye to eye on such questions, as you know, but this time Ciano insists on taking a hand. He plans to use the occasion as a pretext for buttonholing Hitler. The Duce is extremely agitated by Berlin's habit of keeping him in the dark. For instance, our first news of the occupation of Denmark and Norway came from radio reports. Ciano is worried about Axis co-operation. He intends to tax Hitler on the subject.'

'But Denmark accepted German protection,' Wüster objected feebly.

Attolico waved the remark aside. 'Denmark is secondary, Wüster. What matters is the state of German-Italian co-operation. When do you think I can get Ciano a secret interview with Hitler?'

Wüster was astonished. 'You mean your Foreign Minister won't be paying an official visit?'

'There's no time to arrange one. Ciano wants to see the Führer in the next three days.'

'This is a little disconcerting, Your Excellency,' Wüster said. 'I'll gladly speak to the Chancellery and request an appointment, but I naturally can't guarantee anything. . . .'

'What if you spoke to Ribbentrop?' suggested Attolico. 'He's reputed to have the Führer's ear at the moment.'

'I'll do my best, Your Excellency.' Wüster couldn't bring himself to say more.

Attolico laughed. 'Very well, let's devote ourselves to the joys of existence. This place seems perfectly equipped to banish the cares of every-day life.'

Wüster nodded and rang the bell. Kitty answered it in person, a chore which she would not have relinquished to Elvira at any price.

'Well, gentlemen,' she said with a disarming smile, 'have you finished your secret negotiations?'

Wüster raised his eyebrows but took her flippant remark in good part when he saw Attolico smile.

Kitty submitted her albums and the choice was quickly made. She withdrew to telephone, dispatched Elvira with another bottle of champagne, and sat down to await the agents' arrival.

The two girls, whose cover names were Brigitta and Barbara, appeared within five minutes.

'Your clients are the Italian ambassador and a senior official from the Foreign Office, ladies,' she told them briefly before conducting them to the drawing-room.

The gentlemen approved. Champagne flowed and canapés were served. There was a general retreat to the bedrooms and everything went off swimmingly.

As the two men were leaving, Attolico said to Wüster: 'I'm sure this place would appeal to Count Ciano.' That was as far as he went. Being a diplomat, he was used to expressing himself with delicacy.

They parted in the Kurfürstendamm. The Consul-General hurried to his office in the hope of catching Ribbentrop. He could not have known that things were already on the move.

It took the SD men on listening-watch only a few minutes to grasp the potential importance of the conversation between Wüster and Attolico.

While they were recording it, the duty NCO telephoned Meineckestrasse. He got through to Schwarz immediately and informed him of what was coming over the wire.

'Bring the disks here at once,' Schwarz ordained.

He employed the ten-minute delay to notify Schellenberg. By the time the Italian ambassador and his German companion were disporting themselves with Brigitta and Barbara, their preliminary conversation was issuing from a record-player in Schellenberg's office.

Schellenberg reacted promptly. He and Heydrich notified Himmler, who got in touch with Ribbentrop by phone. Within an hour, they had all assembled at the Chancellery for a conference with Hitler.

Attolico and Wüster were just saying goodbye in the Kurfürstendamm.

The Salon Kitty had passed its first test with flying colours.

During the early 1940s, most of Berlin's embassies and legations, trade missions and consulates were situated in Rauchstrasse.

In the midst of such illustrious company, Rauchstrasse boasted a 'salon' which claimed the Gestapo's particular interest and attention. Its proprietors gladly arranged introductions between pretty but impecunious young girls and well-heeled but lonely foreign diplomats, though they took good care to ensure that no intimacies occurred on their own premises.

The proprietors were a cheerful, sociable couple with a healthy bank balance (each 'introduction', as they termed it, brought them an advance payment of ten marks, and it was testimony to the loneliness of foreign diplomats in Berlin that they arranged as many as a hundred contacts daily). They were not averse to a friendly chat, and the relaxed atmosphere that reigned in their establishment soon made it a rendezvous for habitués who were prepared to do more than discuss the weather over a thimbleful of sherry. Their conversation was not confined to hints. They swapped personal experiences, and it was only natural that these experiences, most of which involved Nazi bigwigs, should not have been invariably favourable. In short, many of their exchanges betrayed a certain dissatisfaction with the régime—yet another reason for the Gestapo to infiltrate their circle with undercover agents who could steer the conversation and elicit items of interest.

German Military Intelligence under Admiral Canaris had likewise developed an interest, albeit minor, in the Rauchstrasse 'salon', and Major-General Egbert von Bentivegni, head of counter-espionage, had instructed Colonel Rohleder of Department IIIF to keep an eye on the diplomats' home-from-home.

Department IIIF, it should be noted, styled itself officially 'Defence against Foreign Services—Counter-Espionage' and was to some extent an independent secret service with its own agents and methods. The department's main field of activity was counter-espionage against openly or putatively hostile military intelligence services and their command centres. IIIF deliberately infiltrated enemy intelligence and counter-intelligence services with the aim of detecting, combating and neutralising such organisations, their methods, plans, agents and communications networks, also the traitors who were in contact with them. It sometimes managed to 'turn' an agent and enlist him in its own ranks. IIIF was, so to speak, an anti-secret-service secret service.

From that aspect, the Rauchstrasse 'salon' represented a sort of social club for friendly adversaries.

Lljubo Kolchev, the Rumanian embassy's new deputy press attaché, was aware of all this when he emerged from 26 Rauch-strasse after lunch on 16 April 1940. Having just reported to his future superior, Raoul Bossy, the Rumanian ambassador in Berlin, and exchanged a few inconsequential civilities, he was bound for the German-Rumanian Chamber of Commerce at 38 Unter den Linden, Berlin NW7. It must have occurred to him to pay the neighbouring 'salon' a quick visit, because he was spotted there that afternoon. He evidently met a friend there, too, because he left the building relatively early—towards 5 p.m.—in the company of an unidentified stranger. The two men strolled casually across to the Tiergarten and were soon lost from view among the greenery.

'How are things, Roger?' the stranger asked quietly. 'I get the impression you're doing all right.'

Roger Wilson, alias Lljubo Kolchev, nodded. 'I'm the Rumanian deputy press attaché. It took a bit of arranging, but here I am. My cover's pretty good, I reckon. What's new with you?'

The other man was Spencer Brown, head of Wilson's operational group. Brown had been in Berlin for a month, carefully reconnoitring in the guise of an engineer employed by the Borsig Corporation.

'I won't be able to survive long as a civilian,' he murmured. 'The Huns are putting everyone into uniform. I'll try and acquire a safer identity, but don't worry about me. Richard and Charles are still in Paris. They've made two attempts to get in over the Swiss frontier, so far without success, and the Siegfried Line is buttoned up tight. We'll have to go ahead without them.'

Brown paused and looked round.

'Something's in the air—I don't know what, exactly, but I can smell it. The Germans have been wallowing in triumph since the occupation of Denmark and Norway. Even their senior government officials aren't immune to the virus. They think Hitler's the greatest warlord of all time—an infallible genius who can't help winning. He's obviously contemplating a blow in the West, but where and when? It's our job to find out.'

He looked round again.

'We won't meet in future. Not a sign of recognition if we bump into each other. If we're thrown together by chance, we'll speak German like a couple of strangers, no matter what happens. Got it?'

Wilson nodded. 'How shall we swap information?'

'Via SOE in London. Watch your security check—it's our only form of insurance. Any questions?'

'No questions.'

'In that case, good hunting.' Brown made sure they were unobserved, then turned and strode off.

Escorted by Attolico, his ambassador in Berlin, Count Ciano conferred with Hitler, Ribbentrop and Himmler. The Italian Foreign Minister was not a man to beat about the bush. He voiced his worries without ceremony. He was concerned about the lack of consultation between the two dictators, about developments in Scandinavia, about rumours that Holland was to be invaded, about the attitude of the Japanese. Everything Ciano said betrayed his fear that Hitler might deprive Italy of her jackal's share of the feast.

For his part, Hitler made a long and noncommittal statement assuring the Duce of his eternal and undying friendship. He dismissed the Italian Foreign Minister a good hour later, having conveyed no more than he intended to convey, which was precisely nothing. Although Ciano was quite aware of this, it gave him a certain satisfaction to have imposed his presence on Hitler at short notice and without long-winded diplomatic preparations. He was therefore in high spirits when he returned to the Italian embassy and joined Attolico in his study.

'Well, Bernardo, and what does Berlin have to offer a poor overworked mortal like me?'

This was just what Attolico had been waiting for. A few discreet questions convinced him that, in his present mood, the Foreign Minister would find a visit to the Salon Kitty just to his taste.

They wasted no time. Attolico phoned Wüster and Wüster phoned Kitty Schmidt. When Ciano's party reached Giesebrechtstrasse at about 7 p.m., not only had the drawing-room been reserved for the occasion, but a bevy of girls were swaying rhythmically to the background music of a piano. Champagne corks popped, glasses frothed, and caviare and lobster canapés helped to mellow Ciano's mood still further.

He politely asked where the ladies had acquired such fluent Italian and was intrigued to learn that they were all of German blood. Less than an hour later he slipped away, taking one of the girls with him.

Kitty showed him into No 7, the best room in the house, and Elvira brought another bottle of champagne. That met the Italian Foreign Minister's requirements, at least where room service was concerned.

While Ciano and his companions were retiring to bed with their hostesses on the third floor of No 11 Giesebrechtstrasse, an atmosphere of tense expectancy reigned in the cellar.

Untersturmführer Schwarz had come to supervise his team in person. His best men had been detailed for duty that evening— every one an expert in the field of communications, radio engineers or signallers with an ear so acute that they could isolate and understand one of six voices talking simultaneously.

The first scraps of conversation came down the wire from Room No 7. Ciano and his girl were speaking Italian.

'What's he saying?' Schwarz asked the SS interpreter whom he had taken the precaution of bringing along.

The man made a few short-hand notes. His face was grave.

'Well, what is it?' insisted Schwarz.

'You want me to translate verbatim?' asked the interpreter.

'Fire away, man! That's an order!'

' "Your Führer is a two-faced hypocrite," ' the interpreter began to recite in a monotone. ' "I forced him to see me. I know exactly what his plans are, but the Duce won't believe me. He's in for a rude awakening one day. . . ." Now the girl: "What's going to happen?" Ciano: "He'll invade Holland and bring the world in against him." The girl: 'Will he win?" Ciano: "Luck's on his side at the moment, but Germany doesn't have the resources. Where's Hitler going to get the men and equipment to occupy the whole of Europe? Forget it—you're a pretty little thing." '

Schwarz silenced the interpreter with a gesture and turned to the duty NCO. 'These disks must go straight to the Central Security Office. I want them transcribed and translated, even if we have to work all night. Obersturmführer Schellenberg must have the German transcript on his desk first thing tomorrow morning, is that clear?'

Heydrich had every reason to be pleased with his intelligence chief when the latter called to submit his report on Ciano's visit to the Salon Kitty. He came to meet Schellenberg with both arms extended.

'Congratulations, Sturmbannführer. . . .'

Schellenberg's eyes widened at the last word.

'Yes,' Heydrich went on, waving Schellenberg into a chair. 'I intend to promote you on 20 April. I've no doubt Himmler will give his approval.'

This meant that Schellenberg had skipped the rank of Hauptsturmführer. 20 April was the Führer's birthday, a day when decorations were conferred and promotions announced.

Schellenberg deposited his Ciano material on Heydrich's desk. 'The Salon Kitty is developing into a mine of information, Gruppenführer. Visitors from the Foreign Office, the War Office and the Propaganda Ministry are positively queuing up to unload their intimate secrets. Our monitoring centre can hardly continue to operate from 11 Giesebrechtstrasse without detection.'

'What do you suggest?' asked Heydrich.

'I'd like to transfer it to Meineckestrasse. We've already explored the technical problems involved. The necessary cables and line amplifiers could be installed by the Post Office. The connections inside the building would have to be made by our own people for security's sake. All in all, I don't see any real problem.'

Heydrich stroked his jaw for a moment. 'How long do you think the place can continue to operate?'

'So far, only three people are acquainted with the full set-up. You, Gruppenführer, myself, and Untersturmführer Schwarz, our technical supervisor. I see no need to widen the circle. From that angle, there's no reason to suppose that our source will ever run dry.'

'And what will the Post Office authorities say if they're asked to lay a heavy cable in an unimportant area of the city? They'll smell a rat and start nosing around.'

'I've thought of that too, Gruppenführer. Fortunately, Brigade-führer Kaltenbrunner lives at 12 Giesebrechtstrasse, next door. Being a Reichstag member and head of the entire Austrian security service, why shouldn't he require direct lines to a large number of official departments? Even a Post Office engineer should swallow that idea. I'd like to use it as an official pretext.'

Schellenberg's keen intelligence was a constant source of wonder to Heydrich. He literally seemed to overlook nothing.

'Very well,' he agreed. 'But you're personally responsible to me for the maintenance of absolute secrecy.'

The newly fledged Sturmbannführer rose. He knew Heydrich inside out. At the door he paused and froze to attention with his arm raised. 'Heil Hitler, Gruppenführer!'

Chapter 7

On 10 May 1940, Hitler issued the following proclamation to his troops on the Western Front:

> Soldiers of the Western Front!
> The hour of the most decisive struggle for the future of the German nation has struck. . . .
> The struggle that is beginning today will decide the fate of the German nation for the next thousand years.
> Now, do your duty.
> The German people and its good wishes go with you.

Fanfares and special communiqués spewed from the Greater German Radio. Hitler's run of victories appeared to be continuing, this time in the West.

The Rumanian embassy in Berlin registered this fact with concern. Hodos, chief of the cultural and press section, together with press councillor Pintea and his new attaché Lljubo Kolchev, carefully compiled all the news and information available to them.

As a trained British Intelligence agent, Kolchev did not find it hard to form a swift assessment of the situation in Berlin. His personal documents revealed that he had been educated at Eton, so many diplomats and hostesses in the German capital welcomed the new arrival as someone who had interesting things to say on the subject of England, the English, and their possible future behaviour. In less than three weeks, Kolchev had a fair idea of whom he could trust and whom he could not.

He quickly found a smart flat in the Kurfürstendamm, too small to allow him to throw parties on a grand scale but large enough for the entertainment of individual guests, some of whom visited him under cover of darkness and stayed the night.

He also cast an eye over fashionable haunts such as Freddy

Horstmann's, the Osterroth residence, other Berlin 'salons', and —needless to say—the Salon Kitty.

Having learnt to look and listen before opening his mouth too wide, Kolchev introduced himself to the Salon Kitty under the pseudonym 'Baron von Itter'. He was surprised to meet such a wide selection of Berlin notabilities there—surprised and professionally intrigued. This prompted him to concentrate his attention on the Salon Kitty and spend more time there than anywhere else. Casual conversations with Kitty Schmidt yielded nothing of note. Then, through an acquaintance in the German Foreign Office, he was given the code word 'Rothenburg'. In the course of time he slept his way through both Kitty's special albums and became suspicious.

Roger Wilson, alias Lljubo Kolchev, alias Baron von Itter, never exposed himself or did anything to threaten his false identity. He was invariably polite and disarming, but his tentative inquiries got him nowhere because the notorious 'salon' seemed to be surrounded by an impregnable wall of silence.

This intrigued him still more. He suspected that the Salon Kitty was an intelligence clearing-centre of the first order, but the key to the problem evaded him.

Then chance came to his aid.

Shortly after the start of the German campaign in France, he tripped over a cable outside 11 Giesebrechtstrasse and would have fallen if a strong hand hadn't caught him by the elbow.

'Much obliged to you,' Kolchev said. He brushed some dust off the hem of his coat and raised his hat. 'Thanks a lot.'

The strong hand belonged to none other than Schwarz. Kolchev's training told him that the man was in some way connected with the cable-laying operation. Nothing in his manner betrayed it, but at that moment a bell rang in his central nervous system and he knew that he had bumped into a colleague. In fact, Schwarz had only dropped by for a few minutes to check on his men's progress.

Kolchev strolled leisurely to the Kurfürstendamm, where his steps quickened. He sought out one of the few available taxis, dangled a banknote under the driver's nose and directed him to a corner where he could keep Schwarz under observation.

It wasn't long before Schwarz climbed into his little Opel P4 and drove straight to Meineckestrasse.

Kolchev could only wag his head at Schwarz's carelessness. He didn't like dealing with amateurs because they were dangerously unpredictable, and this man was an undoubted amateur.

He chewed the matter over. The helpful stranger belonged to the German Security Service, and cables were being laid outside the Salon Kitty. Kolchev was a quick thinker. Within seconds, several pieces of the puzzle fell into place. Of course! The brothel's exalted clientèle, the codeword, the choice girls with their over-intelligent conversation and keen interest in current affairs, the Post Office engineers and their SD supervisors—everything fitted.

Thoughtfully, he returned to his flat and drafted a message for London. It was a hot piece of information. The SD were even more dangerous than he had been led to expect. Only gifted amateurs like the members of the SS security service could have devised and executed such a plan.

Kolchev could hardly wait to transmit his news to London and request further instructions. He passed the message via a dead letter-box. The answer came back four days later, during which time he maintained an unobtrusive watch on the Salon Kitty. Suspicion yielded to near-certainty as he noted the excellent quality of the materials used and the men who carried out the final connections. He would have bet anything that they were soldiers in disguise. In fact, they were SS signallers in civilian clothes.

He also noted the fact that Ernst Kaltenbrunner lived next door at 12 Giesebrechtstrasse—a pure coincidence which at first confused him.

London's reply took the form of an order: 'Avoid doing anything which may impair the Salon Kitty's value as an intelligence source. Try to establish closer contact and tap the flow of information.'

Kolchev-Wilson's instructions were as clear in theory as they were difficult to carry out in practice.

Fortunately, he received some moral support. A few days later his door-bell rang. There was a beggar outside, an old man who stood with his head slightly bowed, looking up at him from under his brows. His cupped hand contained a coin.

Kolchev nodded at him. 'Hungry? Come in and have a bowl of soup,' he said loudly, in German. One could never tell.

It was Spencer Brown.

'We're all alone,' said Kolchev-Wilson. Brown straightened up and looked round.

'Nice place. I hear you've struck lucky. London sent me. What exactly gives at this Salon Kitty of yours?'

Wilson told him as much as he knew.

'Interesting,' Brown said ruminatively. 'What's your plan of campaign?'

'I'll try and endear myself to one of the girls. After all, I'm young, unattached, and friendly to the German cause—the perfect partner for a patriotic German girl, even if she is an agent.' Wilson chuckled.

Brown sank gratefully into an arm-chair and massaged his eyes, as he always did when he was thinking hard. He seemed to reach a decision. 'I like the idea, but ease yourself in gently or you'll attract attention—and your niche here is safer than mine.'

'How about the other two?' Wilson asked. 'Haven't they reached here yet?'

'They're back in England—they never made it. Our bosses in London are so worried by the German advance they ordered them home. I'm afraid we're on our own.'

Wilson said something unworthy of an ex-public school boy.

Heydrich, Schellenberg and Schwarz had acquired two unwelcome partners—two professionals who were determined to profit from the intelligence business without investing anything in return.

The transfer of the monitoring centre was completed by 18 May 1940.

Untersturmführer Schwarz reorganised the Salon Kitty operation, which continued to expand under the auspices of Department VI, Central Security Office. It fell into the following categories:

1. Intelligence source, meaning the Salon Kitty itself.
2. Personnel. All agents lived in the immediate vicinity of the Salon Kitty and could, if necessary, reach the place on foot within ten minutes.

Every agent had to submit a written report immediately after completing each 'assignment' and deliver it to the cover address.

The agents had no idea that all their conversations were

monitored by microphone and, if important, recorded on wax disks.

Each agent had to report once a week for a medical examination and once a month for routine briefing at the cover address.

All letters addressed to agents were opened and examined at headquarters prior to delivery. In the case of 'official correspondence', answers were usually dictated by the authorities.

Every agent was aware that failure on her part would mean liquidation.

In their spare time, agents had to undergo further training, improve their knowledge of foreign languages and study Party directives.

All leave was cancelled until further notice, and very few exceptions were made.

Agents were forbidden to contact each other. They only met on duty, viz. at the Salon Kitty.

All social intercourse with Salon Kitty staff was prohibited, the only exception being Kitty Schmidt herself.

In the event of illness or other special circumstances, an agent had at once to notify the cover address.

3. The monitoring centre was now located at 10 Meinecke-strasse, headquarters of Department VI, Central Security Office, where premises were adequate to the maintenance of a permanent listening-watch.

The monitoring centre was manned by two dozen trained SS signallers divided into three regular watches and a stand-by shift. The latter was available for special use when traffic was particularly heavy or members of the regular watches went on leave.

The listening-post had maximum security rating and was disguised as a switchboard. Each technician was individually sworn to secrecy on the subject of his duties.

The listening-post continuously monitored all conversations conducted in the reception rooms and bedrooms of the Salon Kitty.

In doubtful cases, conversations were recorded live. Pick-ups and wax disks were available to all personnel on listening-watch, whose duty it was to make a brief note of the subject of each recorded conversation, insert it in the record sleeve, and hand it to the duty NCO before going off watch.

Any SS technician who thought he had recorded information

of particular urgency was instructed to alert the duty NCO forthwith. The latter then decided whether or not to notify Schwarz's department.

Personnel were strictly forbidden to discuss what they overheard.

4. The Control Section, later called the Records Section, kept an inventory of disks and agents' reports, made transcripts of important passages and translated them where necessary.

The contents of disks were checked against the contents of agents' reports. Any discrepancies were carefully noted and added to the personal file of the agent concerned. Major discrepancies were reported to Schwarz's department on a special form.

The Control Section also maintained a card index of particulars relating to the persons whose conversations were monitored.

5. Schwarz's department, which was directly and exclusively subordinated to Sturmbannführer Schellenberg, undertook the preliminary evaluation of incoming material and submitted a daily report on its probable significance and importance.

It also wielded executive authority over the girl agents, the SS listening-post technicians and Control Section personnel, supervised the cover address, organised medical examinations and issued all relevant orders.

All written correspondence, in so far as any proved necessary, was checked at regular intervals and destroyed.

Schwarz's department was not authorised to report direct to any office other than that of Schellenberg or, in his absence, Gruppenführer Reinhard Heydrich.

This rigid administrative framework was essential to the success of the Salon Kitty venture.

Chapter 8

Unobtrusively and under conditions of the strictest secrecy, the Salon Kitty had been dovetailed into Walter Schellenberg's large but close-knit intelligence network.

Besides attracting information from all quarters, it offered a means of checking on diplomats, Party officials, members of the government and armed forces. Schellenberg hoped that it would soon lead, in addition, to the exposure of enemy espionage networks. He was shrewd enough to realise that brothels, and especially brothels like Kitty Schmidt's, were bound to attract agents of other nations. No rendezvous could have seemed more innocuous, secure or informal than an establishment of this nature.

As for Kitty herself, she had come to terms with the new situation. Business boomed and her 'salon' became the haunt of pro-German diplomats, German generals and other senior officers, Party bosses and government functionaries.

She knew, or at least guessed, that some of her girls were SD agents. She also knew that she must carry out the orders of Walter Schellenberg and Untersturmführer Schwarz to the letter, but she herself received no fresh instructions worth mentioning.

Kitty still felt worried sometimes. She itched to confide in someone and discuss the whole matter with a third party, but the threats of the SS were too deeply etched into her mind for her to unburden herself, even to a relative or close friend.

So she let matters take their course.

Life was kind. Consignments of food and drink continued to arrive regularly, and there were no shortages. The girls selected by Schwarz proved quiet, sober and pleasant to work with. There was never a squabble over money, never any jealousy or ill-will over a client. Commercially, things could not have been better. Kitty regularly received her licence from the brothel surveillance department of the CID. Her knowledge of politics was limited to what she heard from clients. She knew most of what was going on in war-time Germany, but it did not affect her greatly either way.

She consorted with her friends as before, rising steadily in their estimation as her clientèle became more distinguished. She had a lot of acquaintances, not all of them patrons of her establishment, but kept them at arm's length. The risks of intimacy were too great, and she had no wish to expose herself to attack by Schwarz and his henchmen. This did not present many problems because everyone acknowledged that the proper supervision of her establishment left her little time for personal relationships.

Fifty-eight years old but still 'pushing forty' in appearance, well-groomed and charming, helpful and good natured, tactful and discreet—such was Kitty Schmidt in the spring of 1940.

On 10 May 1940 Hitler embarked on a new series of successes. The German air force launched simultaneous raids on 72 enemy airfields in Holland, Belgium and France. The surprise effect of these mass attacks was such that it took the Air Force High Command a fortnight to quantify the damage inflicted. 389 enemy aircraft had been destroyed on the ground, many runways put out of commission and hangars set ablaze. The air bases at Metz, Nancy, Reims, Romilly, Dijon and Lyons were particularly badly hit.

The same day brought a change of government in London. Reuters announced from the British capital that Chamberlain and his colleagues had resigned. Churchill became premier and made Parliament his famous offer: 'I would say to the House, as I said to those who have joined this Government, "I have nothing to offer but blood, toil, tears and sweat." ' It was clear to him and the British people that the United Kingdom had entered the firing line at last.

Baron von Itter was a welcome guest at the Salon Kitty. He was courteous, forthcoming and open-handed, a dazzlingly handsome young man who could have wormed his way with ease into the bed and affections of any respectable German girl but preferred sexual variety instead—or so it appeared from his frequent visits to the Salon Kitty.

Itter made a point of chatting to Kitty every time he patronised her establishment. The subjects they discussed were trivial, but a casual friendship gradually grew up between them.

Itter made a particular impression on the Rothenburg girl known as Brigitta. Brigitta, who was twenty-two and equipped not only with fluent French and English but a superb figure, tried to claim his exclusive interest.

It was hard, at first. Whenever she got the young baron alone in one of the bedrooms he came straight to the purpose of their encounter and seemed reluctant to linger afterwards. Furthermore, he was fickle. Brigitta was a little hurt by this because, despite all her undoubted merits as an agent, she considered herself irresistible as a woman.

Reports on the baron multiplied in Schwarz's files, but nothing important or remarkable came to light. Itter was completely ignored, a fact which he almost resented. He even began to wonder if he had jumped to the wrong conclusion about the cable-laying operation, so he decided to lure his enemies into a trap. He played along with Brigitta, flirted with her madly, and allowed her to detain him for longer periods. At the same time, he couldn't deny that she appealed to him physically.

He tried to pump her about her background, and Brigitta eagerly recited the life-story which Schwarz had invented for her. It was a good one.

'Three years ago I fell in love with a foreigner,' she told him, '—a Frenchman from Paris who was working here. I became infatuated with him. Before he left he said he wanted to marry me and asked me to join him in Paris. Like a fool, I believed him.

'A few weeks later I took the train to Paris. He met me at the Gare de l'Est and suggested that we celebrate over a few drinks. We drove to a gloomy little bar in Montmartre, where we met some friends of his. I must have drunk too much, because I suddenly passed out. Either that or they put something in my champagne—I don't know for sure. When I came to I was in bed in a hotel room with three men sitting there. I was naked and they didn't have much on. One of them said they'd all had me, and I had plenty to learn.

'Next, I was made to "service" Charles—that was my boyfriend. I didn't understand at first, but I soon found out. They held me down and made me do it for him.

'I tried to slip away to the German consulate, but they beat me up so badly I had to stay in bed for three days. Then they sent more men to me. It was always the same. Sometimes I tried to get one of the men to inform the police, but my French wasn't good enough in those days.

'I stuck it for a year, then I escaped. I knew the ropes by that time, and I'd managed to save a little money. Eventually, I got to Berlin. . . .'

Brigitta sobbed a little, overcome by the sad tale and her telling of it.

Baron von Itter patted her arm sympathetically. 'But couldn't you have picked up where you left off?'

'That's what I hoped. . . .' Brigitta sank back against the pillows with her hands clasped behind her head. Her young breasts rose and fell with a steady rhythm, her eyes gazed dreamily into the far distance. 'The first thing I did was to go to my parents and tell them everything—after all, they hadn't heard from me for a whole year—but they threw me out. My father called me a whore and refused to have anything more to do with me. Then I went looking for a job as a secretary. No one would take me on without a recent reference. I was on the streets. I had to find a room and something to eat. Another girl gave me Kitty's address, and Kitty helped me without asking questions. I've been working here ever since. . . .' She smiled rather ruefully. Even the smile was rehearsed.

'And now?' Itter asked. 'Haven't you managed to save anything?'

'A little, but not enough. I want to be completely independent when I make the final break—open a shop or something. If only the war was over. It can't go on much longer, can it?' She pouted seductively, and Itter kissed her.

'Which reminds me,' she said suddenly, 'why aren't you in the army?'

Itter's sweetheart had come to the point at last, but he was as well-rehearsed as she was.

'Know something?' he said. 'I'm not even German.'

'What?' Brigitta's eyes widened with genuine astonishment. 'You—not German?'

'No.' Itter hesitated a little. 'I'm a Rumanian, working at the embassy. That's why I use a false name when I come here—so no one will know. You understand?'

Brigitta understood perfectly, but she knew at the same time

94

that this nice young man might turn out to be a useful source of information, so she said : 'No, not really.'

'It's obvious,' he said, playing along. 'If I patronise this place under my own name it could ruin my reputation—and I can't afford that in my position. It's bad enough having to come here in the first place, just to see you. . . .' Having cast his hook, he waited for the fish to bite.

Brigitta bit. 'You go to bed with the others,' she pouted.

'Of course,' he said, 'but only so as not to arouse suspicion—to make it look like a normal visit. . . .' He turned away and walked to the window. 'Oh God,' he groaned, wringing his hands, 'it's all so complicated. . . .'

Brigitta watched him intently. He seemed to be hooked—after all, how was he to know that she was an SD agent? 'What's complicated?' she cooed.

He stood there like a schoolboy about to be scolded. Brigitta had to admit that he attracted her. She didn't for an instant forget why or on whose behalf she was alone with him, but there was no reason why she shouldn't combine business with pleasure. She put out her hand. 'Come here,' she said huskily, only half playacting.

They made love as they had never made love before.

'What's your real name?' she whispered.

'Lljubo,' Kolchev whispered back.

'Lljubo.' She let the unfamiliar syllables dissolve on her tongue. She liked the name. It was mellifluous but masculine. 'Are you married?' she asked.

Kolchev feigned indignation. 'You think I'd be here if I was?' He rolled away from her.

'But darling,' she cooed, pulling him towards her again, 'I didn't mean any harm—after all, you might have been.' Kolchev grudgingly conceded that she was right. He had come a long way today, and Spencer Brown's orders were to proceed slowly. If the building really did contain monitoring devices, the wires would already be humming and his 'indiscretion' would somehow find its way back to the Rumanian embassy. His false identity and status were well covered, so nothing could go wrong. Even if inquiries were made in Bucharest, everything would stand up to the most exhaustive scrutiny. He was suddenly in a hurry to leave.

'I have to go now,' he said.

Brigitta looked disappointed. 'When shall we see each other again?'

'I don't know, exactly. Can I always get hold of you?'

'Yes,' she said, 'via Kitty.' She felt genuinely sad to see him leave so abruptly, but as soon as he had gone she hurried back to her flat to do her duty. She wrote her report, then went to the cover address and telephoned Untersturmführer Schwarz.

Briefly, she told him of her conversation with Kolchev, little knowing that he was fully informed already.

'Keep in touch with him but be careful—that's an order. Do you understand?'

'Yes, Untersturmführer.'

It was the first official command which had given her real pleasure.

Untersturmführer Schwarz did not take the subject of Baron von Itter more seriously than it seemed to warrant. As a matter of routine, he ascertained that the 'baron' was really Lljubo Kolchev, deputy press attaché at the Rumanian embassy.

Being a member of the SS and attached to the Central Security Office, Schwarz saw himself in the German civil service tradition. He was appropriately thorough.

His first step was to consult the Foreign Office, where the CSO's request was treated with due urgency. State Secretaries Baron von Weizsäcker and Gauleiter Bohle (head of the foreign department) called in the head of protocol, Baron von Dörnberg, and —since the person in question was a press attaché—the Foreign Office press chief, Aschmann.

Together they checked such of Kolchev's credentials as had been deposited at the Foreign Office. They found nothing suspicious, but, just to be on the safe side, Aschmann was deputed to call on the Rumanian ambassador, Raoul Bossy. The visit was unofficial and revealed only that Attaché Kolchev, while not the most diligent of diplomats, belonged to one of the best families in Rumania.

This rounded off the picture. Aschmann reported his findings to Walter Schellenberg, who informed Schwarz that Kolchev was 'clean'. Meanwhile, Schwarz had taken the additional precaution of consulting German Military Intelligence. The inquiry was referred to Department III, headed by Major-General von

Oil painting of Kitty Schmidt made in the early thirties. Born in 1882 in a working-class district of Berlin, she opened her first 'Salon' in 1922.

The third and most elegant 'salon', which was to be used by the SS, was opened in 1932 disguised as 'Pension Schmidt' in Berlin's Giesebrechtstrasse.

Authentic items from Salon Kitty showing the 'refined' bourgeois taste of the establishment.

Right: *Reichsführer Himmler, leader of the SS since 1929 and the German police since 1936. He also became Minister of the Interior in 1943.*

Below: *SS Gruppenführer Reinhard Heydrich (right), General of Police and, since 1934, Chief of the Gestapo.*

Right: *Photo of Walter Schellenberg, SS Brigadeführer, responsible for 'Operation Salon Kitty', taken after his arrest in 1945.*
Below: *During his trial in 1948 (upper row, second from right).*

Gestapo headquarters in Berlin and a picture of a prison cell which later became the monitoring centre for the activities of Salon Kitty.
Below: *After the conquest of Berlin.*

Right: *Admiral Canaris. Until his imprisonment in July 1944, he was chief of counter-espionage of the Wehrmacht and opponent of Schellenberg.*

Below: *Two of the many famous visitors to Salon Kitty: the German foreign minister Joachim von Ribbentrop and the foreign minister of Fascist Italy, Count Ciano. (The former was executed in Nuremberg on 16th October 1946 and the latter was shot in Verona on 11th January 1944.)*

Another 'distinguished' visitor was SS Obergruppenführer Sepp Dietrich, commander of the 'Leibstandarte' Adolf Hitler and one of the founders of the Waffen-SS.

Below: *Well-known meeting place of SS leaders in the thirties, Cafe Kranzler in Berlin.*

Bentivegni, who in turn passed it to Colonel Rohleder of IIIF (Defence against Foreign Services).

Rohleder also drew a blank and notified the Central Security Office accordingly.

Kolchev-Wilson had counted on all these developments, so he was not surprised when Ambassador Bossy summoned him to his office on the morning of 22 May.

After an exchange of courtesies, the envoy came to the point. 'The Germans are expressing an interest in you,' he said lightly.

Kolchev looked mystified.

'Well, what have you been up to?' Bossy insisted.

The press attaché hesitated, then blurted out: 'I think I fell into a Gestapo trap.'

'The Gestapo?' Bossy sprang to his feet. 'How did it happen—anyway, what sort of trap?'

'The thing is, Your Excellency, I lead a pretty hectic social life. I also patronise some of the better-class brothels. I introduced myself to the Salon Kitty under a false name and was stupid enough to confide in one of the girls. That was on Saturday. Today—four days later—you call me in and question me. It's obvious, Your Excellency. The girl must have been an informer or undercover agent.'

The ambassador knit his brow. 'Does anyone else know your false name?'

'Yes,' Kolchev said, after a moment's thought. 'The proprietress of the establishment, a certain Frau Schmidt, and the housekeeper —no one else. But as for being aware that I'm really a Rumanian diplomat, only the girl I was with knows that. Please forgive me, Your Excellency. May I ask how the Gestapo tackled you on the subject?'

'The inquiry came from the Foreign Office,' said Bossy.

'Not the Gestapo?'

Bossy shrugged. 'Not officially. What do you propose to do now?'

'Do, Your Excellency?' Kolchev frowned. 'What am I supposed to do? I haven't committed a crime or betrayed any secrets —what's more, I don't intend to do. This has been an object lesson to me. We ought to warn the rest of the embassy staff. I'll continue to patronise the place, of course—anything else would tip the Germans off that we're wise to them. Who knows, I may even learn something that could be useful to us. Have I your permission?'

The envoy agreed and Kolchev was dismissed, secretly jubilant but thinking hard. He couldn't visualise Admiral Canaris gathering information in such a way—it didn't fit his picture of German Military Intelligence.

Only the SD, Gestapo or SS could be behind the Salon Kitty, and Kolchev-Wilson was firmly resolved to plumb its secrets.

Chapter 9

Kolchev remained on his guard. His training had taught him that the least slip could betray an agent or render him suspect.

The danger that threatened him was all the greater now that he had deliberately drawn attention to himself. Privately, he tried to analyse the enemy's reactions.

If he was right, the Salon Kitty functioned as a place from which to spy on Germans and foreigners alike. This supposition seemed to be confirmed by the fact that he had been an object of official investigation. To that extent, he was on the right track.

How, on the other hand, could he satisfy himself that monitoring devices were built into the Salon Kitty? Everything that had happened so far could have been the result of information passed verbally or in writing. There was nothing to substantiate his suspicion that more sophisticated monitoring techniques were in use.

Kolchev decided to pump Brigitta by all available means, but this could not be done at the Salon Kitty. He would have to court her, meet her outside the brothel—even, to be on the safe side, outside her own flat.

Having reached this stage in his deliberations, he waited no longer. Five days had elapsed since his last visit to the Salon Kitty.

Brigitta was genuinely pleased to see him again. 'You haven't been here for ages,' she complained, but her delight was obvious.

'Oh, I had a spot of bother at the office,' he said casually. 'Aren't you glad I came?'

'Don't be silly,' she murmured.

Kolchev laughed lighty. He looked even handsomer when he laughed. His well tailored suit was a tribute to its wearer's bank balance and good taste. He was well built, too, with a faint tan which seemed to enhance the sparkle in his eyes.

'Shall we?' he asked, gesturing towards the door.

Brigitta stared at him in surprise. Their usual custom was to linger over a drink in the parlour. It was a new departure that the Baron, as he was known at the Salon Kitty, should come straight to the point, but she rose obediently and preceded him down the long passage.

Kolchev had an opportunity to observe her lovely figure while she walked ahead of him, lithe and graceful. A warning note sounded in his head as it dawned on him that he was not indifferent to her.

The passage was about twenty yards long and discreetly, even suggestively, illuminated. It was quiet in the building, and the thick carpet swallowed the sound of their footsteps. Brigitta was wearing a dress that hugged her like a sheath. Kolchev tried to persuade himself that she was a whore. He wondered for a moment if, in her place, he would have hawked his body for patriotic reasons. With something of a shock, he realised that he was seeking excuses for the girl and told himself to stop it. Brigitta was an enemy and a professional opponent—someone whom it was his job to outwit.

By the time they reached the bedroom he was fully in command of himself again.

He closed the door. Brigitta turned to him with a smile and they fell into each other's arms. He felt her body arch passionately against his and could not believe that it was all an act, but he gently detached himself and flopped into an arm-chair.

'How about something to drink?' he asked.

'That would be nice,' she said, smoothing her dress. 'What do you feel like?'

'A bottle of champagne.' Kolchev unbuttoned his collar. It was warm in the darkened room.

Brigitta rang and Kitty appeared in person. He gave his order.

'Champagne at this hour of the afternoon?' Brigitta said. She sat down facing him.

'I haven't seen you for five days,' he replied meaningfully.

She propped her head on her hands. 'Tell me something about yourself,' she said.

He shrugged. 'There isn't much to tell.'

'How old you are, where you were born, why you came to

Berlin, what you do here, how long you're staying—oh, you could tell me plenty of things if you wanted to. . . .'

There was a knock. Elvira brought in the champagne and Kolchev gave her a generous tip. 'Put another bottle on ice,' he joked, 'I'm in for a long interrogation.'

'Interrogation?' Brigitta said indignantly, when Elvira had gone. 'That sounds awful! All right, if you won't . . .' She did not say what would happen then.

Kolchev popped the cork and filled their glasses. 'Cheers!'

They drank to each other. Brigitta put her glass down and began to undress. Standing in front of the big mirror on the wardrobe door, she stripped off one garment after another—dress, slip, bra and panties. Then she turned round, unembarrassed. She stretched, yawned, and walked slowly to the bed.

Kolchev had been watching her with a flicker of excitement. He removed his jacket and draped it casually over the back of a chair, then picked up their glasses and perched on the edge of the bed.

'Date of birth: 2 April 1912. Place of birth: Cernowitz on the Russian frontier. My father was a university lecturer. My mother spoilt me terribly—everyone said I'd end badly. . . .'

'Oh, stop it,' she said, pulling his face down to hers. He gazed into her eyes and felt her breath on his cheek. 'Kiss me,' she whispered.

He kissed her, long and passionately. The scent of her body rose to meet him. 'Just a minute,' he said, when they drew apart.

He undressed quickly and lay down beside her.

'Thirsty?' he asked in a low voice.

She didn't answer, just flung herself at him with a ferocity that startled him. Her tongue explored his eyes, ears and mouth, her lips roved over his throat and chest. Kolchev abandoned himself to the sensations of the moment, reflecting for a fraction of a second that an agent's existence had its pleasanter side. 'You . . .' he whispered, and there was an involuntary note of affection in the word.

They lost themselves in a haze of sensual pleasure and then, when their desire was spent, lay facing one another for a few minutes. Their nipples brushed gently, and they felt their excitement revive as though a charge of electricity were passing between them. They forgot time and space. Brigitta gave herself utterly, and knew, when the mist cleared, that she had fallen in love.

It came to her at the same moment that she was now in danger. She thought of Schwarz and Kitty, or wherever else the source of danger might lie. That sobered her. She sat up and quietly began to weep.

Kolchev, who had not been expecting this reaction, studied her closely. The tears were genuine. He felt sorry for her—she was too young for such a job. He refilled the champagne glasses and handed her one. 'Drink up,' he said. She started to say something but he gently laid a hand over her mouth. 'Not now, sweetheart,' he said, remembering his suspicions. He had no wish to put her neck in a noose.

To distract her, he recited Lljubo Kolchev's life-story just as he had imprinted it indelibly on his mind. He spoke of life in the steppes and at Bucharest, of his school-days in England, that land of arrogant prigs, and of the brief diplomatic career that had washed him up on the shores of Berlin. 'I think they wanted to get rid of me,' he told her. 'They were scared I might sow too many wild oats.'

She smiled through her tears. 'You silly boy,' she whispered, stroking his hair gently. 'Do you have a cigarette for me?'

He lit two cigarettes and put one in her mouth. They lay side by side and smoked, both intent on their own thoughts. Disenchantment came as swiftly as the ecstasy that had gone before. It may have been that the past weighed too heavily—that they had both experienced too much in spite of their youth.

Brigitta knew that she must extract some information from him if she were to avoid official displeasure. She had spent too long with him as it was.

'Tell me,' she said, point-blank, 'what do you do with yourself at the embassy?'

Kolchev was somehow glad to hear her back at work—at least she wouldn't be tempted to make any more mistakes. 'What does a press attaché usually do?' he replied casually. 'I read newspapers, go to parties and receptions, ingratiate myself with the right people and hope they'll let me stay here as long as possible. I like being in Berlin, believe it or not.'

Brigitta took a long pull at her champagne and deposited the empty glass on the bedside table. The extent of her self-forgetfulness suddenly enraged her. She recalled her training. What had they warned her about? Falling in love. Well, she had been half-way there, but that was all over now.

'Get dressed,' she said, almost angrily, and rolled off the bed. She drew one of the curtains, flooding the room with afternoon sunlight.

Kolchev shielded his eyes. 'Must you?' he protested sulkily.

'Yes, Herr Kolchev,' she snapped, 'I must.' He was surprised at how quickly she had regained her composure, also the speed with which she dressed.

He was still knotting his tie when she finished and sat down in an arm-chair to wait. 'A last cigarette?' he suggested politely. He offered his case and she took one. 'Another glass of champagne?' She merely nodded.

Kolchev realised that she was angry and he knew why. She had failed and was brooding about the possible consequences. He decided to brighten her day a little.

'You know, sweetheart, the Rumanian embassy isn't a very important place. The King is weak—he doesn't know his own mind. One day a strong man will come along and save the country, the way Hitler has saved yours. That's what we're waiting for.'

'Anyone in mind?' she asked, off-hand.

He stared at her curiously for a moment. 'Yes, as a matter of fact I have. A man named Ion Antonescu.'

'Never heard of him,' she said. 'Who is he?'

The spirit of the chase had suddenly reawakened in her. She felt that she was on to something—that the young Rumanian might after all prove to be a useful informant.

Kolchev chuckled softly: 'Antonescu? Nobody much—only the chief of the Rumanian general staff!'

He pulled on his jacket. He had scattered enough bait for one day and could see that she was in a hurry to get away. That meant she probably reported by word of mouth, so his theory that monitoring devices were installed here might yet prove to be un-founded. Even so, his eyes roamed over the walls and lamps while Brigitta was renewing her lipstick.

'Lost something?' she asked.

'No, just admiring the décor.'

They made their way back to the drawing-room, where a certain amount of activity was now in progress. A tipsy army officer was playing *Oh, du schöner Westerwald!* on the piano, over and over again, while the rest of the party bellowed the words. A couple of girls burst into strident peals of laughter.

Kitty came over to them. 'Well, you two?'

'The Baron has been telling me all about his love-life,' Brigitta said superciliously.

'That's right,' said Kolchev, 'it's a long story.' His face wore its usual open, boyish smile. 'I have to go now, Kitty.'

He paid his bill and said goodbye to Brigitta. 'I'll come next week, if I may,' he murmured.

And Brigitta, sensible of her duty to the Security Service, said: 'It's always lovely to see you.'

She left exactly five minutes after Kolchev. Emerging from the building, she looked round vainly for a taxi and then set off on foot. She was in a hurry to dispatch her report, so she headed straight for the cover address. If she had glanced over her shoulder she would have noticed a familiar figure following her, but it never occurred to her to look.

Once in the office of the cover address, she telephoned Unter-sturmführer Schwarz direct.

'Heil Hitler, Untersturmführer,' she said crisply. 'I have an important piece of information for you.' She passed on all that Kolchev had told her, starting with his life-story and ending with the reference to Antonescu.

Schwarz listened attentively. 'Well done, Brigitta. Excellent! Keep up the good work.' He replaced the receiver.

A minute later the men on duty at the monitoring centre were subjected to a harangue that singed their ears. For the first and last time, one of Schwarz's agents had beaten them to it.

'This is a bloody disgrace!' yelled the Untersturmführer. 'You're charged with negligence, the lot of you. I'll have you trans-ferred for disciplinary reasons—to the front!' Schwarz had the bit between his teeth. His rage was genuine and so were his threats. The members of the duty watch were relieved at once and posted to France two days later.

Schwarz saw to it that their fate reached the ears of the other duty personnel. From that day onwards, no agents from the Salon Kitty ever stole a march on the listening-post.

Not even SS men were indifferent to the perils of active service.

Kolchev should have been more patient. He thought he had discovered Brigitta's home address and left it at that. Had he guessed the real nature of her destination he would certainly have devoted more time to the place. As it was, he went home feeling pleased with himself.

No one who saw him leave his flat as darkness fell would have given him a second glance.

Dressed in an ill-fitting reach-me-down of the sort worn by tens of thousands of Berliners, he emerged from the building and sauntered along the Kurfürstendamm. He stared incuriously into a few shop windows, drank a beer in a small bar, and took the underground to Stuttgarterplatz, where he sat on a bench and smoked a cigarette.

As soon as the streets cleared he walked round the block, waited in a gateway for some minutes until he was sure nobody had tailed him, then ducked into a bar frequented by respectable card-playing citizens.

He leant against the counter and ordered a beer. Glancing round, he saw Spencer Brown playing *Skat* with a party of other men. Their calls—'Eighteen, twenty, two and zero . . .'—sounded curiously peaceful in comparison with the martial music that blared from the radio. Kolchev gazed meditatively into his glass of beer, drained it and ordered another.

'Don't recall seeing you before,' said the landlord's wife.

'No,' he replied in his best Berlin dialect. 'I live up Lichterfelde way. I don't come here very often.'

'Ah,' she said, 'so you're here on a visit.'

'That's right,' said Kolchev, 'to my sister.' He changed the subject. 'Has your husband been called up yet?'

'Him? He couldn't wait, the bloody fool. He volunteered, and now he's on his way to Paris—at least, that's what he wrote me.'

'Don't worry, it can't last much longer.'

The woman looked sceptical. 'That's what they said in the first war, and we never reached Paris. Still, the menfolk need something to occupy them, I suppose.'

She was interrupted by the radio announcer heralding a news broadcast. A sudden silence descended on the room, and everyone stared spellbound at the radio on the counter. Even the *Skat*-players lowered their cards.

Our break-through to the Channel has been extended (proclaimed the announcer). At Narvik, our troops continue to fight off far superior enemy forces. In the cathedral square at Milan, Count Ciano has proclaimed Italy's readiness to enter the war on Germany's side.

There were two other reports, but the customers had lost interest. Cards were raised and conversation broke out again. Unlike the rest, Kolchev listened intently. The reports were as follows:

> Breslau Fair was today opened by State Secretary Landfried. He referred in his inaugural address to the fact that trade between Germany and South-East Europe has, in the past five years, assumed proportions which many people previously considered impossible.
>
> According to an official Soviet government report, members of the British trade mission to Moscow have urged a reduction of Soviet trade with Germany. On its own submission, the Soviet government responded to this proposal by stating that it intends to maintain and develop commercial links with Germany in accordance with its treaty obligations.

Card-play ceased at one of the tables and the men called for their bill. The landlord's wife bustled over, collected their money and glasses, and returned to the counter.

'I'd like to pay too,' Kolchev said. He pushed a note across the counter and was given some small change. Then he made for the door.

'Watch the black-out!' called the landlord's wife.

There was a chorus of jocular reassurances from the *Skat*-players whose departure coincided with Kolchev's. They all went out. Kolchev crossed to the other side of the street without looking round.

The others took leave of each other. 'See you tomorrow,' said one. 'Heil Hitler,' said someone else, and there was a dutiful murmur in response. The party broke up.

It was a dark night. One of the men crossed the street and quickly overhauled Kolchev.

'Got a light?' asked the stranger.

'Sure,' said Kolchev. 'Better find a doorway first, though. They're getting strict about the black-out these days.'

'You can say that again,' the stranger agreed. He pulled a packet of cigarettes from his pocket while they looked for a convenient doorway.

Kolchev struck a match. 'How goes it, Spencer?' he whispered.

'Here, have a cigarette yourself,' said Brown. 'Cup it in your hand and let's go—and not so much of the Spencer. My name's Karl, okay?'

'*Jawohl*,' said Kolchev.

They walked down the street, keeping to the kerb and whispering so low that it would have been virtually impossible to overhear them.

'What's the news from London?' asked Kolchev.

'Not good. We've lost a lot of agents. Our best ones are practically eliminated. Hitler's unbroken run of luck is giving our German contacts cold feet. Strictly speaking, we're all in danger except you. London wants to recall me. My job at Borsig's is getting shaky—I may be called up any day now, which means I'll have to skedaddle. I don't know how I'll get out, but that's my worry, not yours. The important thing is to discuss future channels of communication.'

'Any ideas?' Kolchev asked. It chilled him a little to think that his last remaining friend would soon be gone, leaving him virtually marooned.

'Yes, we've still a good chance of keeping in touch with you. There's a laundry in Emserstrasse. Take your custom there in future. The people won't know your address, so you'll have to deliver and collect your laundry in person. We've provided you with six dozen handkerchiefs. On them you'll find your instructions encoded in invisible ink. Your own information can be passed the same way. You'll be supplied with the chemicals you need.'

'A live letter-box. . . . Isn't that risky?'

Brown shrugged. 'Of course it's risky, but we don't have much option. The laundry people are safe—good Party members one and all. Their boss acts like a three hundred per cent Nazi. Let's hope they don't rumble him.'

'What if I come up with something really hot?'

Brown handed him a matchbox. 'Thanks for the light,' he said aloud. Footsteps approached them in the darkness, then died away. 'You'll find the new code and three phone numbers in there. If you've something urgent for London, call the first number and pass it direct to the laundry. If you need anything, ring the second number and you'll be told how to get it. If you're in danger, ring the third number and they'll see if they can help you. Never get into conversation on the phone—just state your name and say "What about my laundry?". They'll understand.'

Wilson, alias Kolchev, chuckled grimly. 'Nice prospect!'

'Another thing,' Brown continued in a low voice. 'Commit the three numbers to memory and destroy the matchbox, preferably tonight. And always use public phone booths at least a mile from your flat, is that clear?'

'Perfectly. By the way, I think the Gestapo have run a check on me.'

'And given you a clean bill of health—yes, we know. That was a neat ploy of yours. They think you're a sex-struck playboy, which pretty well puts you in the clear. You fit into their present scheme of things. I wouldn't be surprised if they approach you some day soon and try to enlist your services. If they do, play along. Spill a few beans from the Rumanian can.'

'I already did,' Kolchev cut in. 'I think they swallowed the lot.'

Brown laughed. 'All the better. One more point. If you receive a phone call, either at the embassy or at home, and the caller simply says "Your laundry is ready", collect it the first chance you get—it'll mean there's some urgent information for you. Alternatively, he may say "There's a piece of laundry missing", which means danger. When you hear that, get out as fast as you can. Switzerland might be the best bet because they'll assume you're heading for Rumania. Keep a few basic essentials packed in an overnight bag—you can always pretend it's your air-raid kit. All the Germans are toting their tooth-brushes around these days, so it won't strike anyone as odd. Above all, though, destroy everything that might arouse suspicion. Any questions?'

'Yes, one. What name do I use at the laundry?'

'Baron von Itter.'

Kolchev halted in mid-stride. 'You know?'

'Of course,' Brown said drily. 'Give us credit for a little independent research. Tell me, how are you faring at the Salon Kitty?'

Kolchev described his last meeting with Brigitta and his interview with the Rumanian ambassador. He also gave a brief résumé of the Antonescu story, whose effects he had still to gauge. 'I'm convinced the Germans have installed microphones in the place too, but I've no proof.'

'So you said,' mused Brown. 'Pity we can't tap the wires—it would be a first-class source of information.'

'I'm only guessing at the moment, but even if my suspicions are confirmed I don't see any chance of cutting in without alerting them.'

'All the same, as soon as you know for certain, notify us. Maybe our communications experts will come up with some way of getting at the circuit.'

Kolchev nodded.

'And don't forget, you're the most promising horse in our stable at the present time. We're relying on you for advance notice of Rumanian and German intentions—especially German.'

'I know.' Kolchev smiled wrily. 'I dream about it at night.'

They had reached an underground station.

'Heil Hitler, Herr Meyer!' Spencer Brown raised his arm in the Nazi salute.

'Heil Hitler!' said Roger Wilson, alias Lljubo Kolchev, staring after his friend's departing figure. He would not have bet much on their chances of meeting again.

Untersturmführer Schwarz had been devoting serious thought to the problem of security and the forwarding of information gleaned at the Salon Kitty. Kolchev was not a figure of importance, and Schwarz had virtually dismissed him from his mind, but it was unthinkable that the listening-post should have been beaten to the punch by one of his agents.

He realised that the men in the monitoring room were overworked—after all, no one could have foreseen what a prolific source of information the Salon Kitty would become—but he was still reluctant to widen the circle of initiates by bringing in reinforcements.

The only good point was that he now had his men under strict supervision at Meineckestrasse. Each of them was searched from head to foot before and after every shift. The SS signallers knew the form. Their duties gave them an insight into the private lives of senior members of the Party, government, armed forces and diplomatic corps, so they accepted this discriminatory treatment without a murmur.

Besides, they had all been carefully selected. Schwarz was a good psychologist. He made a habit of singling individuals out for words of commendation which implied that they were the backbone of the entire outfit. This bred self-confidence and gave them pride in their work.

But none of this blinded Schwarz to the realisation that symptoms of fatigue were setting in—human failings which could not be eliminated by a judicious use of stick and carrot. He resolved to tackle Walter Schellenberg and air his problems.

Schellenberg, who was unwilling and unable to dispense with the Salon Kitty as a source of information, considered that the only solution was to reinforce the monitoring teams. On the other hand, he could sympathise with his subordinate's misgivings about letting too many people into the secret.

'Can't you suggest an alternative, Untersturmführer?'

'Well,' Schwarz said hesitantly, 'I did wonder if we couldn't reorganise the system. . . .'

'In what way?'

'Forgive me for going into detail, sir, but here's the situation as I see it. Our customers—for want of a better word—patronise the Salon Kitty with the main aim of having a couple of drinks and enjoying themselves. Our girls naturally have to get them in the right mood. The listening-post monitors all these preliminaries even though they seldom yield anything of value. Experience has shown that topics of real interest and importance are only raised in private conversation. No customer thaws out and gives us an insight into his thoughts until our agent has got him alone and gained his confidence.'

'Go on,' said Schellenberg.

'Well, sir, my idea is to waive direct surveillance until a customer and his girl have retired to one of the bedrooms. Apart from anything else, what really frays our technicians' nerves is a babble of voices. It takes extreme concentration to pick out individual speakers, and most of what goes on in the reception rooms is just small talk.'

Schellenberg raised his eyebrows. 'So you propose to exempt the reception rooms from surveillance altogether?'

'Not necessarily,' Schwarz replied. 'I've been making inquiries at the State Broadcasting Service. For some time now, they've been having moderate success with a recording device which stores speech magnetically on wire spools. If it's good enough, we could simply record conversations in the two reception rooms from start to finish and decipher them at leisure—the most we'd need would be a man to adjust the frequency. The recordings could then be continuously transcribed by the Records Section. We might also have to appoint an editor who'd separate the chaff from the wheat and submit a summary two or three times a day. That's one possibility. . . .'

Schellenberg, who had been listening intently, said : 'Sounds as if you've got something else in mind.'

Schwarz nodded. 'I've also discovered that IG-Farben and AEG have been collaborating on the development of a so-called tape recorder. The State Broadcasting authorities have already been using it for some years as an experimental means of recording and storing transmissions. In view of the Salon Kitty's growing importance and the fact that such a system would enable us to store large quantities of material in a relatively small space, I think we ought at least to explore these techniques further.'

'So do I,' said Schellenberg, secretly amused by the Untersturmführer's passionate devotion to the Salon Kitty venture.

'It'll cost money,' Schwarz added, '—a lot of money.'

'Draw up a list of requirements and a time schedule,' Schellenberg commanded. 'I'll raise the matter with Heydrich as soon as you produce them. Even if your information is only partly correct, both these techniques could be of crucial value to our entire intelligence service, and the Salon Kitty strikes me as an ideal testing-ground.'

Schwarz was more than satisfied with the outcome of this interview. While he was about it, he devoted the rest of the day to a refresher course—an exceedingly rigorous and thorough re-indoctrination of his monitoring teams and the SD agents who worked at the Salon Kitty.

To this end, the Untersturmführer had evolved an effective technique of his own. He never called his subordinates together and addressed them en masse but swore them to secrecy individually, stressed the maximum security rating of their work, threatened them with the death penalty one moment and praised them for doing a good job the next. He also got them to sign an impressive-looking document which drew the individual's attention to his or her duty and the penalties for any breach of security. It was a perfect system of intimidation, and the comparative frequency with which Schwarz performed this ceremony allowed no one connected with the Salon Kitty to forget that the slightest deviation from established procedure might have lethal consequences.

Lljubo Kolchev racked his brains for a quicker way of plumbing the Salon Kitty's secret. His obsession that a monitoring circuit must be concealed somewhere in the building had matured into near certainty, but he could not imagine how and where the necessary devices had been installed.

His first task was to ascertain how the system functioned, his second to discover a way of tapping the flow of information.

It was clear that he must start by trying to endear himself to Brigitta so effectively that she would be willing to divulge more than she was at present. He was still feeding her with titbits about Rumania. He knew that these items were promptly passed on. What he could not prove beyond doubt was whether they were relayed by Brigitta alone or simultaneously picked up by hidden microphones—and this was the point which preoccupied him so unceasingly.

He hit on the idea of wounding the girl's feelings so deeply that she would never mention it to anyone, not even her controller. One breach of faith on her part might lead to another—it would be the thin end of the wedge. The more he considered the plan the better he liked it, but the first requirement was to worm his way into the girl's confidence.

Realising that the so-called story of her life was a pack of lies from start to finish, he made it his first aim to accost Brigitta outside the brothel, get her by herself—even, if possible, persuade her to spend the night with him at a small hotel. A little alcohol and plenty of masculine sympathy might loosen her tongue.

Wilson, alias Kolchev, discovered to his surprise that the prospect titillated him. It was a danger signal, but the plan had crystallised and he was keen to put it into effect without delay.

He paid his next visit to the Salon Kitty the following afternoon. As usual, he began by passing the time of day with Kitty in the drawing-room. Kitty was as amiable and attentive a listener as ever.

'We're doing splendidly in France,' Kolchev ventured.

Kitty smiled mischievously. 'We?' she said.

'Well, in a manner of speaking.' Kolchev produced a card which had long been in play. 'You know all about me?'

'I wouldn't say that,' Kitty replied, and he noticed that she chose her words with care. 'You aren't German, are you? That's all I meant.'

'You're on the ball, Kitty.' They were alone, so he did not lower his voice. 'Brigitta's the only person I've told. Actually, I'm with the Rumanian embassy but I didn't want to broadcast the fact here—you follow? Our countries are linked by more than ties of friendship, but keep that under your hat. Besides, I'm only small fry—just a black sheep in exile, or so my ambassador seems to think. I enjoy myself, though. Life's short enough, God knows, and I don't aim to get myself shot. Better a Berlin posting than a hero's death. This is my favourite place bar none, Kitty. Your girls are absolutely gorgeous.'

'We do our best to please, Baron,' said Kitty. 'May I order you something to drink?'

'By all means,' Kolchev agreed. 'Why don't we split a bottle of champagne?'

Kitty smiled. 'I'm not averse. What about Brigitta—shall I phone her?'

'No, not today,' said Kolchev, working to plan. 'She's a sweet girl, but too many sweet things spoil a man's palate.'

Kitty jumped up and walked to the door. 'I'll fetch you one of my albums.'

She left him alone for a couple of minutes, just as he had hoped. He rose silently, taking it for granted that his every breath could be overheard, and avoided making any untoward noise. He glanced behind the large oil paintings on the walls. Nothing. His keen eyes examined the chandeliers and standard lamps without spotting any suspicious features. Radiators, piano, arm-chairs— nothing seemed to have been tampered with. No tell-tale cables, no bulges, no ventilation grilles, no superfluous lengths of flex. Nothing!

Kitty returned with a bottle and two glasses. The album was clamped beneath her arm.

She found Kolchev in the middle of the room, examining a large portrait of her in oils.

113

'A wonderful likeness,' he said admiringly.

'That? It was painted twenty years ago.' Kitty laughed as she uncorked the bottle. Champagne frothed into the glasses. 'Your health, Baron,' she said, raising her glass.

'Twenty years ago?' Kolchev exclaimed, following suit. 'I don't believe it!'

'Time doesn't stand still,' she sighed. 'All that's left are the little pleasures of life—this, for example. . . .' She took a big sip of champagne. They sat down and she began to turn the pages of her album. 'Have you ever tried Rosemarie?' she asked, rather like a tourist guide extolling the beauties of Rome.

'No, is she new?'

'There's nothing new under the sun,' she retorted with a grin. 'No, she isn't new, but she's a lively little creature. You'll have fun with her.'

'In that case. . . .' Kolchev started to hum *Rosemarie, I love you*. Kitty dialled the girl's number and asked her to join them.

'I envy your way of life, Baron,' she said lightly.

'What's so enviable about it? I have to work like everyone else. The same thing, day in, day out. Read newspapers ad nauseam, cuts bits out, put them on the ambassador's desk, office routine, red tape. . . . Still, it's bearable. We live in an interesting age, and at least there's always something doing here in Berlin. Cheers!'

Kolchev savoured his champagne. He felt he was on the right track. He would soon discover if Brigitta learned of his assignation with Rosemarie and how she reacted to it. Everything depended on that. If she wasn't told, he'd have to tell her himself.

Elvira put her head round the door. She looked nervous.

'Excuse me for a moment, Baron,' Kitty said, obeying the summons. She had a ladylike sense of decorum. 'Rosemarie must have arrived. . . .'

Kolchev had another couple of minutes in which to scan the large drawing-room with a trained eye. It infuriated him that he was unable to discover the slightest thing. He guessed that the leads were concealed beneath the skirting-board in which the expensive wall-paper terminated, but there must be a microphone somewhere, and a microphone wasn't an undiscoverable pin-head. Then his eye was caught by a circular depression in the wall-paper. It might have concealed the former egress of a stove-pipe, except that it didn't coincide with the likely position of a stove.

The almost imperceptible concavity was situated above the door-surround, about nine feet from the floor.

Kolchev began to hum again, delighted with his discovery—relieved, too. His hunch had yielded at least one lead. He still had to follow it up, but he was sure of his facts now.

With a sigh, he returned to the arm-chair and drained his glass. It was good to feel that he had made progress. He caught himself grappling with the problem of how to tap the circuit but told himself to relax and take it easy. First, he must try to detect similar concavities in other rooms as well.

Kitty returned, looking rather less serene than she usually did.

'I'm terribly sorry, Baron,' she said, 'but I'm afraid I can't accommodate you after all. I've just been booked by a large party —I hope you understand.'

It flashed across Kolchev's mind that he might somehow have been spotted. Calmly, he said : 'But I thought Rosemarie was coming.'

'Quite so, Baron, but she isn't available—not today.' Kitty sounded almost imploring.

'Very well,' he said, 'better phone Brigitta instead.'

'But Baron,' Kitty pleaded, 'I just told you—today is out. I'm expecting a big party, don't you understand? I need every room.'

'I see.' Kolchev played the graceful loser. 'Till next time, then. Tomorrow, perhaps?'

Kitty smiled. 'Yes, tomorrow.'

He could almost feel her plucking at his sleeve, so he went.

Kitty slumped into a chair, drained of energy. Untersturm-führer Schwarz had signalled an imminent visit from Heydrich and Schellenberg.

Chapter 10

Two big Mercedes saloons pulled up outside No 12 Giesebrecht-strasse. They carried SS number-plates. A black-uniformed NCO leapt from each vehicle and flung open the rear doors. The house had witnessed many such arrivals in 1940 because it was the home of Gruppenführer Ernst Kaltenbrunner, a man who still had a big part to play in the history of the Third Reich.

The cars disgorged Reinhard Heydrich and Walter Schellenberg, both in civilian clothes. At a befitting distance behind Schellenberg stood Untersturmführer Schwarz.

Heydrich glanced up at the building's grey façade as though checking on the location of Kaltenbrunner's apartment, then strode briskly towards the entrance.

12 Giesebrechtstrasse was a typical upper middle-class Berlin house with long windows and plaster moulding. The tradesman's entrance was in the rear courtyard and could not be seen from the street.

Schwarz raced ahead and swung open the heavy door. 'Through here, Gruppenführer!' he said deferentially. He had never dreamt that Heydrich would deign to inspect 'his' Salon Kitty, and was sweating with anxiety in case something went wrong.

The hall was approached by half a dozen steps covered with red coconut matting. The three men climbed them. Schwarz hurried on ahead, but instead of opening the lift gate he beckoned Heydrich and Schellenberg down the few steps to the tradesman's entrance. The door was open.

They debouched into the courtyard between Nos 11 and 12 Giesebrechtstrasse and covered the thirty yards that separated them from the next tradesman's entrance. Then they vanished into 11 Giesebrechtstrasse, and two minutes later they were inside the Pension Schmidt. Everything had gone like clockwork.

'Dismiss the cars,' Heydrich told the Untersturmführer.

116

Schwarz snapped to attention and withdrew. He realised that his presence was no longer required.

Kitty, wearing her most affable smile, greeted the distinguished guests in person. 'This is a great honour, Gruppenführer,' she said, and led the way into the drawing-room.

'You're looking well, Frau Schmidt,' Schellenberg said admiringly.

'Thank you,' she replied, indicating the most comfortable arm-chairs. 'May I offer you something to drink?' Everything was as usual, except that she knew her fate was in the balance once more. Schellenberg glanced inquiringly at Heydrich; the Gruppen-führer gave a curt nod. 'Bring us a bottle of champagne,' he decreed.

Kitty hurried out.

'Is the circuit switched off?' Heydrich asked.

'Of course, Gruppenführer,' Schellenberg assured him.

Heydrich surveyed the room with grudging approval. 'Very cosy. I can imagine why our Party bosses feel at home here. Wine, women and song—you picked the ideal place.'

Schellenberg nodded gratefully. 'Would you care to see the albums, Gruppenführer?' His tone was discreet.

'Of course,' said Heydrich. 'That's why we're here.'

Kitty returned with some glasses, followed by Elvira, who carried an ice-bucket containing two bottles: French champagne and German sparkling wine. Heydrich identified them at a glance.

'Make it the German,' he said, '—Ribbentrop has to earn a living somehow.' The other two smiled covertly at this sarcastic reference to the German Foreign Minister's former activities as a wine salesman. 'Let's have a look at that album.'

Heydrich studied each photograph in turn, intently but with-out expression. 'A skinny lot,' he said at length. 'Don't they make them with breasts any more?'

'I have another album,' Kitty told him.

'Then get it!' That was Heydrich. Curt, brusque, imperious, happy to ride rough-shod over any form of opposition or human feeling.

Kitty hurried out again.

'How old is the madame?' asked Heydrich.

'Nearly sixty,' Schellenberg told him.

'The life seems to agree with her.'

'Business is booming, Gruppenführer.'

'I can believe it. Berlin is swarming with lounge-lizards—this is the perfect spot for them. Where does she keep her girls?'

'They're always summoned by phone. . . .'

Kitty returned with the second album and put it in front of Heydrich. He leafed through it with the same dispassionate concentration. 'Which one has the biggest tits?' he demanded eventually.

Kitty looked disconcerted. 'I couldn't tell you, Gruppenführer. I don't have their vital statistics.'

'Surely you know your own girls?' Heydrich sneered, but Schellenberg intervened. 'No, she doesn't . . .' he said with a meaningful glance.

Heydrich took the point. He reopened the first of the albums and slowly turned the pages until he came to the photograph of a dark-haired girl. The name underneath read 'Irene'.

'Send for this one,' he said.

Kitty glanced at the album and made to pick up the phone.

'Call her from outside,' Heydrich snapped.

Obediently, Kitty withdrew. There was something about the blond man with the glacial blue eyes which sent shivers down her spine.

'Why don't you pick yourself a girl, Schellenberg?' Heydrich asked his subordinate.

Schellenberg gave a slightly embarrassed smile and began to leaf through the albums himself. 'I congratulate Schwarz on his selection,' he said approvingly.

'Fräulein Irene will be here in a few minutes,' Kitty announced when she returned to the drawing-room. 'Meanwhile, may I offer you gentlemen a bite to eat? Caviare, smoked salmon, lobster?' She looked inquiringly from one to the other.

'Caviare,' decreed Heydrich. It was another order.

As soon as Kitty had left the room, he turned to Schellenberg. 'You mean to say she really doesn't know these girls? A bit implausible, isn't it?'

'It's true, Gruppenführer. The girls are forbidden to engage in personal conversation with her. They're polite to her, of course, so as not to arouse suspicion, but they go home as soon as their clients have left and write their reports. Schwarz tells me that one girl actually submitted her report before the monitoring team submitted theirs. It's a tribute to the girls' training.'

Heydrich laughed. 'We'll soon be able to test their standard of training for ourselves.' He rose abruptly and started pacing up and down the room. 'Are you quite sure nobody's listening in?'

'Absolutely positive, Gruppenführer.' Schellenberg stood up too.

Kitty reappeared. The caviare nestled in a silver dish full of ice-cubes. Several slices of toast lay on a snow-white napkin beside it. 'Can I do anything more for you?' Kitty asked.

'Yes,' said Heydrich. 'Herr Schellenberg needs some female company.'

'It just so happens that Rosemarie is here,' Kitty said tentatively. 'A client from the Rumanian embassy had already sent for her when your visit was announced. If you're interested . . .'

Schellenberg smiled. 'All right, send her in.' He was glad to have his mind made up for him.

Kitty went out and came back with Rosemarie a few moments later. The girl stiffened when she recognised Heydrich, almost as if she were about to come to attention and salute, but Heydrich waved her nonchalantly into a chair.

'Forget it,' he said, 'we're off duty. Sit down and join us.' He filled her glass like a perfect gentleman.

Irene turned up soon afterwards. She too seemed to freeze when she saw the mightiest of her bosses rise to greet her, but it was not long before the wine did its work. The atmosphere became gayer and less constrained with every bottle.

Later, they retired to two separate rooms. When Heydrich and Schellenberg left the building four hours later and strolled to the Kurfürstendamm, the Gruppenführer was more than pleased with his assistant and the Salon Kitty.

'All right, Schellenberg, I'm sold on the place. I'm satisfied that it'll supply us with valuable information—the sort that comes nearest the truth. Those little bitches of yours know their stuff.'

Coming from Heydrich, this was high praise. Schellenberg entered it in the assets column of his professional balance sheet.

Kolchev kept his promise to Kitty and returned next day.

'Well, expecting any more distinguished visitors?' he asked teasingly.

'Not that I know of, Baron. Would you like me to phone Rose-marie?'

Kolchev feigned indecision. He had since received an item of news from Rumania. He knew the German government must already be aware of it, but he wanted it to reach the SD's foreign intelligence service independently. The piece of stale news might serve to dispel any suspicion that still attached to him. It might also prove that he was an object of little interest to the Security Service, merely an irresponsible, well-heeled young Rumanian diplomat of minor importance. An additional factor was his wish to show Brigitta how implicitly he trusted her by confiding any secrets that came to his ears.

He sighed. 'Oh, maybe I'll stick with Brigitta after all.'

'Why not?' Kitty laughed. 'No point in chopping and changing for the sake of it. I'll call her.'

Brigitta arrived less than ten minutes later. Kolchev retired to one of the bedrooms with her at once.

'I was going to sample Rosemarie yesterday,' he said. 'However, Kitty got rid of me to make room for more important customers —top brass, I suspect.'

'I wouldn't know,' she said, and his words hurt her more than she cared to admit. 'I wasn't here yesterday.'

He decided to dangle his first piece of bait. 'There's trouble at home.'

'Really?' she said. 'Is someone sick?'

'I don't mean that. My government has called up three hundred thousand men, which virtually puts the army on a war footing, but the King wants to preserve Rumanian neutrality at all costs. Damned if I know how things'll turn out. . . .'

'I'm sure you'll end up on Germany's side,' she said. There was a hint of wishful thinking in her tone.

He nodded. 'Let's hope so.'

'Why?' she asked flirtatiously, sensing that the words referred to her in some way.

'Because I'll be able to stay on here. I've grown very attached to Berlin.'

'Only to Berlin?'

'And to the Salon Kitty,' he said. 'It's a great institution.'

'You're being horrid,' she said petulantly.

Kolchev laid a finger over her lips and pulled her towards him.

120

He felt her melt into his arms as he kissed her.

'Come,' she whispered, drawing him towards the bed. She had to have him, possess and be possessed by him. It was a moment she had dreamt of for days.

They lay side by side afterwards, fingers tightly interlaced. Silence reigned between them until Kolchev said : 'I have to go now.'

'Must you really, Lljubo?' The question was like a sigh.

They left 11 Giesebrechtstrasse separately, in the usual way. Kolchev unobtrusively trailed the girl to her cover address, intending to see her again somehow, get her alone out of doors where no one could overhear them. With a start of surprise, he remembered that he didn't even know her surname.

He slipped into the hallway and tried to identify her on the residents' name-plates, but none of the names seemed to suit her. Then he heard footsteps and recognised them as hers. He hurried out and secreted himself in a doorway just in time to see her walk off briskly.

He followed at a safe distance. She did not have far to go. A few blocks away she turned into another apartment house. He wondered whether to accost her as she was opening the front door but decided to rest on his laurels. Kolchev's sixth sense told him that he had jumped to the wrong conclusion the first time. This was where she lived, he felt sure. Only someone arriving home would behave as she was doing now. In that case, why had she called at the other address? Of course! Brigitta was an agent—she had been making her report.

He smirked to himself. Things were going his way at last. Suppressing an urge to jump for joy, he slowly and pleasurably lit a cigarette.

Untersturmführer Schwarz smirked too, when he received Brigitta's report.

The news was as stale as a week-old loaf. Reports of Rumania's military preparations had been lying on his desk for the past forty-eight hours. The little press attaché was a dud informant after all.

Schwarz made a crucial mistake. He finally dismissed Lljubo Kolchev—or rather, Roger Wilson of British Intelligence—from his mind. But then, Schwarz was no professional in the field of counter-espionage.

Kolchev put in a spell of really hard work at the embassy, which earned him an ambassadorial pat on the back—the first ever—and reassured him that the ambassador would let him know if the Gestapo, Security Service or German Military Intelligence showed a renewed interest in his activities. That done, he relaxed. Slowly but steadily, he cut down on his official duties and devoted himself more and more to his 'hobby', the Salon Kitty.

It did not concern him that the French government had fled Paris and that Reynaud was appealing to Roosevelt for assistance. He merely noted in passing that King Haakon of Norway had escaped to England and that Italian-Soviet relations seemed to be improving. He headed for the Salon Kitty on 10 June 1940 firmly resolved to take an important step forwards.

Kitty welcomed him with her customary warmth and telephoned Brigitta. The girl arrived a few minutes later and they retired to Room 7, their usual haunt.

Kolchev deliberately confined his conversation to commonplace topics, items which could be read in any newspaper. They drank a good bottle of wine, then some coffee. Kolchev seemed in no hurry. He lounged on the bed half-dressed, chain smoking, and grumbling mildly about the amount of work he had been obliged to do in recent days. He asked Brigitta the occasional question but took care not to lead her into deep water. It was a warm day, in any case, and she showed no undue interest in his work—or hers.

He crooked his arm round her, the wine took effect, and Brigitta dozed off.

Gingerly, he disengaged himself from the girl. He was wide awake now. Keeping one eye on her the whole time, he crept noiselessly round the room in his socks. He knew that he mustn't touch anything, so his eyes scanned the wall-paper, searching for the indentation which any hidden cavity was bound to produce—and he was sure that any such cavity, if it existed, must harbour a microphone.

His experience in the drawing-room told him where to direct his gaze. Sure enough, he found what he was looking for. A small depression here, an almost imperceptible line of dust there, and all repeated at mathematically regular intervals. Then there was a knock at the door.

Kolchev moved quickly. He hopped back on to the bed,

stretched as if he had just been roused from a deep sleep, and called out : 'Yes, who is it?' The door opened and Elvira came in.

Brigitta woke up. 'We dozed off,' she mumbled, yawning.

'You must have,' Elvira said tartly. 'Kitty was wondering where you'd got to. Like something to drink?'

'How about a coffee, Brigitta?' Kolchev suggested.

'That would be nice.' She rolled over and snuggled into the pillows.

'Hey, don't go to sleep again,' Kolchev warned her. 'I'll have to make tracks soon—it's getting dark.'

'Draw the curtains before you switch the light on,' said Brigitta, '—black-out regulations.'

Obediently he drew the curtains and switched on one of the little bedside lamps.

'You look delicious when you're sleepy,' he said, perching on the edge of the bed.

A sudden wave of tenderness and understanding surged between them. Brigitta was just about to confess that she had fallen in love with him when he put a hand over her mouth, then kissed her. She flung her arms round his neck, and he felt her strain against him.

'Not now,' he whispered, 'the girl's coming.'

Elvira entered with a tray. Kolchev slipped her a three-mark piece and she went out, leaving them alone again. He poured two cups, adding milk and sugar the way Brigitta liked. She reached for him again, but he thrust a cup into her hand.

'Here, have a sip of this first.'

Now he knew for certain that every word they said was monitored, he was doubly careful. He must do nothing to endanger the girl because she alone could supply ultimate confirmation of what he suspected. He was almost sure she had no knowledge of the monitoring system, but nothing detracted from his certainty that she was a trained agent. For some minutes he toyed with the idea of enlisting her as a double agent, then realised that she was too inexperienced and new to the game.

He decided to extract an admission that she was working for the SD. It couldn't be done at the Salon Kitty, where the walls had ears. He would have to play for time and convince those ears that all in Room 7 was as it should be.

Kolchev wondered just how sensitive the microphones were.

123

He was naturally aware that the Germans had made considerable advances in this field, so he decided not to run any risks.

He glanced at his watch, started, and rose to leave.

'Anything wrong?' Brigitta asked, looking surprised.

He nodded. 'Yes, I forgot. I'm late for an engagement. Don't be angry, I'll come again the day after tomorrow.'

He kissed her lightly on the lips, straightened his tie and left in a hurry.

In the hall he bumped into Kitty. 'We dozed off and forgot the time,' he said. 'I was due somewhere half an hour ago—may I pay next time?'

'By all means.' Baron von Itter stood high on Kitty's list of credit-worthy clients.

It was dark when Kolchev stepped into the street. He could scarcely see the opposite pavement. Occasional slivers of light from masked headlamps swept up and down the Kurfürstendamm, but there was little traffic.

Soft music drifted through open windows. A number of local citizens had turned out their lights and were enjoying the cool night air. Kolchev recognised the danger and made allowances for it. He crossed the street and leant against a tree. He did not have long to wait. Brigitta emerged from the front entrance about ten minutes later—he recognised her footsteps.

He tailed her, blessing the inventor of the rubber soles which enabled him to follow her so unobtrusively. She went straight to the cover address as usual but remained there less than five minutes. Of course, he reflected, she had little to report. Then she headed for home.

Now was the time.

He quickened his pace until he caught her up. 'Brigitta,' he called softly.

The girl swung round. 'Lljubo!' she gasped. 'How did you get here?'

'Ssh, darling,' he said soothingly, taking her arm. 'I simply had to see you again.'

'But what about your appointment?'

'I'd never have made it,' he said. 'I followed you instead.'

'Yes, but—I don't understand. . . .' Brigitta was genuinely dismayed. It was obvious that he must have followed her to the cover address as well.

'Brigitta,' he said, 'I'm crazy about you.'

They paused beneath a tree and he took her in his arms and kissed her. Both of them realised that they were playing with fire, exposing themselves to a greater risk than they had ever run. Brigitta's only certainty was that Kolchev wielded a spell over her which it would be vain to resist. She didn't even want to try.

Equally, she knew that her life would be at risk if Untersturm-führer Schwarz or one of his myrmidons found out. Schwarz had warned his agents often enough that they would be under constant surveillance. Her heart pounded.

'We mustn't be seen together,' she whispered, '—not in the open.'

'I know,' he said. 'Can I come to your place?'

She shook her head fearfully. 'No!'

'What's the matter, scared?'

'Yes.' She kissed him again and he felt her tremble. 'I love you,' she said.

'I know, that's why I have to speak to you. Some place where no one can overhear us.'

'Why not come to Kitty's tomorrow?' she suggested.

He couldn't help smiling in the darkness. So she didn't know that all they said was monitored. Privately, he paid homage to the originators of the system. It seemed to function perfectly. The SS and SD must be behind it—he knew for certain but he couldn't prove it. Here, in this girl, lay his chance to do so.

'Come on, let's take the underground,' he said, propelling her along by the elbow.

'Where to?'

'The embassy. I'll borrow a car and we'll go for a drive.'

'I ought to go home,' she said. 'They may check . . .' She stopped short, aware that she had given herself away, and clapped a hand over her mouth.

'Not tonight,' he told her. 'Your bosses are probably celebrating the imminent fall of France.'

She stared at him in the gloom. Whoever he was and however much she knew, Brigitta loved him. She allowed him to steer her along, almost bereft of personal volition.

They were in luck. There was an embassy car free and the porter had the key. Kolchev took it, telling the man that he would be back in two hours.

While they drove through the Tiergarten, via the Kurfürsten-damm and Halensee, to Grunewald, Kolchev did the talking on Brigitta's behalf.

'I know you're an agent whose job it is to pump foreign diplomats. I know more than you think, but I love you—that's why I'm putting myself in your hands. You can denounce me tomorrow if you like. The Gestapo will arrest me and lock me up in a concentration camp. That's one course of action, but you won't take it because you love me too. And because we love each other we'll have to find a way of meeting outside Frau Schmidt's establishment. It's crazy, having to pay every time I want to be with you—can't you see that?'

Brigitta was overwhelmed by a sudden sense of absolute security. She would have given anything to go on driving through the night with him, oblivious of all that lay behind her, but she knew that she was inextricably enmeshed in the toils of the SD —that there was no escape.

All at once she started to cry. The tears streamed down her cheeks. She rested her head on his shoulder, and the pent-up pressures of the last few months erupted in a storm of weeping. Her shoulders shook as she fought to control herself.

Kolchev pulled a handkerchief from his breast pocket and gave it to her. 'Carry on,' he told her gently, 'don't mind me.'

A few minutes later, out in the leafy suburb of Grunewald, he found a suitable spot. He backed the car close to a wall so that no one could steal up on them unobserved.

'Tell me everything,' he said quietly, 'if you want to, that is.'

She blurted it all out—the training course at Sonthofen, the methods used to coerce her into her present form of activity, her duty to write a report on every client, the constant pressure and admonitions of the Central Security Office, the ceaseless surveillance. 'I betrayed you like all the rest,' she concluded, physically sickened by the thought.

'You didn't betray me because there was nothing to betray,' he said. 'Anything I get from Rumania the SD know at least three days in advance. Your people are far better informed than junior diplomats like me. Anyway, who cares about my measly job? I just kill time and thank God for every extra day I'm allowed to spend here in Berlin, so forget it.'

Brigitta started to cry again, but he kissed her tears away until she laughed despite herself. 'I'm so happy,' she murmured.

'Me too,' he said. 'That's why we've got to be doubly careful. I've discovered something you must keep to yourself at all costs. Don't breathe a word to anyone, but everything that's said at the Salon Kitty is picked up by concealed microphones. You're under constant observation, not only there but possibly elsewhere as well—never forget that. So watch your tongue when I come visiting. I'll always bring you a couple of items of information so they won't stop you from seeing me. Apart from that, I'll try and find some way of meeting you on neutral territory.'

'Why don't we meet at your place?' she asked ingenuously.

'Be sensible, sweetheart! How long do you think it would take them to discover that you were having an affair with a Rumanian diplomat, and what do you suppose they'd think then?'

Brigitta was experienced enough in the ways of the SD to know what the inference would be. 'I'm sorry,' she said, 'that was stupid of me.'

He thought for a moment. 'In future, if I want to tell you something I'll write it down. You can do the same, but we must always destroy the pieces of paper at once, agreed?'

'Agreed.' She nodded happily. Then they kissed, and for a few short moments Brigitta became a young girl in love.

The visit from Heydrich and Schellenberg left Kitty in a pensive frame of mind. Berlin friends of long standing who saw her at this period noticed that a change was taking place in her.

They asked her what the matter was but didn't press her. The mood of national euphoria was such that no one really wanted to delve into other people's problems, so Kitty was absolved from the need to find excuses.

Untersturmführer Schwarz only contacted her by phone now. She had not seen him for many weeks, but that puzzled her less. It was the personal visit from Heydrich and Schellenberg which really gave her cause for concern. Did they mistrust her? Was she regarded as a security risk? She found no answer to these and many other nagging questions.

The worst of it was, she couldn't discuss them openly with anyone. Her fear of fresh reprisals was so great that she didn't even confide in her daughter, who had recently come to live with her.

Kitty had naturally heard some of the rumours that proliferated in Berlin. People spoke in hushed voices of this or that person —usually a Jew—who had vanished overnight and never been seen again. There was talk of concentration camps and the brutalities that were perpetrated there, but all of it nebulous.

Kitty had many friends among Berlin's Jewish community. She sometimes wished she had stayed on in London after her royal welcome from Samuel Levy and his fellow-exiles.

The more she thought about it, the more she became obsessed with the desire to shut up shop and leave Berlin. But did she have the slightest control over her own future? Kitty was shrewd enough to know that she had none. She was forced to run with the pack. There was little chance of outwitting Schellenberg. On the other hand, she lived better than many of her compatriots. She lacked for nothing. If she needed something she rang Untersturmführer Schwarz and it arrived within a few days. Besides, she often managed to convince herself that what was going on in her house was a nightmare which she would one day shake off like any bad dream. She still imbibed coffee and schnapps whenever gloom descended on her, but she never gave up hope. Resignation would have meant surrender and a threat to her survival—and Kitty loved life, even now.

And yet. . . .

There was something she had never managed to overcome. Her thoughts returned again and again to the same subject—the possibility of escape. Although she knew how such experiments could end, she started to tick off possible places of refuge. Switzerland was the obvious one, but who could guarantee that Hitler would not one day overrun this small oasis of neutrality? Anywhere else was too remote. England seemed a world away, and as for America—it was far beyond the scope of her wildest dreams.

The fact remained that her present mode of existence was intolerable. The girls who now came to the house were no trouble, but she had little contact with them. She didn't know who they were, why they did what they did, or what was really going on. Sometimes she yearned for her old girls, who came less and less often. It wasn't that she had frozen them out. It was simply that even her existing clients had grown so accustomed to the Rothenburg girls—as she privately called them—that the demand for her 'regular personnel' had dwindled steadily.

At least there had been the occasional scene in the old days—the occasional argument over a client, over money or a dress. Unimportant little squabbles though they were, Kitty found herself missing them more and more.

She now had a high-class clientèle—exalted gentlemen of exalted rank—and everything took place on the refined and elegant plane that had been her ambition in times gone by. But Kitty had dreamed of building up such an establishment differently, on lines evolved by herself, not dictated by the Central Security Office.

She could not, with the best will in the world, imagine that Heydrich and Schellenberg had visited the place for their personal delectation. She might have slept better if she had known that their motive was nothing more sinister. As it was, she continued to be gnawed by doubt, uncertainty and fear.

Which was precisely what Untersturmführer Schwarz hoped and expected.

More fanfares blared from the radio, heralding a special announcement: 'The High Command of the Armed Forces has issued the following communiqué: victorious German troops are now entering Paris!'

Paris. . . . Kitty's mental image of Paris was a city like London, teeming with people, throbbing with life, aglow with a myriad lights. Although she had never been there, she felt a sudden yearning to go. She debated whether to request Schwarz for a transfer to the French capital.

Transfer? She rebuked herself for thinking like an NCO, but nothing could dispel the charm of the idea.

Claustrophobia overcame her. She put on a light coat, told Elvira to take charge, and left the house on foot. Aimlessly, she strolled through the streets of Berlin. The longer she walked the freer she felt—almost guiltily free. Everyone who hurried past her seemed to be grave-faced and intent on reaching a set destination.

She didn't know how she got there, but she suddenly found herself standing outside the building which housed Superintendent Kuhn's office.

How much of a friend was he? At least he was a contemporary —sixty or so. In a sort of trance, Kitty climbed the stairs to his office and knocked.

It was her first visit, and Kuhn was perceptibly surprised to see her.

'Kitty Schmidt! What brings you here?' He came to meet her with both arms outstretched, genuine delight written all over his face. 'I can't offer you any champagne, I'm afraid.'

Kitty sank into a chair. 'It's good to see you again, Superintendent. You've been avoiding me lately.'

Kuhn looked embarrassed. She was right. The people who now patronised her establishment were out of his class. Kuhn couldn't afford to risk official displeasure so soon before his retirement. He told her so, more or less.

'Don't you keep anything to drink in this place?' she asked.

'Nothing alcoholic.' He chuckled ruefully. 'This isn't the Gestapo.'

So they sat over two watery cups of office coffee and chatted about old times. When Kuhn escorted her downstairs an hour later, she knew she had at least one friend she could rely on.

He arrived soon after lunch, clearly in high spirits. Elvira opened the door to find him brandishing a bottle of wine in either hand. He smiled broadly, good teeth white in a tanned face, and said simply: 'It's me. Kitty at home?'

Elvira recognised him at once. He had been a regular customer before the war—a generous one, too. Elvira's pocket had suffered from the absence of his tips. She gave him a welcoming smile in return.

'Come in, I'll tell the mistress you're here.'

She ushered him into the parlour and went to fetch Kitty. He laughed when he saw her.

'Still the same old ritual, I see.'

'My God, Richard, it's been ages! Where have you been all this time?'

'Where every true German belongs when Führer and Fatherland call,' he replied flippantly, '—at the front, of course. Well, here I am, home on leave and champing at the bit.'

Kitty wagged her head. 'You're incorrigible, Richard. There's been a lot of changes here. . . .'

'What?' he exclaimed in mock alarm. 'No more girls?'

'Yes, yes, don't worry.' She smiled. Richard was one of her old customers, a nice boy, always good-humoured, always full of devilment and thirsting for something new in the way of female company. She decided to take a risk and introduce him to one of her Rothenburg girls. 'I've got a real delicacy for you today —Leni, her name is. Let me know afterwards how you get on together.'

'A virgin?' he demanded eagerly.

'Not exactly—more the hot-blooded type. She's new. . . .'

'I'm all for novelty. Wheel her in, Kitty. How soon can she be here?'

'You won't have to wait long,' Kitty said drily. She rang for Elvira. 'Take the gentleman to No 6 and bring him something to drink—anything he fancies. Book it to me.'

Richard laughed and waved his brace of bottles in the air. 'No need, Kitty, I came equipped.'

'Take them with you when you go,' she told him. 'We aren't short.'

She went to phone Leni, who arrived ten minutes later. Richard had already downed a couple of quick ones in the interval. It was always the same with him. First curiosity, then a touch of nervousness until the ice was broken. Finally, the determination and ability to make love until his partner wept for sheer delight.

'So you're Leni,' he said, eyeing the new girl with pleasurable anticipation.

Leni nodded and launched into her usual routine, but Richard seized the initiative. He didn't wait for her to make the running. It was clear that his needs were sexual rather than conversational.

'Come on,' he said, pulling her up out of her chair. 'That's a pretty dress, but I bet you look even prettier without it.' He undid the poppers and propelled her ahead of him to the big wall-mirror, where he slid the dress very slowly off her shoulders until she stood there in her bra and pants. 'My God,' he whispered appreciatively, 'I was right. . . .'

The girl shot him a smouldering glance in the mirror.

'If your breasts are half as good as I think they are, this is going to be a day to remember.' He unhooked her brassière. Her breasts came to light, young and firm, the nipples encircled by big rosy moons. Richard cupped them in his hands. She leant back and gave him her lips to kiss. He felt the warmth of her skin and inhaled its musky fragrance. His fingers moved down her body until they slipped inside her panties and found what they were seeking—the moist and expectant cleft of a woman ripe for the act of love.

131

Richard picked her up effortlessly in his strong arms and carried her to the bed. He laid her down, bent low over her and kissed her breasts, one hand busy with his tie and shirt buttons. 'Just a moment, sweetheart,' he said, and undressed with lightning speed.

'Anyone would think you were a quick-change artist,' she said teasingly.

And then he was with her again. His hands roved over her young, tanned body. He feasted his senses on the feel of her magnificent breasts, on the kisses from her full lips and the flame of lust that darted from her to him when he felt her touch his erect and urgent penis, which was ready to explode with suppressed desire.

Brutally, he tore her panties over her knees and entered her with all the force of a sex-starved man. He raised himself on his elbows to look into her face, a mask of sweet and dreamy surrender which seemed to grimace with pain at every thrust of his body. She lay there with her eyes closed, emitting low moans of pleasure.

'Play with my nipples,' he whispered hoarsely.

Her long slender hands groped for his hirsute chest. With gentle circular movements, she began to rub the nipples between her thumb and forefinger as she goaded him on. 'You randy swine,' she hissed, 'come, damn you, fill me to the brim, come deep and hard inside me, you sweet bastard, do it now, come . . .' Her whispered words gave away to moans which rose in volume until her body arched ecstatically beneath him. 'Aah!' she cried. 'I'm coming. . . .' And he felt her come, dissolve, melt, suck him dry, then suddenly relax. Limply, she wound her arms round his neck and drew him down to her. Her lips clamped themselves to his throat as she uttered little whimpers of delight and fulfilment. 'You, you . . .' she gasped. Desire flared up in her again, and again her body twitched convulsively with excitement. And Richard stayed inside her, clawing her against him, clasping the softness of her in his powerful arms, feeling the sweat flow between her breasts and weld their bodies into a seemingly indissoluble whole.

Suddenly he rolled off her and jumped out of bed, dragging her after him. He pulled a stool in front of the mirror and took her from behind, she resting her elbows on the stool while he played with her breasts. Their gaze met, charged with erotic tension, as they watched one another in the mirror and waited for the rhythm of their animal movements to unleash another orgasm. She writhed in his grasp until, woman that she was, she surrendered to his potent masculinity and sank to the floor. Richard just managed to catch her.

'I told you it would be a day to remember,' he whispered in her ear as he carried her back to the bed.

'You're a marvel,' she murmured, 'but you finish me. If every client was as strenuous as you are, we'd be entitled to danger money.'

He laughed. 'It's those breasts of yours—they inspire me. I rated as an expert on breasts, even at school. The thing was, I'd evolved a theory about them. It earned me a lot of prestige.'

'You mean you're a bosom-fetishist?'

'Not exactly, but I still like women with curves in all the right places. I told my schoolmates that if you could see a girl's nipples through her dress she was a virgin—if not, she'd already been with someone and got them squashed flat. They believed me for ages.'

'But you can't see a girl's nipples under her bra,' Leni objected, giggling.

'Sure, but I didn't know that at the time. I was curious to see if my theory worked.'

'You must have been quite a lad.'

'I still am.' He tapped his head and genitals in turn. 'Brains plus brawn, that's me.'

'You're great,' Leni sighed. She made a half-hearted attempt to draw him out, but Richard seemed to have no political or military views whatsoever. They didn't emerge from No 6 until four hours later. Leni swayed a little, and he solicitously took her arm.

'That was gorgeous,' she sighed as he was leaving. 'Couldn't you manage another visit before your leave ends?'

'Another visit?' Richard shook his head reproachfully. 'I aim to come every day.'

Leni almost crossed herself in pleasurable alarm. 'For God's sake,' she said, 'you'll put me in hospital!'

Kolchev's revelations had come as a shock to Brigitta. For days she wavered between love and duty. Sitting around idly in her small apartment, waiting for Kitty to call, she longed for Lljubo's presence. Then, remembering what he had told her, she embarked

133

on a thorough search of her room. Brigitta was well trained enough to avoid making any suspicious sounds. She was horrified to think that her apartment might be bugged and angry with Untersturmführer Schwarz for showing so little faith in her and her fellow-agents, especially as her own faith in Hitler and the German cause remained unshaken. On the other hand, she didn't want to lose the man she had come to know and love. Realising that she was in a blind alley from which there could be no escape, she solved the problem in a typically feminine way by delegating all decisions to her lover.

Once she had reached this stage in her deliberations and satisfied herself that the apartment contained no monitoring devices, she risked calling Kolchev at the Rumanian embassy, not from her apartment but from a telephone kiosk some distance away.

'Where are you speaking from?' he asked at once.

She reassured him and could hear the relief in his voice.

'I think you can safely come to my place,' she told him. 'You know what I mean. . . .'

She gave him an address in Nestorstrasse.

'I'll try and drop by this evening,' he said. 'Listen for three short rings, then you'll know it's me.'

Brigitta glowed with pleasure, though she might not have done so if she had known of his current activities. He had passed her information to London and received an important message by return: 'Technicians will contact you Monday 24 June.'

And today was Monday.

Kolchev left the embassy building in Rauchstrasse just before 5 p.m. No one had contacted him so far, so he drank a coffee—or what now passed for one—at Kranzler's and went back to his apartment.

He switched on the radio but turned it off again after a few minutes because the heroic marches got on his nerves. Listlessly, he tidied up the flat for something to do. He had to admit to a certain uneasiness. He sensed that London was on the verge of taking a crucial step and knew the dangers associated with it. The risk of detection would be greatly increased once his helpers arrived.

Unable to endure the suspense, he walked over to the laundry in Emserstrasse.

The shop was already shut, so he knocked at the back door.

134

A fat and genial Berlin housewife opened it. 'Oh, it's you, Baron,' she said loudly, as though eager to advertise the rank of her customer to the entire building. 'I tried to ring you just now. Please come in—your laundry is waiting for you.'

She pulled him inside and slammed the door.

'In there,' she continued, nudging him into a darkened room. The curtains were drawn, even though it was still light outside.

Three men were sitting at a table. One of them, evidently the proprietor of the laundry, rose and went out, bidding Kolchev 'Heil Hitler!' as he left the room.

'Heil Hitler,' Kolchev replied. He glanced at the other two inquiringly.

'He's all right,' said one of them. They didn't introduce themselves. 'Where's the job?' asked the other, point-blank.

Kolchev, who was drilled in his Secret Service catechism, knew that the two men were fellow-agents but double-checked to make quite certain. Then he briefed them on the set-up.

'And your theory is that the cable runs through a normal Post Office conduit?'

Roger Wilson, alias Lljubo Kolchev, reported on his observations of recent months, on his talk with Brigitta and the clients who now patronised 11 Giesebrechtstrasse.

The two men listened attentively.

'Even if we managed to tap the wires without anyone noticing, we'd have to establish a listening-post of our own and man it almost continuously. It's a problem, but we'll have to solve it somehow. . . .' They discussed various possibilities without reaching any definite conclusion.

The elder of the two said : 'We could always blow up a house during an air-raid and move into the ruins when the dust has settled.'

'Too conspicuous,' said Kolchev. 'Besides, they'd patch it up immediately, if only for prestige reasons.'

'What about the sewers?'

'My guess is, they patrol them regularly.'

'Perhaps we could get the RAF to plaster the surrounding area.'

Kolchev grimaced. 'They'd have to be pretty accurate. One bomb in the wrong place and our best source of information goes up in smoke.'

'There's this place too,' said the younger man. 'The man's a

135

loyal Party member—nobody would think of suspecting him.'

They debated the proposal and rejected it. The laundry rendez-vous was too valuable to jeopardise. No other solutions suggested themselves.

'The first thing is to find out for certain if the place is bugged from the outside and, if so, whether we can get at the circuit.'

They spread a street map of Berlin on the table and Kolchev pin-pointed the places outside Nos 11 and 12 Giesebrechtstrasse where he had seen engineers at work. The two strangers made detailed drawings on an overlay. Every now and then they ex-changed confirmatory glances, nodded or asked questions. After half an hour's intensive work, they sat back.

'We'll contact you in due course,' said the senior of the two.

'In that case, Heil Hitler!' Kolchev grinned at them and got up to go. As he was leaving, the plump woman thrust a small parcel of laundry into his hand.

He went home and opened it. There were several snow-white handkerchiefs inside, neatly ironed and packed in tissue paper.

He prepared a bowl of solution and immersed the handkerchiefs. A long list of instructions took shape as he watched, all to do with the Salon Kitty. He memorised them, then stuffed a copy of the *Völkischer Beobachter* into his tiled stove and reduced the nice new handkerchiefs to ashes. That done, he set off to see Brigitta.

Chapter 11

Walter Schellenberg would have been furious if he had known that, from 2 July 1940 onwards, he had been supplying the British Secret Service with items of intelligence from the Salon Kitty.

The communications experts from London actually managed to cut in on the land-line to the listening-post in Meineckestrasse. Although they only succeeded in tapping a few cores under cover of darkness, the fact that Wilson-Kolchev had been correct in his suppositions meant that they could go ahead with plans to monitor the entire circuit.

From Kolchev's point of view, it was satisfaction enough to know that his suspicions had been confirmed. His visits to the Salon Kitty became less frequent—so much so that Kitty tackled him about it.

'What's the matter, Baron? We hardly see you these days.'

Kolchev gave a wry smile. 'Pressure of work, Kitty. I hate to say it, but I think I'm finally growing up. Never mind, bring me something to drink and send for one of your girls.'

'Brigitta?' she asked.

He shrugged expansively. 'I don't mind.'

'I'll go and call her right away. She's pining for you—at least, that's my impression.'

'If you say so. . . .' Kolchev's tone was indifferent, but his ears burned. If the hidden eavesdroppers took Kitty's remark seriously, Brigitta would be in deadly peril. He called Kitty back. 'Look,' he said, 'you can send for her, but this is the last time. After today, I'll have to look around for someone new. I don't like emotional entanglements.'

'You're a smart young man, Baron,' said Kitty. There was something about the Rumanian which appealed to her maternal instinct.

A few minutes later everything was as usual. Brigitta and

Kolchev found themselves alone in Room 7. He handed her a scribbled note. It read: 'We mustn't meet here any more. I'll stage a walk-out. In future, see you at your place.'

'Know something?' he said aloud. 'My liege lord, King Carol the Second, has made another of his unilateral decisions. The Front of National Revival—as we call it in Rumania—has become the country's sole political party. In future, it's to be called the Party of the Nation. Nice name, don't you agree?'

Brigitta laughed. 'Sounds interesting, Lljubo. Party of the Nation. . . . What's the matter with that?'

'Nothing,' he said, 'except that it'll operate under the King's supreme command. Guiding the moral and material life of the nation and the Rumanian State—that's the official description of its function. The King will appoint party bosses responsible to him alone. The whole thing is a right-wing plot.'

Brigitta deftly took her cue. 'I still don't see what you're grumbling about. Better right-wing than communist.'

'Maybe, but it won't work,' he snapped, signalling to her to follow his lead. 'Another few months and we'll all be up the spout.'

She injected still more irritation into her voice. 'How can you say such things about your king and country?'

'Rumania isn't Germany,' he retorted angrily. 'I wish I was a German so I could fight on your side, and plenty of Rumanians think the same way. Carol's turning the country into a circus.'

'But Lljubo,' she said, 'what sort of attitude is that?'

'I'm strung up, that's all,' he fumed. 'I'd better go—I'm not in the mood today. Besides, you're getting on my nerves. Why the hell do you think I come here? Relaxation's what I need, and you spend the whole time needling me. I'm sick of it, do you hear? I've had enough!' He stormed out and slammed the door loudly behind him.

'Brigitta's getting on my nerves,' he told Kitty. 'I'm tired of the girl. Next time I come, find me someone else—someone less interested in politics.'

'By all means, Baron,' Kitty said soothingly. 'Leave it to me.'

Kolchev allowed himself to be pacified. He even gave a chuckle. 'You're an angel, Kitty. If it weren't for you I'd despair of the whole human race.'

Kitty described a mock curtsy. 'Thank you, kind sir.' She escorted him to the door and said goodbye.

Kolchev wondered as he left the house whether his act had gone down well. He hoped so. His parting shot had been an attempt to explain, for the benefit of the microphones, why he would not be patronising the Salon Kitty so often in weeks to come. He was pretty sure that the authorities charted all clients' visits with Prussian precision. They might reprimand Brigitta, but he had prepared her for that.

The man who arrived in Berlin on 4 July 1940 to supervise security measures for the forthcoming visit of Adolf Hitler, Führer and Supreme Commander of the German Armed Forces, was a member of the Waffen-SS, or military SS. To be more accurate, he was—by deed if not by intention—its originator.

Sepp Dietrich had the temperament of a rugged sergeant-major, even if he now wore the insignia of a Gruppenführer, or major-general in the SS. Born in 1892, Dietrich had done everything and been everything—farm labourer, waiter, tank unit NCO in World War I, policeman, tobacco factory foreman, customs officer and petrol-pump attendant. He was a man of action, crafty but not insidious, a sociable, gregarious type who could tackle any practical problem and be relied on to solve it.

Dietrich joined the Nazi Party in 1928 and was rewarded with a job in the Party-owned publishing house. He rose quickly through the ranks of the SS, whose devil-may-care aura appealed to him. By 1930 he was commanding the SS in South Bavaria, by 1931 the North Hamburg district. Himmler and Hitler were both impressed by his huge stature, resolute bearing and genial manner—the latter enhanced by a broad Bavarian dialect. It may have been this combination of qualities which convinced them that he was the right man to protect the Führer from his enemies. In 1933, Dietrich was appointed to command the SS-Leibstandarte, or SS bodyguard, later awarded the honourable suffix 'Adolf Hitler'. This laid the foundations of the Waffen-SS, a fully militarised organisation which ultimately provided 40 divisions in World War II.

Dietrich's absolute loyalty and devotion to Hitler assured him of a meteoric career, while his popularity with subordinates and superiors alike helped to boost his reputation as a tough all-German swashbuckler—an image which he glorified in and cultivated with care.

On 4 July 1940, however, Sepp Dietrich had other worries. His job was to organise and safeguard the Führer's triumphal return to the capital of the Greater German Reich. Being a practical man, he felt undismayed by the prospect of completing his arrangements in a single day. He turned up towards evening, although the Führer was due to be welcomed with pomp, ceremony and popular acclaim only two days later.

Dietrich paid his respects to Goebbels, issued instructions to Count Helldorf, the City Police Commissioner, got in touch with the trusty members of his local SS headquarters, and still found time to visit the Salon Kitty, which had often been recommended to him.

His first impression of the place was profoundly satisfactory. Cold beer and a warm welcome seemed to hold promise of greater delights to come.

'Right,' he said bluntly, 'where are the women?'

'We have our own special system, Gruppenführer,' Kitty told him. Sepp Dietrich was in uniform, and she had learnt to distinguish the various insignia of rank. She brought out her albums of prospective partners and politely suggested that he might like to pick one.

'One?' Dietrich threw back his head and guffawed. 'One?' He slapped his thigh with undisguised merriment. 'Parade the whole bloody lot!' he commanded, taking a hefty swig of beer.

'As you wish,' said Kitty, and started to phone.

'Did you hear that?' Dietrich demanded of his companions, a pair of young officers on his staff. 'One!' he repeated, still unable to contain himself. Then he began to inspect his surroundings. 'Some place!' he said appreciatively. 'She's even got a piano. How about it, Franz? Come on, let's have a tune!'

His young aide jumped up and went to the piano.

'What'll it be, Gruppenführer?'

'Something to put us in the mood. Fire away!'

Franz opened fire with a salvo of popular ballads. By the time the first girls arrived, each member of the threesome had sunk four half-litres of strong German beer—quite enough to banish any lingering inhibitions.

The girls joined in with a will. They felt drawn to the black-uniformed officers, if only by the esprit de corps which it would have cost them their lives to mention.

140

Sepp Dietrich was the first to make a move. 'Right,' he told Kitty, 'all I need now is a woman, a bed, and a bottle of bubbly.'

Kitty gave him an understanding smile. 'Which of my young ladies do you fancy?'

Dietrich didn't take long to make up his mind. 'That one over there,' he said, '—the brunette.' Kitty followed the direction of his extended forefinger. 'Fräulein Hildegard,' she called, 'I wonder if you'd mind. . . .'

'Mind be buggered,' Dietrich cut in. 'Come on, girl, let's get cracking.' He grabbed Hildegard by the elbow and towed her into the passage. 'Which way?' he asked.

Elvira materialised with two clean hand-towels over her arm. 'Follow me, please.'

'We'll follow you, all right,' roared the Gruppenführer, leering over his shoulder at the captive Hildegard.

'Would you like something to drink, sir?' Elvira inquired when they reached the bedroom.

'Sure, bring us a bottle of fizz,' Dietrich told her. 'This is my night out—money's no object.' Contentedly, he unbuttoned his uniform tunic, tossed his ceremonial dirk on to a chair and snapped his braces.

'All right,' he told Hildegard, who was sitting demurely in an arm-chair, waiting for some of the champagne which Elvira had just brought in, 'get that clobber off.'

'Don't be in such a rush,' the girl said coquettishly, mindful of her agent's duties. 'Let's have a glass of champagne and get to know each other first.' But her usual gambit was lost on Sepp Dietrich.

'The hell with that!' he roared. 'I didn't come here to talk. Come on, move, or I'll rip the clothes off you myself.'

'But Herr Sepp,' she protested.

'Less of the Herr—plain Sepp, understand?'

Hildegard did her best. 'Tell me a bit about France,' she said. 'What was it like?'

'I'll show you in two minutes—it'll make your hair curl. All right, cut the cackle. I came here for a fuck, not a school debate.'

He hauled the girl out of the chair and unbuttoned her dress. She made a last desperate effort to extract some information, however little, but the giant SS man was too much for her.

With incongruous elegance of movement, Dietrich pulled off his soft leather boots and leapt into bed like a panther, naked. 'Right,' he yelled, 'come here. . . .'

'I'd like to wash, if I may. . . .'

'Ho-ho-ho!' His raucous laughter filled the room. 'Good,' he said, 'very good. Cleanliness is next to godliness—is that what they taught you in Sunday school?' He put the champagne bottle to his lips and drank greedily, then gave a contented belch and shouted : 'What's keeping you?'

'Just coming,' Hildegard called back. She joined him on the bed, aroused despite herself by his animal temperament. Her fingers insinuated themselves into the bush of hair on his chest. Dietrich lay back, enjoying the sensation.

'You were asking what it was like in France,' he said with a smirk. 'I'll tell you. French, that's what it was like.' He took another swig. 'Those women know their onions. They've got a natural talent for sex, believe me. You ought to take a few tips from them.'

'Teach me something,' Hildegard said.

'Who, me?' Dietrich smirked again. 'Well, for one thing, why leave out the hors d'oeuvres? That's half the fun. What's your mouth for? Not just for necking. There are plenty of other things you can do with it. Have a go.'

He stretched out and waited to see what the girl would do.

Hildegard was perplexed. Until now, her clients had always made the running. She had helped a little sometimes, of course, but mostly with elderly gentlemen who were having difficulty. Confronted by this hulking bull of a man, she felt utterly at a loss.

'Carry on, kiss me,' he said. 'From head to toe, I mean, and mind you don't leave anything out.'

Hildegard tried. She started on his eyelids.

'Poof!' he grumbled. 'Don't lick, suck. Suck like a baby and do it with feeling, so I get a kick out of it. Have a nibble if you like— I'll sing out if you overdo it. Either that or I'll knock you silly. You'll soon know if you're getting it wrong. All right, get cracking!'

He lay back and closed his eyes. Hildegard tried again.

'Bravo!' he commended her. 'That's better. What did I tell you? You girls better pull your fingers out when our lads get back from France. They're used to being spoiled.'

Success was only moderate until Sepp Dietrich fell on her

and worked off all he had been storing up for weeks. He had plenty of stamina and the girl enjoyed it. It wasn't until they were lying side by side, pleasantly fatigued, that she remembered her duties.

'Are we going to invade England next?' she asked, lighting a cigarette.

'How should I know?' Dietrich said. 'Ask the Führer—he makes all the decisions. I'll tell you this much : if we attack the British we'll crush them the way we crush anyone who gets in the Führer's hair.'

'What exactly do you do in the SS?' Hildegard asked.

'What's it to you?' Sepp Dietrich emitted a low rumble of laughter. 'Pumping me, are you?'

'Of course not,' she hastened to assure him.

'Belt up, then.' His tone was kindly but firm.

There was nothing to be done, Hildegard could see that. She wondered what to put in her report. Recalling the events of the past hour, she had to smile. Sepp Dietrich didn't notice—he had blissfully dozed off. She couldn't even detach herself from the hairy, muscular arm that encircled her, so she fell asleep too.

They woke up several hours later, almost simultaneously.

'Shit!' said Dietrich. 'I could use a beer.'

'Hang on.' Hildegard jumped up and rang the bell beside the door. Elvira, who never seemed to sleep, shuffled in.

'Anything I can do?'

'Yes,' said Hildegard, 'the Gruppenführer would like a beer.'

'And make it snappy!' bellowed Dietrich.

Elvira brought three bottles to be on the safe side.

'Smart girl,' Dietrich told her approvingly. He emptied the first bottle without drawing breath. 'That's better!' he said, thumping his chest. 'Got a tough day ahead of me,' he added as he started to dress. With his uniform tunic buttoned and his ceremonial dirk buckled on, he once more looked what he was reputed to be : one of the boys—a man's man. The second bottle of beer went the way of the first.

'I may drop by in the next couple of days,' he told Hildegard. His hand shot up in a Nazi salute but halted mid-way. Even he realised that it was a little out of place.

'Anyone can make a mistake,' he muttered to himself as he marched down the long passage.

The German News Agency reported on 6 July 1940 that the Führer and Supreme Commander of the Armed Forces had returned to Berlin after directing operations on the Western Front since 10 May. The inhabitants of Berlin gave him jubilant welcome.

Goebbels's propaganda machine was firing on all cylinders.

Sepp Dietrich rode on the running-board of the Führer's car. The Gruppenführer felt tired but happy. If a sniper had drawn a bead on his master, Sepp Dietrich would have been powerless to stop him—but then, who was likely to assassinate Hitler on that glorious, victorious day in 1940?

The next day Hitler received Count Ciano, the Italian Foreign Minister. There were a few arguments over how the cake should be divided. As Ribbentrop noted later : 'I never saw the Führer so adamant as he was in his rejection of the Italian demands.'

On 10 July 1940 Rumania left the League of Nations. The official declaration issued by the Rumanian Foreign Office did not land on Lljubo Kolchev's desk until 15 July. The news was so stale that he decided against dropping it into Schellenberg's 'canal' and refrained from visiting the Salon Kitty.

Chapter 12

Reinhard Heydrich, all-powerful head of the Central Security Office in Berlin's Prinz Albrechtstrasse, returned from the French campaign with a chestful of medals.

In spite of Schellenberg's failure to abduct the Duke and Duchess of Windsor from Lisbon—an elaborate scheme which went awry—Heydrich knew that his subordinate was a man whose goodwill was worth retaining. Accordingly, he recommended Schellenberg for promotion to Obersturmbannführer, a rank corresponding to that of lieutenant-colonel in the German army.

The SD foreign intelligence service continued to be Heydrich's major source of information. As for the Salon Kitty, it supplied him with an up-to-date picture of the views held by the Third Reich's potentates and their allies—one which gave him a better insight into the real state of morale than any other source could have yielded. He even gave items reaching him from the Salon Kitty precedence over 'SD Reports on Domestic Questions', which were compiled by SS-Obersturmbannführer Otto Ohlendorf, head of the SD Inland Intelligence Service, with the help of numerous spies and informers. These reports were, in effect, an early form of opinion poll. Doctors, schoolmasters, artists, scientists, university teachers and civil servants all contributed to them in their capacity as confidential advisers to the SD. They were expressly instructed to avoid optimistic distortions and paint the attitude and morale of the population as it really was. The intimate revelations which Heydrich derived from the Salon Kitty made him indispensable to Himmler, with whom he shared a strange sense of affinity.

Himmler, already Reichsführer-SS and head of the German police, aspired to become Minister of the Interior. With this end in view, he strove to accumulate as much personal power and authority as he could. Heydrich was one of his most important henchmen. Although Himmler always distrusted him and felt that he was secretly undermining his position, he could not dispense with his help and advice.

Heydrich, whom even his subordinates accused of a ruthless and unbridled lust for power, treated Himmler with almost doglike devotion. He never contested any of Himmler's orders, even though his keen intellect told him that many of them were senseless as soon as they were issued.

For his part, Himmler hated and admired Heydrich for the clear and concise way in which, with a minimum of verbiage, his briefings managed to give an objective picture of any given situation.

Although Heydrich's manner towards Himmler was almost typical of the Nazi subordinate, he nonetheless excelled at playing off his own subordinates inside the Central Security Office in such a way that each of them was stimulated to give of his best.

In turn, Heydrich's close links with Schellenberg derived solely from the latter's ability to drop choice items of intelligence on his desk. Only this accounted for his indulgent attitude towards blunders and extravagant behaviour on Schellenberg's part which he would have punished unmercifully in anyone else.

It seems likely that the Salon Kitty played an important part in this. Heydrich's human weaknesses included a reputedly insatiable appetite for sex which made him a regular patron of brothels and high-class prostitutes. The fact that the Salon Kitty was, in a sense, 'SD-manned', and that frequent visits could be disguised as 'tours of inspection', may likewise have fostered his special relationship with Walter Schellenberg, although Heydrich simultaneously suspected him of conducting a clandestine affair with his wife, Lina.

Nor did it worry Heydrich, during his 'inspections' of the Salon Kitty and other brothels, that the girls tended to smile on his most frequent companion, Schellenberg, and merely tolerated his own attentions. Perhaps it was the fault of his unpleasant falsetto voice and the ice-cold aura for which he was famed.

Whatever the true circumstances, Heydrich automatically approved all expenses incurred in connection with the Salon Kitty —another factor which helped to strengthen Schellenberg's hand.

146

Schellenberg soon grasped this situation and took full advantage of it. Whenever he was in Berlin he made a point of visiting the listening-post at least once a week. He devoted close attention to the recording procedure itself, also the Records Department where the wax disks were transcribed, conveying by his presence that all personnel engaged in this maximum security project were constantly under the supervision of a senior officer.

It did not, of course, escape him that the monitoring centre was becoming more and more cramped. The wax disks now ran into thousands and vast numbers of files had been opened, so there was a patent need for reorganisation.

Schwarz, who had since been promoted Obersturmführer on Schellenberg's recommendation, was urged to speed up his experiments with wire- and tape-recorders and explore the possibility of transferring the monitoring centre to an alternative site. He was also instructed to draw up a list of the Salon Kitty's clients, classified under various headings. German visitors were to be listed according to membership of Party, government or armed forces, foreign visitors according to country, diplomatic status and political importance.

This assignment tied Schwarz to his desk for weeks, because it was a task which he had to undertake personally if he did not wish to jeopardise the Salon Kitty's security rating. It may well have been this which saved the lives of the British technicians who were currently at work on the monitoring cable. The system was thus at risk from an unknown quarter; at the same time, danger threatened the entire Security Service from the highest quarter of all : Hitler himself.

Rumania had been hugely impressed by Germany's great victory in the West, and King Carol sought closer ties with the Axis powers. His bargaining counter was oil, which Germany and Italy badly needed in order to continue the war. On 26 June 1940, the Soviet Union presented Rumania with an ultimatum demanding the cession of Bessarabia and Northern Bucovina. Ribbentrop's Foreign Office, when consulted, advised Rumania to yield to Soviet pressure.

The annexation of these territories brought the Russians close to Rumania's oil-producing regions, and their success prompted the Hungarians to reclaim territory surrendered after World War

I. The danger of hostilities between Rumania and Hungary compelled Germany and Italy to intervene.

It transpired in the process that the SD foreign intelligence service was involved in some rather peculiar intrigues. The SD had for years been backing Horia Sima and his Iron Guard organisation, whose avowed aim was to topple the conservative prime minister, General Ion Antonescu, because Himmler and Heydrich saw the Iron Guard as a sort of Rumanian SS.

Horia Sima's intermediaries actually persuaded King Carol to arrest Antonescu, but the latter—who enjoyed the backing of Hitler and Ribbentrop—was released under German diplomatic pressure. Ribbentrop thus supported Antonescu's intention to become dictator of Rumania.

After a further loss of Rumanian territory, this time to Hungary, and the swift disintegration of a temporary alliance between Antonescu and Horia Sima, a national crisis broke out.

On 4 September 1940 King Carol conferred full powers on Antonescu and appointed him head of government. On 6 September Antonescu forced Carol to abdicate in favour of Crown Prince Michael, his virtual puppet.

Meanwhile, the SD foreign intelligence service continued to back Horia Sima and the Iron Guard, who were still preparing to rise against Antonescu in the expectation of German assistance promised them by SD intermediaries.

Antonescu increased his dependence on the Axis powers, however, and announced that he would visit Hitler in Berlin to negotiate an expansion of German military and air force missions, their task being to modernise Rumania's armed forces.

Ribbentrop, who had meanwhile learned of the SD's machinations in Rumania, gave an exaggerated account of them to Hitler. The dictator flew into one of his celebrated fits of rage and vowed to wipe out 'the black plague' (i.e. the SD) if it did not come to heel. Ribbentrop delightedly seized the opportunity to strip the SD foreign service and intelligence network, at least temporarily, of its influence on foreign policy—something for which neither Himmler nor Heydrich ever forgave him.

Future developments in Rumania became a matter of interdepartmental prestige. It was in this context that Schellenberg recalled to mind a small and insignificant figure whom the Salon Kitty had brought to his notice a few months earlier. His excellent memory became a sudden and immediate threat to the Rumanian deputy press attaché, Lljubo Kolchev, alias Baron von Itter.

Kolchev recognised the danger very quickly. Being broadly acquainted with current developments in his ostensible country of origin, he realised that the Germans were kept fully informed, not only by their diplomatic representatives but also by their various intelligence services. There was no further point in feeding them stale information.

On the other hand, Wilson-Kolchev was a trained agent with a capacity for logical thought. As such, he recalled that the SD had once shown an interest in his person. It was obvious that the Military Intelligence and Foreign Office inquiries about him had been inspired by the Gestapo, also that they stemmed from his conduct at the Salon Kitty. It could only be a matter of time before they approached him, and it was wiser to be prepared.

He knew that he would have to put Brigitta at least partially in the picture. Research on the SD's part could not fail to unearth the relative frequency of his visits to their agent in the past. Kolchev was quick to steal a march on his adversaries. On 31 August 1940 he called at Brigitta's Nestorstrasse apartment.

'Forgive me for staying away so long,' he said. 'It's this chaotic state of affairs in Rumania.'

She flung her arms round his neck. 'I was afraid you'd forgotten me, darling. I've no one to talk to, that's the trouble. There was the air-raid, too—something might have happened to you. . . .'

The first bombs had fallen on Berlin nearly a week earlier. A force of 81 British bombers had raided the German capital during the night of 24-5 August 1940. Only forty of them reached Berlin itself, the rest having been driven off by anti-aircraft fire and German fighters, but they did inflict minor damage on the centre of the city and kill a handful of civilians.

The raid made a profound impact on the capital's inhabitants. Although there had already been a dozen uneventful air-raid alerts, German victories in the West had lulled people into a false sense of security. Now, for the first time, the city had come face to face with the horrors of a war which, for Berlin, was only just beginning.

Kolchev laughed. 'Nothing can happen to me, sweetheart—

the embassy has a nice deep air-raid shelter and I've hardly left my office for weeks.'

'What about Kitty's?' she pouted. 'Haven't you been there either?'

'Of course not, you should know that as well as I do.' He frowned. 'What's the matter, jealous?'

'Yes.' Brigitta sat there with her hands in her lap, looking like a sulky little girl.

'You've no reason.' Kolchev pulled her to her feet and kissed her. For a moment he forgot why he had come, but only for a moment. He held her at arm's length and gazed into her eyes. Would he be able to trust her? Would she summon up the courage to play for high stakes? She was an agent—that much she admitted —but she was an SD agent, an amateur who had been pressed into service by unscrupulous SS men. Could he trust her? Wouldn't her doubts revive if he burdened her with confidences and was then prevented from seeing her for a considerable time? As long as he was near her and could convey that he loved her, as long as he could talk to her, all would be well. After weighing the odds with care, he decided not to take her fully into his confidence. At the same time, he would have to go on playing the game and prepare her for what, in his view, was a near certainty.

'Remember when I first told you I was a Rumanian diplomat?' he asked.

Brigitta nodded, eyes shining, Of course she remembered. That was when she realised that he had ceased to be a mere client and was showing a personal interest in her. She had loved him from that day on.

'All right,' he said, 'what I'm going to tell you now must remain strictly between the two of us. I had a suspicion, even then, that the Salon Kitty was bugged. I was right. Immediately after I left there, the Gestapo took steps to check on everything they'd overheard.

'Now that Rumania has become a focus of interest and the Germans need our oil more than ever for their planned invasion of England, your bosses are bound to remember me. It's possible they'll put you to work on me again—in fact you can bet on it.

'Naturally, they'll also discover that our last meeting at the Salon

150

Kitty ended in a row. Tell them you know me pretty well and feel sure you can put matters right between us, but only if they allow you more freedom of movement.'

Brigitta wasn't slow to understand. 'If only they would!' she said joyfully.

Kolchev could see why British Intelligence employed so few women. Emotions were unpredictable, and feminine emotions doubly so.

'It would be marvellous,' he said, feeling sure that the scheme was a sound one.

Just at that moment, with a sense of timing so perfect as to seem almost suspicious, Brigitta's telephone rang. It was Obersturmführer Schwarz.

'Kindly report to my office at 9 a.m. tomorrow.'

'Certainly, Obersturmführer.' For safety's sake, Brigitta added : 'Not at the cover address?'

'No, Meineckestrasse,' said Schwarz.

Kolchev chuckled. 'You see, darling? Lucky I managed to brief you first.'

He stayed with Brigitta for another two hours—two hours which left him convinced that she was fundamentally a damned nice girl. Somehow, he felt sorry for her.

Brigitta entered Schwarz's office in Department VI, the foreign intelligence section, to find him ensconced behind a mountain of files. The newly promoted Obersturmführer was still busy compiling the lists requested by Schellenberg. He waved her into a chair and began leafing through a capacious folder.

'You used to have a frequent visitor at one time—a young Rumanian diplomat who introduced himself to the Salon Kitty as Baron von Itter. Is that correct?'

'Yes, sir. His real name is Kolchev, but I don't think he holds a very important post.'

'Deputy press attaché,' Schwarz said drily. 'What's your present relationship with him?'

'We haven't seen each other for some time,' she lied, 'but I doubt if he's still annoyed with me. He was irritable the last time we met. Perhaps I asked too many questions.'

Schwarz thumbed through his papers. 'Think you could re-establish contact without arousing his suspicions?'

'I could certainly try, Obersturmführer.'

'Good. In that case, get in touch with him—try and lure him back to the Salon Kitty. If you can't do that, meet him elsewhere. I'll make an exception in this case. He seemed to be very taken with you at one time, or am I wrong?'

Brigitta shrugged. 'You could put it that way. Obersturmführer.'

'And you?' Schwarz scrutinised her for a moment, keenly.

'I played along, naturally. He likes the sound of his own voice. If there's anything to be got out of him, I'm sure I'll manage to extract it. . . .'

'It isn't a question of information,' Schwarz said coldly. 'We want him to work for us. For that, we need his entire confidence. We plan to win it through you. Sooner or later, you'll be told to introduce him to one of our agents—I can't tell you when.' Schwarz paused. 'What about his political attitude?'

'He once said he wished he was German and could fight on our side.'

Schwarz commended her memory and went on to commend her work in general. He spoke of pay increases and promotion.

Brigitta thanked him gracefully and took her leave with a crisp 'Heil Hitler!'

On 4 September 1940 Kolchev paid his first visit to the Salon Kitty for many weeks.

Kitty had missed him. 'You're a rare visitor, Baron,' she said. 'I hope you haven't been ill?'

She showed him into her snuggery and sent for a bottle of champagne.

'What's been the matter?'

'Nothing fatal,' he quipped, lapsing into his usual boyish manner. 'I've had my nose to the grindstone, that's all. I don't know who invented hard work, but it isn't my cup of tea.'

They laughed and clinked glasses.

Kitty fetched her albums and put them in front of him. 'How about Rosemarie?' she suggested, and added a glowing recommendation.

To her surprise, Kolchev declined. 'You know how it is, Kitty,' he said, deliberately off-hand. 'A man needs to work up an appetite. Call Brigitta. I think I was a bit hard on her. She talks too much, but so do most women. In other respects she's a damned

nice girl. Who knows? Maybe we'll patch things up and celebrate.'

Kitty obeyed with alacrity. 'I get the impression there's something between you,' she said.

'I like her a lot,' he confessed, not having to lie.

Elvira knocked. 'There's a party of air force officers outside.
Raring to go, from the look of them.'

'Business seems to be booming,' Kolchev said approvingly.

Kitty chuckled. 'I'll soon spoil their fun if they get too
rowdy.'

'What's your special technique?'

She glanced at her watch. 'Like a demonstration?'

'I can hardly wait.'

'Come along, then.' Kitty led the way into the drawing-room.
The party was in full swing, even though no girls had been sent
for. Eight young fighter pilots, some of them highly decorated,
were firing off champagne corks like cannon. They greeted Kitty
with a rousing cheer.

'Bring on the dancing-girls!' bellowed one.

'You seem to be doing pretty well on your own,' she retorted.
'Don't worry, leave it to me.'

Kitty had stopped submitting her albums in such cases—it was
a waste of time. She simply phoned a series of girls and told them
to get there fast.

Kolchev went over to her. 'What about this demonstration you
promised me?'

'Only five minutes to go.' She gave a sly grin and consulted her
watch again. Then she walked to the radio and turned it on.
Military marches blared from the loudspeaker.

The young flyers protested. 'What's that in aid of? Turn the
thing off and let's have some records.'

'Gentlemen,' said Kitty, 'the Führer is due to speak in two
minutes. I take it you're all interested?' She stared challengingly
round the silent circle.

Kolchev couldn't suppress a smirk. He was spared Hitler's
rhetoric because Brigitta turned up just in time. They withdrew
—as of old—to Room 7, where they officially celebrated their
reunion for the benefit of Obersturmführer Schwarz and his
monitoring team.

Not that Kolchev was there to witness it, but Kitty's method

153

flopped disastrously. The young air force officers listened spell-bound to their idol's words and broke into frenzied applause when he promised them reprisal raids against the British. The only effect of the broadcast was to whip the party into a lather of enthusiasm. There was much drinking and love-making at the Salon Kitty that night.

Obersturmführer Schwarz, who had been following the recon-ciliation between Brigitta and her supposed Rumanian diplomat with approval, switched repeatedly to the drawing-room channel. Today was a day after his own heart—one when everything went like clockwork. Profoundly satisfied, he drafted a report for Schellenberg which spoke of new Rumanian sources to be tapped and devoted several pages to extolling the morale of the German air force.

But the major assault on Britain hung fire. By the time Dunkirk fell on 4 June 1940, Lord Gort had managed to salvage most of his expeditionary force, together with many thousands of French soldiers and General de Gaulle. Vast quantities of arms and equip-ment fell into German hands, but nearly 350,000 men survived to fight another day.

German armoured formations had been prevented from follow-ing up the enemy and wiping them out by Hitler's astonishing standstill order, which was largely inspired by Hermann Goering's promise to cut off and annihilate the retreating troops from the air. The commander of the Luftwaffe failed utterly to honour his undertaking, not least because the RAF screened the British evacuation with skill and success. Logistical problems arising from the rapid German advance rendered the Luftwaffe too weak to overwhelm its dogged and determined adversary.

There was little RAF activity over the Continent once evacua-tion was complete, while German air force units were tied down by the occupation of France, which progressed steadily.

Having concluded the war against France, Hitler gave orders for 'Operation Sea-Lion'. Its principal strategic aim was: '. . . to eliminate the British homeland as a base for carrying on the war against Germany and, should it become necessary, occupy it entirely.'

The Battle of Britain opened.

The inhabitants of Berlin waited for peace to descend on their city. Their surprise and dismay were all the greater when enemy air-raids grew more frequent.

The High Command of the Armed Forces tried to play down these raids. 'Enemy aircraft,' it announced on 7 September 1940, 'again attacked the capital of the Reich during the night and inflicted some damage and casualties by indiscriminate bombing of non-military targets in the centre of the city.'

By contrast, German raids on London were writ large. A special communiqué issued by the German News Agency on 8 September stated :

> Our air force has so far dropped 1,000 tons of bombs of all calibres on London. These attacks are in reprisal for the night raids—begun by Britain and intensified in recent weeks—on residential quarters and other non-military targets in German territory. Marshal Goering is personally directing the attack from Northern France.

But by 9 September the High Command was already conceding that 'British planes are raiding Berlin almost nightly', and on 11 September :

> A few enemy aircraft succeeded in reaching Berlin and dropping bombs there. Two hospitals in the centre of the city were hit. In the diplomatic quarter, some buildings had to be temporarily evacuated because of the danger of collapse. One bomb fell on the parliament building and another on the Academy of Arts. The numerous incendiary bombs would have inflicted greater damage had it not been for the strenuous efforts of security and ancillary services and the self-defensive measures of the Berlin population.

None of which helped to raise public morale.

Almost every night, people were roused from their beds by air-raid sirens and spent hours in their shelters, most of them wretchedly equipped, until the All Clear allowed them to emerge for a hard day's work. The morale barometer, which had hitherto been set fair at 'Victory', slowly but steadily dropped. Sceptics were listened to once more, also the BBC.

Goebbels and his men worked overtime to convert defeats and

losses into victories and gains, but it was the people of Berlin who first lost faith in the Minister of Public Enlightenment and Propaganda. They saw their city burn too often, were too often confronted with the spectacle of death and destruction, to swallow his statistics for ever.

Chapter 13

The Salon Kitty was not immune to the changed situation. Where boisterous parties had once acclaimed every new German victory and success, clients now scurried in and spent little time in the reception rooms before getting down to 'business'. Where drinks and canapés had once loosened their tongues and prompted them to confide in the girls of the house, an atmosphere of haste now reigned.

Schwarz was naturally among the first to notice this change. The reports from his agents and the listening-post became steadily shorter and the flow of information less copious. Many reports stated simply that sexual intercourse took place, whereupon the client departed without more ado.

Schwarz reacted promptly. He reported to Schellenberg.

'Obersturmbannführer,' he said, 'the Salon Kitty isn't what it was. I think we ought to do something at once.' He gave a brief summary of the situation.

Schellenberg studied the previous fortnight's list of visitors, then looked up.

'I note that diplomats seem to be avoiding the place as much as anyone. Why is that, Schwarz?'

'Read the transcripts and you'll see for yourself, sir. The fact is, they're shit-scared. These incessant air-raids are spoiling the whole set-up.'

'But there's a first-class shelter, isn't there?'

'Yes, sir, but not many of them know that. No one bothered to make for the cellar during the early raids, and it's too late to inform them now. We can hardly send out a circular!'

Schellenberg pondered the problem. The absentee diplomats must somehow be lured back to the Salon Kitty. He knew that Serrano Suñer, the Spanish Foreign Minister, was expected in Berlin on 22 September. Although his own standing with Ribbentrop had been badly damaged by the Rumanian affair, he had by some means to entice the Spanish Foreign Minister into the Salon Kitty. Antonescu was also scheduled to visit Berlin before long.

'That reminds me,' he said. 'What about the Rumanian press attaché?'

'Everything's fine. Our agent has him firmly in hand. Shall we tackle him?' Schwarz was happy to be able to report something positive.

'Not yet,' Schellenberg decreed. 'We must feel our way carefully if we want to avoid another row with the Foreign Office, but I'll let you know in good time.'

Schwarz was dismissed, but Schellenberg at once tapped his private line to the Foreign Office. He had plenty of informants there who disagreed with Ribbentrop's foreign policy and were secretly on the side of the Central Security Office.

He proceeded to relay some confidential information given him weeks earlier by the German ambassador in Madrid. This he passed on in exchange for a guarantee that Suñer would visit the Salon Kitty. His confidants in the Foreign Office promised to do their best.

Serrano Suñer landed at Tempelhof airport on 21 September 1940, having flown there in a German Junkers 52. Ribbentrop welcomed him in style and personally escorted him to the Foreign Office, where the two ministers conferred in private.

On 22 September Hitler received the Spanish Foreign Minister with Ribbentrop in attendance. Himmler's request for permission to be present at the interview was expressly rejected by the Chancellery.

The official purpose of the visit was to discuss trade relations between Spain and Germany. Hitler, who wanted to bring Franco into the war on his side, hinted at the availability of substantial economic aid. He also pointed to the two countries' comradeship-in-arms during the Spanish Civil War and the decisive contribution to Franco's victory made by German 'Condor Legion'.

Ribbentrop revelled in his triumph over Himmler. He generously allowed the Reichsführer-SS a talk with Suñer but simultaneously insulted him by arranging a prior interview between Suñer and Dr Ley, director of the German Labour Front.

Himmler finally got to see the Spaniard, but their talk was limited to trivialities. He fulminated about this to Heydrich, who sought to pacify him by hinting at Suñer's prospective visit to the Salon Kitty. While not explicitly mentioning the brothel, he conveyed to Himmler that he would soon be acquainted with the real reasons for the Spanish Foreign Minister's presence in Berlin.

23 September 1940 was probably the most successful day in the Salon Kitty's history.

Kitty received a call from the Foreign Office informing her that a distinguished guest wished to visit her establishment with several companions. She was to hold the drawing-room in readiness, also—to be on the safe side—half a dozen ladies. A knowledge of Spanish was desirable.

The party arrived just before 9 p.m. Kitty was astonished to find herself shaking hands with Joachim von Ribbentrop, the German Foreign Minister. Accompanying him were Foreign Minister Suñer, the Spanish ambassador in Berlin, a Foreign Office interpreter, and an embassy official.

She ushered them straight into the drawing-room and saw to it that they were plied with the drinks of their choice. Ribbentrop took such a fancy to the Salon Kitty's décor and service that he often paid private visits thereafter. The Spanish Foreign Minister was equally charmed.

'I'm sure,' he said jocularly, 'that we could have conducted our secret talks better here than at your ministry, Excellency.' Even though his supposition could not have been further from the truth, Ribbentrop laughingly—and unwittingly—agreed. Down in the Meineckestrasse cellars, Walter Schellenberg strained to catch every word that came through the headphones.

'The Führer,' Ribbentrop said, 'is counting on your influence with the Caudillo to win his approval of our plans for Gibraltar.'

'I can't venture an opinion at this stage,' Suñer replied diplomatically, 'but do you really think the British will surrender their key position without a fight?'

'Your Excellency,' Ribbentrop assured him, 'with Spain's assistance, we shall succeed. We propose to move some of our best troops to the frontier dressed in Spanish uniforms and take the Rock from the landward side. The Führer has selected General Dietl, the hero of Narvik, to command the operation.'

'And what is the Führer's underlying aim?'

'To compel the British to negotiate. The capture of Gibraltar would rob them of their dominant position in the Mediterranean and seal off the Western approaches. You must be familiar with the text of the Führer's speech to the Reichstag in which he strongly advocated an end to bloodshed. The British flatly rejected this last generous offer and are now bombing German cities night after night. The holocaust will spread to the whole of Europe unless we bring the war with Britain to a peaceful conclusion. The Führer regards the capture of Gibraltar as an urgent strategic step on the road to this objective.'

'I understand that perfectly,' said the Spaniard. 'However, I'm sure that our firm consent to your plan will have to be preceded by another conference designed to specify what Germany is willing to offer in return . . .'

'A share of the French colonial territories,' Ribbentrop put in.

'We've long had your approval on that point,' Suñer countered. 'What we need at the moment is grain and fuel.'

'We'll work something out,' Ribbentrop said soothingly. 'In the meantime, I'd be grateful if you could at least set a provisional date for the operation on your return to Madrid.'

'You're still thinking in terms of 10 January 1941?'

'For the moment, yes. Our preparations are going ahead under the code name Operation Felix, as you know. It might be advisable for us to use that name in our future correspondence on the subject.' Abruptly, Ribbentrop turned to more immediate things. He raised his glass to the Spanish Foreign Minister and drank to their joint prosperity, then rang for Kitty and suggested that the ladies might join them.

The night was a total success, unlike Operation Felix, which was never put into effect. On 23 October 1940, Hitler met Franco at Hendenge on the Spanish border. At this meeting, Franco made no secret of his belief that Germany would never defeat Great Britain, and the two dictators parted without reaching agreement.

Hitler was offended by Franco's refusal and had plans drawn up for the capture of Gibraltar without Spanish connivance. Being still receptive to the arguments of his military commanders, who talked him out of the venture on the grounds that Spain's help was indispensable, Hitler renewed his request for co-operation. Franco finally rejected the idea in December 1940, and Operation Felix was shelved.

Schellenberg immediately had a transcript made of the recorded conversation. He considered the information sufficiently important to justify his rousing Heydrich in the middle of the night.

The two men met at 4 a.m. in Heydrich's Dahlem villa. Schellenberg started to give a brief summary of what had been said, but Heydrich interrupted him.

'Do you have a transcript?'

The Obersturmbannführer removed the text from his briefcase. 'I listened in on the conversation myself—it's a monstrous plan!'

Heydrich carefully read the handful of typed sheets. 'I shall inform the Reichsführer-SS at the earliest opportunity,' he said curtly.

Schellenberg was dismissed. Not a word of thanks or commendation. From Heydrich's point of view, Schellenberg had merely done his job.

Himmler received Heydrich first thing next morning at the latter's urgent request.

'Herr Reichsführer,' Heydrich said, 'Ribbentrop and the Foreign Office have worked out a crazy scheme which would severely prejudice our own efforts in Spain. I request your instructions.'

Then, in his terse way, he outlined the principal features of Operation Felix.

Himmler was beside himself with rage. 'I'll pay Ribbentrop back for this,' he said eventually. 'Where did you get this information, Gruppenführer?'

'From an absolutely unimpeachable source,' Heydrich replied. 'May I now request the Reichsführer for his instructions?'

Himmler had no instructions for Heydrich. On the contrary, he would rather have had Heydrich's suggestions on how best to exact revenge for Ribbentrop's high-handed behaviour. However, this was no time to show weakness or publicise the chinks in his armour.

'I'll let you know my decision in due course,' he said, rather more brusquely than he had intended.

'Certainly, Herr Reichsführer.' Heydrich raised his arm in the Nazi salute and withdrew.

He knew that he was leaving Himmler in a quandary. On the other hand, he had no wish to bring down Ribbentrop's wrath on the Central Security Office—it wasn't firmly enough established yet. As far as he was concerned, Himmler could look around for other allies. . . .

Hardly had the Salon Kitty survived its 'Spanish soirée' when it was patronised by clients of an entirely different hue, namely, Japanese.

Kitty was in a cleft stick. She had heard too much about offences against racial purity not to take out some form of insurance. Having ushered her first Japanese visitor into the parlour, she offered him a drink for courtesy's sake—he asked for fruit juice—and excused herself for a moment.

In extreme haste, she telephoned Schwarz. The Obersturm-führer, who had just returned to his office after being highly commended by Schellenberg, was friendlier than usual.

'What's the trouble, Frau Schmidt?'

Kitty told him in a few words. 'Is it all right,' she asked ingenuously, 'about his race, I mean?'

'Don't worry, he must be an embassy official. Does he speak German?'

'Like a cross between a turkey and a goose,' she said with a chuckle, '—he gobbles and hisses. What shall I do, introduce him to one of the Rothenburg girls?'

Schwarz thought for a moment. 'By all means,' he said, and hung up. He rang the listening-post and summoned the duty NCO. 'We've got a special visitor today,' he announced, 'a Jap. I want you to pay extra attention to him, and pass that on to the relief watch too. Right?'

The duty NCO clicked his heels. 'Received and understood, sir!' The Japanese diplomat yielded little information of value. It transpired that he was a member of the delegation which had negotiated the Tripartite Pact with Germany and Italy.

All Schellenberg's efforts to inject new blood into the Salon Kitty proved abortive. Schwarz, who had obtained his subsequent approval of the decision to admit a Japanese, was equally devoid of ideas. In spite of claimed successes in the Battle of Britain, RAF bombers were nightly bombing German territory, including Berlin itself. The effect on a German population which had yet to taste defeat was demoralising and depressing.

Schellenberg sensed the danger that threatened his pet project. The Salon Kitty, which had once been such an abundant source of information, now yielded only a weak and feeble trickle.

Most of the patrons were officers on leave eager to unburden themselves of their petty grievances. German and foreign diplomats came less and less often despite the now widespread rumours that Kitty had entertained the Spanish Foreign Minister and a number of Japanese delegates. Berlin industrialists and businessmen preferred to spend the night in their own air-raid shelters rather than risk unwelcome exposure at 11 Giesebrechtstrasse.

Another factor was the growing scarcity of men in Berlin. Many respectable married women now welcomed temporary protectors to their empty beds, solely to dispel loneliness. Last but not least, there were the winter nights, the black-out—which for the first time wielded an inhibiting effect on Schellenberg's regular clientèle—and the increasing shortages which slowly endangered even the Salon Kitty's supply of luxuries, hitherto one of its chief attractions.

The end of the Salon Kitty seemed imminent.

The only people to benefit from the situation were Kolchev and his girl-friend. Brigitta, still acting under orders and armed with her special dispensation, concentrated on her 'victim' with all the singlemindedness of a woman in love.

Obersturmführer Schwarz had exempted her from normal duties at the Salon Kitty and left her free to devote all her time to the 'Rumanian question'—and that, to her, meant Lljubo Kolchev.

Their usual rendezvous was her apartment, where they could now meet undisturbed with the blessing of the Central Security Office. Kolchev had naturally submitted the place to a thorough search rather than accept Brigitta's assurance that it had not been tampered with. Once he was satisfied, they spent many enjoyable hours together, and slowly, step by step, he extracted the whole truth from her.

He also supplied her with regular dollops of confidential information about Rumania, a breach of faith which did not trouble his conscience overmuch. For her part, Brigitta dutifully composed a daily report which usually ended with the words: 'I continue to enjoy the full confidence of Lljubo Kolchev, Rumanian citizen and deputy press attaché at the Rumanian embassy in Berlin.'

Kolchev had dictated that formula himself. He also helped to edit most of her reports. There were times when he came close to confessing that he was a British agent, but patriotism and training held him back. In so far as they could, under the circumstances, the young couple pursued their personal happiness and private interests.

Kolchev had heard virtually nothing from London for weeks now. Only once on his visits to the laundry, which he continued to patronise regularly, did he encounter one of the communications experts dispatched by London, but he refrained from speaking to him. He was pretty certain that the German air-raids on Britain had helped to curtail the flow of information.

Kolchev still communicated with London by way of dead letter-boxes. He passed on the fruits of his own observation, together with items gleaned from the diplomatic representatives with whom he came into contact, always striving to convey a picture of the current mood in Berlin. He never knew if his superiors received the reports he sent them at this time.

Regularly, at prearranged intervals, he tuned in to BBC London. Because this was forbidden by law, he had devised a safe but laborious method. Taking his radio into bed with him, he turned the volume down low and listened to it beneath a thick canopy of blankets and eiderdowns. This made him sweat like a pig but insured against the risk of being overheard and denounced— although he knew that he was only one of many thousands who nightly defied the Goebbels propaganda machine and listened to news from 'the other side'.

There were never any coded messages for Roger Wilson, alias Lljubo Kolchev.

From Schellenberg's point of view, the year 1941 began badly. Half-way through January he received a call from Gruppen-führer Reinhard Heydrich, who wanted to carry out another inspection of the Salon Kitty. He expressly ordered Schellenberg to ensure that the monitoring circuit was switched off for the duration of his visit to Giesebrechtstrasse.

Schellenberg notified Obersturmführer Schwarz, who duly alerted Kitty Schmidt.

Kitty dreaded these inspections because they were a continual reminder of the inescapable pressures exerted on her, but she made her preparations with the care and tact for which she was renowned. The drawing-room and parlour were reserved, random visitors politely but firmly turned away, bottles chilled, canapés prepared, and a number of Rothenburg girls warned by phone to hold themselves in readiness.

Heydrich turned up early that evening, towards 7 p.m. He wasted little time on preliminaries. Kitty introduced him to several girls and he picked Leni. He disappeared with her into one of the bedrooms and remained there for about two hours, then departed as unobtrusively as he had come.

Leni was instructed not to submit her usual report and all seemed to be in order.

By the time Schellenberg reached his office next morning, Heydrich had already left word that he was to phone on arrival. The Obersturmbannführer did so and was immediately summoned to Prinz Albrechtstrasse.

Schellenberg felt uneasy, because Heydrich's manner on the telephone had been one degree chillier than usual. His memoirs describe what happened :

> Considering Heydrich's propensities, it did not surprise me that he occasionally visited this intimate establishment for 'inspection' purposes, as he put it. Beforehand, however, he expressly ordered me to ensure that the entire technical apparatus was switched off. After one such inspection he sent for me and accused me of failing to comply with his directive. He had, he said, already complained to Himmler about it. The Reichsführer was extremely annoyed and wanted me to submit a written explanation. I at once sensed that Heydrich was hatching a plot against me— possibly because he suspected me of conducting an illicit affair with his wife. He declined to accept my explanation that the apparatus could not be switched off that evening because electric cables were being transferred, whereas Himmler at once pronounced himself satisfied. This incident was my first warning to be on my guard against Heydrich from then on.

Heydich's parting shot was : 'I order you to transfer the entire monitoring installation, complete with all files and equipment, to Prinz Albrechtstrasse. At once, do you understand?'

'Certainly, Gruppenführer!' said Schellenberg, realising as he spoke that he would have to step up his efforts to restore the Salon Kitty's attractions.

Next day, Schellenberg issued instructions for the entire monitoring and surveillance apparatus to be transferred to Prinz Albrechtstrasse. He had previously carpeted Obersturmführer Schwarz and was secretly toying with the idea of replacing him. However, Schwarz was second to none in his knowledge of the Salon Kitty set-up, so he decided to wait until the man had supervised the move with his usual efficiency and attention to detail.

On 17 January 1941, German post office engineers began to lay a heavy multi-core cable from Meineckestrasse to Prinz Albrechtstrasse. Unfavourable weather conditions notwithstanding, the task was completed within a week. It took SS technicians and signallers another week to connect the Meineckestrasse cable to its extensions, dismantle the monitoring equipment and complete the whole move.

Preliminary experiments indicated that line amplifiers would have to be installed because the distance from Giesebrechtstrasse to Prinz Albrechtstrasse exceeded the cable's capacity to give perfect reception. Thanks to the SD's habit of doing the impossible, Schellenberg was able to report completion by 31 January.

Fortune smiled once more on Schellenberg and his minions.

On 1 February, an Italian embassy official patronised the Salon Kitty and, more particularly, the SD agent named Hildegard. He poured out his heart, which was evidently full to overflowing. By phrasing her questions skilfully, the girl agent managed to elicit not only his name but an abundance of information.

'This war is going to ruin Italy,' he complained. 'Mussolini should have played the honest broker and left it at that. Now he's turned into a megalomaniac.'

'What makes you say that?' asked Hildegard.

'The madman thinks he can wage a war of his own with the French loot Hitler gave him for declaring war on England and France. But the Führer wasn't content with that. He badgered the Duce into joining the Tripartite Pact and embroiled Italy in a world war as well.'

166

Hildegard continued to stoke the blaze. 'But we're winning on every front, surely?'

'You may be, we're not. Presenting Greece with an ultimatum was the act of a lunatic. As if we didn't have enough on our plate already in Cyrenaica and British Somaliland, not to mention Abyssinia and the Egyptian frontier!'

'How are things going in Greece?'

The Italian gave a mirthless laugh and showed himself admirably well-informed. 'Going?' he exclaimed. 'From bad to worse! Hitler wasn't interested in helping us—he didn't want to extend the war to the Balkans for fear of disrupting German economic links with South-East Europe. However, we conquered Albania in 1939 and Mussolini decided to build on that success so as to restore his crumbling prestige. Our troops invaded Greece at the end of October, but we didn't have Germany's luck. The British intervened. They occupied Crete, mined Greek waters and sent combat units to the Albanian front. Things have progressed all right, but in favour of the Greeks. So far, they've reconquered a third of Albania.'

Hildegard tried to console the despairing Italian. 'I'm sure the Führer won't leave you in the lurch.'

'No,' he replied with a sudden revival of optimism, 'thank God Operation Marita is under way. That should relieve the pressure.'

'Marita?' Hildegard smiled. 'Sounds like a girl's name.'

'It's the codename for a relief attack on the Balkans by German troops, so as to counter the threat to their south-east flank and prepare for deployment against Russia.'

'Against Russia?' The girl's tone was incredulous. 'But we signed a non-aggression pact with Russia, didn't we?'

The Italian gave a full-throated laugh. 'You women are all the same—you still have faith in signed documents and written promises. Believe me, little Signorina, politics is a dirty business but war is downright lunacy. All the rules of human behaviour go out of the window—the lie reigns supreme. The player who bluffs best and draws the highest cards, wins. You Germans are real experts in that field.'

Hildegard steered the conversation to another theatre of war. 'What about Africa?' she said.

'Things couldn't be much worse,' the Italian grumbled, downcast again. 'Last August the Duke of Aosta occupied British

167

Somaliland. Very nice, except that our Tenth Army under Marshal Graziani proceeded to cross the Libyan border and advance as far as Sidi Barrani. The British couldn't tolerate that, of course. Their counter-attack has been in progress since December. We lost 38,000 men in the Sidi Barrani area alone. Sollum fell in mid-December and Bardia on 5 January—25,000 men were taken prisoner there. But the worst thing was the capture of Tobruk, a week ago. The British snapped up another 50,000 Italian soldiers. Now they're hammering at the gates of Benghazi and El Agheila. It'll end in disaster if we don't get some help soon.'

'Have a drink,' Hildegard suggested soothingly. She was finding it hard to memorise such a deluge of details. 'Excuse me a minute,' she added, '—call of nature.' Closeted in the bathroom, she hurriedly made some written notes. Then she rejoined the Italian and gave him what he had come for.

The senior NCO on duty at the listening-post judged the conversation important enough to rouse Obersturmführer Schwarz from his slumbers. He earned himself a pat on the back. The Records Section worked all night to produce a transcript for Schellenberg.

Reading it next morning, Schellenberg was less interested in the details of Italian defeats and successes than in the Italian's references to the Soviet Union.

'Is that all the man said about Russia?' he demanded.

'Yes, Obersturmbannführer!' Schwarz reported smartly. He had another welcome announcement to make. 'By the way, sir, I've completed my analysis of the Salon Kitty's visitors' list for 1940.' He fumbled in his briefcase and produced a bulky file bearing the ominous 'Top Secret' stamp.

'Thank you, Obersturmführer.' Schellenberg put it aside for the moment. 'It occurs to me that we obtain virtually no information about Russia from the Salon Kitty. Do Soviet diplomats avoid the place?'

'I've been wondering that too, sir. The fact is, the Russkis aren't good mixers. They bury themselves in their embassy and hardly ever show themselves in public. Since Molotov's visit last November, their attendance at official functions has been limited to a handful of representatives. One can't get at them, I'm afraid.'

'Thank you, Schwarz. That's all.'

As soon as he was alone, Schellenberg reached for the thick

folder and leafed through it. His findings satisfied him profoundly. More than ten thousand customers had patronised the Salon Kitty in 1940—an average of over thirty a day. It was a lucrative business, to say the least, and he made a mental note to run a check on Kitty Schmidt's finances in the near future.

Of even greater interest to him were the names of those who had indirectly been his customers. The list swarmed with notabilities. Diplomats, generals, politicos, ministers, Gauleiters, artists—all were represented, from Sepp Dietrich to Joachim von Ribbentrop, from Ferdinand Marian to Hans Albers, from Reich press chief Otto Dietrich to Labour Front leader Robert Ley, from Foreign Minister Ciano of Italy to Foreign Minister Suñer of Spain. Only the Russians and Americans were missing.

Their absence gave him food for thought.

Kolchev found himself in constant demand during this period. He was able to supply the SD daily with valuable items of information about Rumania via Brigitta, whose reports were read by Schellenberg and Schwarz with mounting satisfaction.

'We couldn't have a better contact with the Rumanian than Brigitta,' Schwarz said firmly, and recommended that the original plan be dropped. Kolchev was not, after all, to be introduced to an SD middleman, nor would there be any attempt to recruit him for espionage against Rumania—he was doing quite well enough already.

SD agent Brigitta was summoned yet again to Schwarz's office, now in Prinz Albrechtstrasse. Schwarz relieved her of her Salon Kitty duties until further notice and gave her full authority to deal with the Rumanian contact, Lljubo Kolchev, as she deemed fit. She also received a pay rise.

Schwarz's instructions revived Brigitta's pleasure in her work as an agent because they accorded perfectly with her own inclinations. One of the Obersturmführer's remarks made a particular impression on her: 'You, and you alone, are responsible to me for this man Kolchev.'

'Rumania is safe in German hands, Obersturmführer,' she replied proudly—and, in her view, she had never been compelled to lie once.

She could hardly wait to tell her lover the glad tidings. Kolchev was reassured to note that the SD had fallen for his line. On the other hand, the latest development was a renewed indication that his opponents were amateurs and, as such, dangerous despite their apparent readiness to be led by the nose. It never occurred to him to relax or drop his guard.

Chapter 14

In the early hours of 22 June 1941, Hitler launched his attack on Russia and thereby transformed the whole of Europe into a battlefield.

To Walter Schellenberg, Germany's early successes in Russia coincided with the high-water mark of his career to date. Victory fanfares rang out once more, filling the Germans with renewed exultation and blinding them to the fact that their country was now involved in the one thing Hitler had dreaded most : a war on two fronts. The Salon Kitty again swarmed with officers and diplomats eager to live it up and open their hearts to Schwarz's SD girls. As for the latter, they gave of their best in a mood of euphoria. Hitler seemed to be achieving the impossible, and they were glad to make their own small contribution to his success.

More concretely, Schellenberg was promoted SS-Standartenführer, or full colonel, and appointed head of Department VI, the SD foreign intelligence service.

Reason enough for Schellenberg to treat himself to a good time; reason enough, too, for him to submit the Salon Kitty to another personal inspection. He got Schwarz to notify Kitty of his arrival.

Kitty greeted the man who was responsible for her predicament with the affability which was second nature to her, whatever the circumstances. She had naturally deployed the best her kitchen and cellar could offer and warned the prettiest girls to stand by for duty. Having ushered Schellenberg straight into the drawing-room, she offered him a chair and politely inquired if a little female company would be in order.

Schellenberg was, as ever, astonished by her dazzling appearance. 'Why not sit down for a moment?' he said. 'Won't you join me in a glass of something?'

Kitty accepted his invitation, and a minute later they were sipping champagne. She was a little apprehensive of what might be in store for her, but Schellenberg was in a good mood. 'The place is going great guns,' he said. Kitty couldn't quite determine whether it was a statement or a question.

'Thank you,' she said, 'I'm satisfied.'

Schellenberg gave an approving nod. His eyes turned to the paintings on the walls.

'You're fond of art?'

'Extremely,' she replied. 'I like the Italians best—Tintoretto, for instance, and Leonardo da Vinci, but I'm afraid they're beyond the reach of ordinary mortals like me.'

He cocked an eyebrow as if to imply that brothel-keepers and Tintoretto didn't mix.

'You sound well informed,' he said drily.

It was Kitty's turn to play a minor trump. 'I know as much as a person of average education ought to know,' she replied, doing her best not to seem provocative. 'For instance, take Tintoretto's *Crucifixion* in the Scuola di San Rocco, or da Vinci's *Mona Lisa* and *Last Supper*—they're more than just world-famous works of art. Quite apart from their artistic merit, they show that painting can compete with music as an international language.'

Schellenberg couldn't believe his ears. He had expected her —however genteelly—to sing the praises of sex, and here he was, suddenly involved in a conversation which left him slightly at sea. He switched to music and was treated to some equally articulate comments on Bach and Beethoven, Chopin and Debussy. To hide his embarrassment, he cut her short and came to the real reason for his visit.

'Do you have any nice girls on call, Frau Schmidt?' He sounded quite subdued, and Kitty was profoundly gratified to note that she had shaken his composure. She rose to fetch her albums, but the newly fledged Standartenführer stopped her.

'I'd be grateful if you'd recommend someone.'

Kitty told him that Barbara was on the premises.

'Fine,' Schellenberg said. 'In that case, let's have a look at her.'

His inspection of Barbara lasted two hours and was an unqualified success. When Schellenberg and his companion emerged from their room, Kitty was astonished to hear them swapping Christian names.

'Hey,' said Barbara, 'why don't we split another bottle with Kitty?'

'Good idea,' Schellenberg replied. He had not felt so pleased with life for a long time. 'His' Salon Kitty was a splendid institution after all. His experiences of the past three hours had finally made it clear to him why he had managed to lure so many distinguished visitors to the Pension Schmidt and why they so often came back for more.

When he left after another two hours, Kitty was privileged to address him by his first name.

Although not entirely overjoyed by this mark of favour, she took it as a sign that the immediate threat to her person had receded. And so she accepted it calmly, like everything that had descended on her since the outbreak of war.

Next day she was surprised to receive a visit from Barbara, Schellenberg's partner of the previous night.

'You're not supposed to come unless I call you, Barbara—you know that. I'd sooner stick to that arrangement if you don't mind.'

'I know,' the girl said, twisting her hands together, 'but I've got a personal problem—one I can only discuss with another woman ...'

Her hangdog expression stirred Kitty's sympathy. 'All right, let's have it.'

'I've been drinking rather a lot lately,' the girl stammered, 'so I put it down to that. . . .'

'What are you talking about?' Kitty demanded, although she already had an inkling.

'Well, I've been feeling so queazy these last three weeks, and this is the second time I've missed a period. It looks as if . . .'

'Pregnant?' Kitty asked sternly.

The SD girl nodded. She had ceased to be the tough, hard-headed agent, trained in unarmed combat and pistol-shooting. She was just a girl in trouble.

'A nice mess,' Kitty said. She sat down and called for Elvira. 'Make us some coffee and bring a couple of schnapps as well.' Elvira had been with Kitty long enough to know that she was on the verge of an important decision.

Kitty inhaled the fragrant steam from her coffee-cup and pondered. 'Well,' she said, 'have you got any ideas?'

The girl, who seemed quite desperate, didn't reply. Kitty continued to ponder. Strictly speaking it was her duty to report the incident to Obersturmführer Schwarz—in fact it was the only way of keeping her own nose clean. She was ignorant of the rules which governed Schwarz's contacts with his agents but could not imagine that the girl would be able to hide her condition indefinitely. Equally, an abortion might put her out of commission just when her services were required.

'I'll have to think it over,' she said at length. 'I'll work something out by the next time you come.'

Barbara gave her a tearful smile. 'Thanks, Kitty—it isn't the sort of thing you can discuss with everyone. Please help me.'

'Run along with you,' Kitty said.

Turning the matter over in her mind when the girl had gone, she still couldn't see any way of helping her without endangering herself, so she picked up the phone and called Schwarz. She described the incident in a few short sentences, not omitting to point out that Barbara had come to her on her own initiative and not in response to a telephoned summons.

'Very good, Frau Schmidt. Heil Hitler!' Obersturmführer Schwarz slammed the receiver down impatiently. He rang the SD medical section to inquire if the girl had reported her condition and received a negative answer. Schwarz swore, but that didn't solve the problem.

Then he had a brainwave. He telephoned SS-Obergruppenführer Karl Wolff, who was chief of Himmler's personal staff and head of the *Lebensborn*. This SS maternity organisation, whose name meant literally 'Fount of Life', had been summoned into existence by Himmler on 13 September 1936. Its functions were as follows:

1. To support racially and genetically valuable families.
2. To accommodate racially and genetically valuable mothers in suitable maternity homes.
3. To care for the children of such families.
4. To care for mothers of the same.

All senior SS officers were in honour bound to join the association. As Himmler told his masseur, Felix Kersten:

'My first aim in setting up the *Lebensborn* was to meet a crying need and to give unmarried women who were racially pure the chance to have their children without expense. . . . Privately, I let it be known that any unmarried woman who was alone in the world but longed for a child might turn to the *Lebensborn* with perfect confidence. The Reichsführung-SS would sponsor the child and provide for its education. I was well aware that this was a revolutionary step. . . .'

Obergruppenführer Wolff bent a sympathetic ear to Schwarz's request, and two days later SD agent Barbara was admitted to a *Lebensborn* maternity home.

Roger Wilson, alias Lljubo Kolchev, alias Baron von Itter, had a hard time serving his various masters during the period up to September 1941. In spite of revolutionary upheavals in Rumania and the incessant bombing of London and other British cities, however, he succeeded in passing his messages without interruption. This made him a key figure in the British intelligence network and one whom the Secret Service was reluctant to endanger at any price.

Although several dead letter-boxes were destroyed as air-raids on Berlin multiplied, 'Baron von Itter' was promptly informed whenever his 'laundry' was ready and could thus arrange to drop his information at other points.

Kolchev always proceeded with the utmost care, and his punctilious observance of precautionary measures was such that he had few qualms about the integrity of his cover.

He was not, therefore, unduly surprised when he returned home after a duty call on Brigitta to hear the telephone ring and a voice inform Baron von Itter that his laundry was ready for collection. Although it was nearly 10 p.m. by this time, he set out for Emserstrasse and rang the back-door bell. As usual, he was conducted into the darkened room where he had conferred with the SOE (Special Operations Executive) communications experts.

Once his eyes were accustomed to the gloom he made out the figure of a man who was sitting across the table from him with his coat collar turned up. The man performed his first security check and Kolchev followed suit. Once they had exchanged a second security check and the question of mutual identification was settled, the stranger began to speak in a low voice.

'It's my duty to inform you that inquiries are in progress in Rumania into your identity as Lljubo Kolchev. Quite how immediate the danger is, we still don't know, but we're trying to find out. The real Kolchev has been living in London, as you're aware. Stupidly, he was recognised by some fellow-émigrés. The SD is bound to get wind of it sooner or later, so you'll have to operate with even greater care in future. Be prepared to vanish any time.'

Kolchev-Wilson asked how the situation had arisen, and the stranger elaborated.

He recalled the trouble which the SD had brought upon itself by supporting the Iron Guard against Antonescu. Horia Sima and fourteen of his lieutenants had been smuggled out of Rumania into Austria and from there to Germany with SD assistance. Admiral Canaris, the German Military Intelligence chief, heard of the venture and managed to get one of the Rumanian fugitives on his side. Canaris, who was in close touch with the Siguranza, or Rumanian security service, interrogated the former Iron Guard officer and learned that the SD's foreign intelligence service was being continuously informed of developments inside Rumania through one of its agents, a woman known as Brigitta. It would not, therefore, be hard for Canaris and his men to trace the source of her information, namely, Kolchev.

The stranger concluded : 'SOE hereby instructs you to break contact with this SD agent of yours, however valuable your relationship may have been until now. Take my word for it, Wilson, you're in danger of detection, and that would destroy your value to us. Keep on your toes and be ready to go underground at a moment's notice.'

Kolchev-Wilson had got the message. He wondered how to break it to Brigitta.

'I can't very well visit the girl again,' he said.

'Do you have her telephone number?'

'Yes, but if what you say is true, they're bound to be tapping her line already.'

'Quite so, and opening her mail. Any other ideas?'

Kolchev-Wilson had a plan—a bold one. 'What if I tell the SD that their competitors are crowding me and place myself under their protection?'

The stranger glanced up in surprise. He seemed to ponder for a moment. 'That sounds promising, but how long will it be before they rumble you?'

Kolchev shrugged. 'We don't have much option.'

'You'll be risking your neck,' the stranger said.

'It might be worse if I simply vanished. I'd have everyone on my heels—SD, Military Intelligence, the Foreign Office and maybe the Rumanians as well. From where I stand, the SD and the Gestapo look the lesser of two evils.'

'I'm authorised to suggest an alternative,' the man said. 'Why not duck out altogether? We could still smuggle you back to London with comparative ease. Things may get tougher later on.'

It was a tempting proposal, but Wilson was young enough to rise to a challenge. 'Thanks, I'll hang on for the time being. How can I get hold of you in an emergency?'

'By handkerchief, preferably. If it's really urgent, use your phone numbers.'

They spent a few more minutes discussing future channels of communication, then Kolchev took his leave.

He wondered as he slipped out of the building whether Canaris's men were already watching Brigitta and had shadowed him to his apartment or the laundry. To be on the safe side, he made a detour and dropped into two bars en route, keeping a weather eye open for potential tails. He got home just before midnight without spotting anything suspicious.

But he was not destined to enjoy a quiet night's sleep. Just as he was undressing, the door-bell began to ring insistently.

Kolchev had enough sang-froid to flush his invisible ink away and drop his tell-tale handkerchiefs into the stove. Then he spun the tuning knob of his radio, pulled on a dressing-gown and shuffled to the door.

'Who is it?' he called.

It was a chauffeur from the Rumanian embassy. 'You're wanted at once, sir—H.E.'s orders,' said the man. 'I've got a car waiting outside.'

Kolchev yawned loudly. He debated whether the Rumanians could be on to him yet but came to the conclusion that they would have sent the Gestapo. His adopted country must be in the throes of yet another crisis.

'Coming right away,' he called back. 'I'll just put a few clothes on.'

The chauffeur sat in the hall and waited while Kolchev dressed with more than usual care. A quarter of an hour later they were in the car, and a few minutes later in Rauchstrasse. No lights showed in the big embassy building, but once they were through the black-out curtains Kolchev could see at once that the place was in a state of full alert. The chauffeur took him straight to Raoul Bossy, the Rumanian ambassador. Bossy seemed to be in a genial mood.

'Ah, our professional man-about-town has turned up at last,' he said tartly.

'I was collecting my laundry, Your Excellency,' Kolchev replied, by way of apology. A quick glance told him that every senior embassy official was present, but none of them looked hostile. On the contrary, they laughed at his explanation. The air was still clear.

'Laundry, at midnight?' Bossy joined in the laughter, then continued what he had been saying before Kolchev's arrival.

'Marshal Antonescu will fly to Oberschöneweide in a special German air force plane, land there just before midday and be driven straight to see the Führer and Reich Chancellor. The meeting with Hitler is scheduled to last an hour.

'Herr von Ribbentrop informs me that the Führer plans to invest the Marshal with the Knight's Cross of the Iron Cross in recognition of the notable victories won by the Rumanian 3rd and 4th Armies. Afterwards there will be an official luncheon to which several members of the diplomatic corps have been invited. On the German side, Field Marshal Keitel, Marshal Goering, Reichsführer Himmler and Herr Goebbels will be in attendance.

'The SS-Leibstandarte Adolf Hitler will mount a guard of honour. Responsibility for security measures will rest with the police and Gestapo. . . .'

The envoy continued to speak for several more minutes. Various points were discussed and embassy officials assigned to specific duties.

Kolchev itched to leave the embassy and convey the news to London by the quickest possible route. Like the rest, however, he was compelled to stick it out till dawn, making notes, nodding portentously or otherwise feigning an interest proper to his official position.

At least it gave him an opportunity to think out a way of contacting Brigitta without writing to her, visiting or telephoning her. The idea that came to him was not without its dangers, but it seemed the best bet. Weary as he was when he left Rauchstrasse just before 7 a.m., he realised that he would get no sleep that day.

He made for the nearest telephone kiosk and dialled one of the three numbers which had been Spencer Brown's parting gift. Without stating his name, he relayed the news of Antonescu's forthcoming visit. He had no idea who was at the other end of the line, but the message was urgent and he knew of no quicker way to pass it on.

Then he walked to Meineckestrasse and asked to see Standartenführer Schellenberg as soon as he reached his office.

Schellenberg betrayed no outward surprise at Kolchev's unheralded visit.

'To what do I owe the honour of your company, Herr Kolchev?' he inquired, after a routine exchange of introductions and courtesies.

Kolchev was well rehearsed. He spoke of Brigitta and his deep affection for her, of his repeated requests to her that she should pass information about the Iron Guard to Schellenberg in his capacity as head of the SD foreign intelligence service, of his admiration for the Führer and his wish to join the Rumanians fighting alongside the Germans in Russia—a wish frustrated by the diplomatic activities which kept him tied down in Berlin. Then, with an air of mystery, he came out with what he knew.

'Just lately, I've been under surveillance by Military Intelligence. I'm half-afraid that Brigitta may be in danger too. . . .' Kolchev's tone was meaningful. He sat back in his chair, crossed his legs and nervously lit a cigarette.

Schellenberg had listened attentively and in silence. Kolchev's manner suggested that he dreaded not seeing his girl again and hoped to enlist Schellenberg as a fairy godmother. On the other hand, Schellenberg had a clear recollection of Kolchev's file. Knowing how much important information he had already given the SD—unwittingly, in his opinion—he only half-believed the Rumanian's story. But then, all was fair in love, war and espionage. He was not unduly surprised.

'How would some good French cognac appeal to you?' he asked with a smile.

Kolchev smiled back. 'Plus coffee? I've been up all night.'

Schellenberg instructed his orderly accordingly. The tray arrived, the heavily padded doors closed once more, and the two men sipped in silence for some moments.

'Tell me,' said Schellenberg, 'how would you like to work for us?'

Kolchev registered interest. 'I don't quite follow,' he said. 'If Canaris's men are after me I won't be worth much to anyone.'

Even Schellenberg found it hard to resist this argument.

'Nevertheless,' he said after a moment's thought, 'it isn't beyond the bounds of possibility that your embassy will receive information which could be useful to us—if we learn of it in good time.'

'I see,' Kolchev replied lightly. 'So you'd like me to pop it in the post to you, is that it?'

Schellenberg smiled. 'That won't be necessary, Herr Kolchev. We have an interest in a certain establishment well known to you —one which is barred to Military Intelligence. You can pass your information there, to an absolutely reliable intermediary. You know where I mean. Can you suggest a better address?'

'The Pension Schmidt, you mean?'

'Precisely. The name of the reliable intermediary is Brigitta. How would that arrangement suit you?'

Kolchev stood up. 'I'm your man,' he said.

'If you need money . . .' drawled Schellenberg, but Kolchev brushed the suggestion aside.

'I don't want payment,' he said loftily.

'All the better.'

Each thought he had trapped the other, and each knew that he knew more about the other than had emerged during their brief interview. They sealed their pact with a firm handshake.

'Will you be attending the Antonescu reception?' Schellenberg asked.

'It'll certainly keep me busy,' Kolchev replied. 'Whether I'll get to see the Marshal is another matter.'

Schellenberg's tone became official. 'For all that, I'd appreciate a report on the subject.'

'As you wish, Standartenführer.' Kolchev smiled faintly. 'Heil Hitler!'

Marshal Antonescu, the Rumanian head of state, arrived in Berlin on 27 September 1941, as planned. He was greeted on the broad steps of the Chancellery by the newly appointed acting 'Protector' of Bohemia and Moravia, Reinhard Heydrich.

Heydrich owed his appointment to Hitler's poor opinion of his predecessor, Baron von Neurath, who had allegedly been lax in his attitude towards growing Czech resistance. Von Neurath was sent on indefinite leave and Heydrich received express orders to carry out liquidations on a grand scale. With the Central Security Office as his instrument, Heydrich proceeded to establish a reign of terror which soon made him the best-hated man in the Third Reich, not only among the Czechs but even among his associates in the SS.

Hitler greeted Antonescu with a pomp and ceremony normally reserved for his friend the Duce.

Lljubo Kolchev, who was present at most of the official functions, assiduously made notes for the benefit of his three employers: the Rumanians, the SD and British Intelligence. The next two days were spent in relaying his information, which he carefully double-checked, complete with a personal assessment of each item.

His 'official' report for the embassy he dictated to a hard-working secretary. It was on Bossy's desk within four hours of Antonescu's departure and earned him a commendation for unwonted diligence. A copy of this report, augmented by a few marginal notes, he slipped into his briefcase with the firm intention of handing it to Brigitta the same evening.

His 'unofficial' report he typed at his apartment an hour after leaving the Rumanian embassy. Having encoded it, he left it in a dead letter-box which he had designated days before the event with the request that anything deposited there should be passed to London with extra speed.

He did not reach the Salon Kitty until just before 11 p.m., but the drawing-room hummed with activity despite the lateness of the hour.

'Private party?' he inquired, when Kitty came to greet him.

'No, Baron, a mixed bag. Officers on leave and a few civilians, but I'll naturally have you shown to a room at once, if you prefer to be alone.'

'That would be nice. You might phone Brigitta, too.'

Kitty smiled. 'Better the devil you know, eh? It must be at least six months since I last saw you, Baron.'

'Is it really as long as that?' Kolchev seemed astonished.

'If not longer. Wait two minutes and I'll call Brigitta. Let's hope she's at home. . . .' Kitty clapped a hand over her mouth. 'I'm so sorry, Baron, I'd completely forgotten—Brigitta doesn't work here any more.'

'You can't mean it!' Kolchev simulated surprise, although he knew from Brigitta that she had been assigned exclusively to him. His private conclusion was that the amateurs of the SD had boobed yet again. 'Never mind,' he said, 'give me her number.'

'No, I can't do that.' Kitty shook her head firmly. 'She may not want to be disturbed.'

Kolchev grinned. 'Look, Kitty, will you do me a favour?'

'That depends,' Kitty said suspiciously.

'Dial a number for me—I'll tell you which. All you have to do is say I'm here and anxious to send Brigitta my regards. Just that, nothing more.'

Kitty made doubly sure. 'And I don't have to ask her to come here?'

'Certainly not.' Kolchev laughed. The situation tickled him, even if it did demonstrate the strictness of the Schellenberg-Schwarz régime.

Kitty dialled the number he gave her and said her piece, then hung up without waiting for a reply.

'Guess what'll happen now, Kitty?' Kolchev said teasingly.

She shrugged. 'No idea. I've done you a favour, Baron—I can't do more.'

'Except find me a room.'

'A room?' Kitty raised her eyebrows. 'I don't follow.'

'Brigitta will be here in ten minutes, want to bet?'

Kitty flushed with annoyance. 'Out of the question! I won't have her in the house, Baron. That wasn't fair of you.'

'Take it easy,' he said, patting her gently on the shoulder. 'I didn't realise you'd had a row. I promise I'll leave with her as soon as she arrives, all right?'

'Very well,' she said relucantly, but there was a note of fear in her voice.

'Word of honour,' he added.

Brigitta arrived five minutes later. Kolchev met her at the door and repeated Kitty's account of the situation. Brigitta slipped past him into the snuggery. He heard a murmur of voices, then she was back again.

'It's all right,' she said, 'we can have No 7.'

They were alone at last. Kolchev had written on a slip of paper : 'Be extra careful !' Aloud, he said : 'Here's my report—better pass it on tonight.' Brigitta, who had received advance warning from Schwarz, made a move to turn on her heel and go, but Kolchev caught her by the arm. 'Half an hour won't make any difference,' he said softly, and started to unbutton her dress.

They made love as they had not done for weeks. Brigitta clung to him afterwards as if she would never let go, but he gently released himself. With his mouth almost touching her ear, he whispered : 'See you outside.'

They were confederates with no chance of meeting again. Kolchev toyed with the idea of inviting her back to his flat but abandoned it immediately. The counter-espionage agents of Canaris's department weren't novices like Schellenberg's men. They would never be shaken off—he realised that—however hard he tried. He was sure they knew of Brigitta's SD status, and her meetings with him smacked too strongly of espionage for a trained agent not to smell a rat. He realised that he must not see Brigitta again, that their personal relationship was at an end. The only favour he could still do her was to refrain from endangering her further. Canaris's men would undoubtedly leave her alone once they discovered that contact between them had ceased.

He told her all this when he met her outside in the street. Brigitta, who was reluctant to accept the inevitable, wept. They walked down Giesebrechtstrasse to the Kurfürstendamm, holding hands like children, and even Kolchev had to admit that the parting grieved him.

'This is a dirty business,' he said. 'Get out of it as soon as you can.'

'But we'll see each other again after the war, won't we?' she said.

Kolchev dried her tears on his handkerchief. 'Of course we will,' he replied, almost believing it.

He didn't kiss her, merely squeezed her hand. By the time the air-raid sirens wailed, he had vanished into the entrance of an underground station. He felt a sudden void inside him, and stared at the hurrying, apprehensive crowds as though Brigitta's face might swim into view at any moment. But all that came was a spate of fire and devastation as more bombs rained down on the German capital.

As for Brigitta, she reached the cover address and reported to Obersturmführer Schwarz, in a voice drained of emotion, that she had an important written report to give him.

Chapter 15

On 8 October 1941, the close personal links which Schellenberg had long maintained with members of Admiral Canaris's counter-espionage network paid dividends once more.

The call reached him at 8 a.m., just as he entered his office. The caller did not give his name, simply said : 'You are employing an informant from the Rumanian embassy. He calls himself Lljubo Kolchev. The man is not Rumanian, nor is that his real name. We can't supply proof, but there's reason to believe that he's a British agent. That's the extent of our information. Heil Hitler!'

Schellenberg replaced the receiver with a puzzled frown. He had sensed from the outset that Kolchev was a shrewd operator, but the notion that a British agent should have offered his services to the SD foreign intelligence service in the guise of a Rumanian diplomat with pro-German leanings aroused the Standarten-führer's reluctant admiration.

He debated whether to try and use the man as one of his secret contacts with London but dismissed the idea. Canaris was on Kolchev's track and wouldn't hesitate to arrest him as soon as he obtained the smallest shred of evidence against him. Schellenberg's sole problem was how to steal a march on Military Intelligence.

He sent for Obersturmführer Schwarz and told him as much as he needed to know.

'Very well, Schwarz, take him into protective custody at once.'

Schwarz ventured to demur. 'But Kolchev has a diplomatic passport, Standartenführer.'

'Did I ask you to state the obvious?' Schellenberg said acidly.

'What do you want done with him, sir?'

'Take him to Prinz Albrechtstrasse and notify me when he's there.'

'Certainly, Standartenführer!' Schwarz saluted, turned on his heel and withdrew.

He took two reliable men and drove straight to the Rumanian embassy. He learned from the receptionist that the deputy press attaché seldom put in an appearance before 11 a.m.

'Could you give me his private address?' Schwarz asked amiably. 'I'm a relative. I'd like to catch a glimpse of him, but my train leaves at midday.'

The girl saw no reason why she shouldn't give Lljubo Kolchev's address to a relative who was so eager to see him.

Kolchev's phone rang at 10 a.m., just as he was sitting down to a leisurely breakfast. It was the laundry in Emserstrasse. The voice said : 'There's a piece of laundry missing.' Then the phone went dead.

Kolchev abandoned his breakfast. He threw the last remaining papers which might have incriminated him into the stove, picked up the overnight bag which always stood ready beside the door, and made his way downstairs without a backward glance.

The car containing Schwarz and his assistants drew up outside the entrance as he emerged. Schwarz recognised Kolchev at once. He leapt out of the car, nimble as a stoat, and strode swiftly towards him.

'Herr Kolchev?' Schwarz said politely, raising his hat. Kolchev recognised the SS man in spite of his civilian clothes—the long leather overcoat was unmistakable.

'I beg your pardon?' he said.

'Is your name Kolchev?' Schwarz demanded, rather less amiably now.

Wilson, alias Kolchev, told the truth without blinking. 'No,' he replied. 'Herr Kolchev lives above me on the second floor.' He started to walk off, but Schwarz barred his path. The other two SS men had also got out by this time.

Schwarz produced a warrant card from his pocket and held it out. 'Gestapo. May I see your papers, please?' It was an order, not a request.

Kolchev glanced round. The situation was hopeless, so he reached into his breast pocket and brought out his diplomatic pass. 'I'd point out that I'm a foreign national. You're asking for trouble.'

'That's our problem. Come with me, please.' Schwarz led the way to the car with Kolchev and the two SS men following behind.

'I insist we drive to the Rumanian embassy first,' Kolchev said firmly, but Schwarz didn't deign to reply. The black Mercedes drove straight to Prinz Albrechtstrasse, where Kolchev was made to surrender his bag in exchange for a receipt and deprived of his personal belongings, tie and braces included. All his protests were in vain. As a last resort he demanded to speak to Standarten-führer Schellenberg.

Even Schwarz cracked a smile at this. 'That's one request I can grant. Standartenführer Schellenberg will be here shortly.'

They locked Kolchev in a cell in the basement of Prinz Albrecht-strasse, He had an hour in which to consider possible ways of wriggling out of his predicament. It was clear that they would have no qualms about killing him—a risk which had often been pointed out to him in training. It was equally clear that the Rumanian embassy would not lift a finger to save him. Heaven knew how the Germans would explain his disappearance, if they bothered to do so at all.

Roger Wilson, alias Kolchev, was not a nervous man. He had known this would happen sooner or later. His principal emotion was annoyance at having fallen into German hands so easily. Self-reproach being futile, however, he resolved to make life as difficult for his captors as he could.

An hour later he was taken to see Schellenberg, who politely offered him a chair.

'Your report on the Antonescu visit was first-class, Herr Kolchev. I'd like to take this opportunity of expressing my grati-tude.'

Kolchev-Wilson eyed him warily, wondering if there was still a chance of saving his neck.

'Thanks for the compliment,' he said.

'By the way, if German comes hard to you we can always speak English. . . .'

Kolchev-Wilson smiled. 'By all means, if you prefer.'

'Are you English?' The question was razor-edged.

'Of course not, but I went to school there. Surely you have my curriculum vitae in your files?'

Schellenberg produced his next card. 'Look, Kolchev, we never fail to extract the truth in this place. I admire you. You've stuck your head into the lion's den regardless of the fact that you could get it bitten off. Congratulations on your courage, but now tell me who you are. Take my advice and come clean—it'll be better for you in the long run.'

'You have my papers. You know who I am.'

'The Lljubo Kolchev whose papers we hold is alive and well and living in a nice apartment—in London. That being so, who are you?' Schellenberg spoke quietly. Patience was one of his chief assets.

Kolchev-Wilson shrugged. 'I'm afraid I can't help you, Standartenführer. I can only suggest that the man you refer to is an impostor.'

Schellenberg was no novice when it came to interrogating spies, so he knew that he would make no progress for the moment. Each agent required a special technique, and this one was a professional. He could have used a dozen like Kolchev in his own foreign intelligence network.

'We'll meet again tomorrow,' was all he said as he got up to go. He paused at the door and handed Kolchev a packet of cigarettes and some matches. 'Don't tell anyone I gave them to you,' he said lightly.

The guard who had been waiting outside conducted Kolchev-Wilson back to his cell. As the heavy door swung to and the bolts crashed into place, he realised that his only hope was to stand firm. He was in good physical condition and determined to resist the myrmidons of the SS for as long as his strength held out. Fortunately, he had burned his security checks. They would find it hard to prove that he was an Englishman.

He slept soundly that night.

Schellenberg kept Lljubo Kolchev at Prinz Albrechtstrasse for nearly a month, regularly supplying him with cigarettes and dispensing with the use of 'intensified interrogation', the official euphemism for torture.

Early in November he sent the self-styled Rumanian to Sachsenhausen concentration camp. There he was confronted with two British Intelligence agents, Major Stevens and Captain Best, whom Schellenberg had been instrumental in capturing soon after the outbreak of war. There was not the slightest sign of recognition on either side.

Schellenberg gave instructions for the three men to be housed in the same block and kept under surveillance, but none of the reports he received from Sachsenhausen suggested that their acquaintanceship antedated Kolchev's detention. Their conversations were confined to trivia such as the sharing of washing facilities, fetching rations from the cookhouse and similar subjects.

Schellenberg would have bet a month's pay that Kolchev was an Englishman, hence his determination to keep him at Sachsenhausen. Concentration camps were outside the jurisdiction of the regular courts, and 'protective custody' was the magic formula which enabled the SS to imprison people there without trial.

It was also Schellenberg's hope that time would work on his behalf. His steadily expanding field of duties prevented him from devoting much attention to the mysterious Herr Kolchev, so he played a waiting game.

The Rumanian embassy received a more or less plausible memorandum from the Rumanian Foreign Office to the effect that its deputy press attaché, Lljubo Kolchev, had been unexpectedly recalled.

Nobody asked about him any more. Brigitta still hankered occasionally for a speedy end to the war and Lljubo's return, but that soon changed when her duties at the Salon Kitty brought her into contact with a young major on the air force general staff who, quite apart from his handsome face and heroic chestful of decorations, had the added advantage of being German.

Chapter 16

Obersturmführer Schwarz was a pedant. Having submitted his comprehensive dossier on the Salon Kitty's customers during 1940, he proceeded to tackle the second of his assignments.

This was a review of the monitoring techniques so far employed at the listening-post. When the SD embarked on its Salon Kitty venture, all conversations were recorded on disks. These disks were monitored by the Records Section, which produced transcripts of the more important passages. It soon became apparent that the filing of these disks and transcripts would in itself require so much space and the initiation of so many personnel that the project's maximum security rating would, in the long term, be jeopardised.

Accordingly, Schwarz considered what other recording processes might be more suitable for use by the SD's foreign intelligence service, and, in particular, which of them would permit storage of the Salon Kitty's vast output of material in the smallest possible space. To have destroyed any of it, however seemingly trivial, would have offended his sense of professional propriety, so he turned again for advice and assistance to the State Broadcasting Service, which briefed him on two likely devices.

The first was an apparatus invented by the Danish engineer Valdemar Poulsen and capable of recording speech on steel wire. Known as the 'Telegraphon', it had first been publicly demonstrated in 1898 but failed to make its mark until the outbreak of World War II.

The second process stemmed from experiments begun during 1934 by the firms IG Farben and AEG. These were aimed at producing neutral plastic tapes coated with particles which could be magnetised by a recording head and subsequently 'read' by a scanner. By 1936, the two firms had managed to interest the State Broadcasting Service in becoming a potential customer.

In collaboration with IG Farben and AEG, the State Broadcasting Service proceeded to develop this new 'Magnetophon' device. In 1940, its technical director, Walter Weber, succeeded in evolving the so-called high frequency magnetisation process. In simple terms, this meant that the background noise inherent in any recording tape could now be appreciably reduced. The new development stimulated official interest in the Magnetophon recording process to such an extent that it slowly but steadily ousted wax-disk and sound-track recording processes from the studios of the State Broadcasting Service.

By the time Obersturmführer Schwarz began to contemplate using the Magnetophon process at his Salon Kitty monitoring centre in December 1941, Radio Berlin technicians could proudly demonstrate the new recording process for his benefit but were unable to supply information about delivery dates for recording apparatus from AEG and tapes from IG Farben.

The results of Schwarz's prompt inquiries were discouraging. Even if the ten recording machines ordered by Schwarz via the Central Security Office were given top priority, AEG could not guarantee to deliver them before summer 1943. As for the tapes, IG Farben could give him no firm delivery date for the many thousands of metres he required. Shattered by the news, Schwarz submitted a lengthy written report to Schellenberg and requested an interview.

'We're inundated with wax disks, Standartenführer,' he announced. 'Our monthly output is running at nearly three thousand, of which only two or three hundred carry valuable information. The rest is just military gossip and self-important blathering on the part of civil servants and Party officials—nothing we can use.'

'I read your report, Schwarz,' Schellenberg said. 'I gather there's no hope of obtaining the equipment before late 1943. That's nearly two years hence. On the other hand, I attach great importance to the recording of seemingly unimportant conversations. Taken as a whole, they give us a picture of military and civilian morale. I do see, however, that something must be done to tighten security. Any suggestions?'

Schwarz, a staunch and indefatigable champion of his pet project, sensed that his job hung in the balance. As usual, he had an idea. 'I suggest we modify our monitoring procedure, Standartenführer,' he said crisply.

191

'In what way?'

'Why don't we hold the recording devices in constant readiness, as before, but refrain from cutting every word that's said? All conversations in bed are much the same—they hardly bring a blush to the cheeks of the girls in the Records Department, not any more. My idea would be to train SS women auxiliaries as short-hand typists and give them basic instruction in the use of recording equipment. That way we could continue to record all conversations of importance. It would be a great advantage, especially where the big drawing-room is concerned, because the human ear has greater powers of discrimination. We'd get less of the babble that spoils so many of our disks.'

Schellenberg considered the proposal and found that it had certain merits. 'In other words, you plan to dispense with all male personnel?'

'Yes, sir,' Schwarz replied smartly. 'A lot of my men are itching to see some active service. As it is, they feel they're shirking.'

This was an exaggeration, but nobody could blame the Obersturmführer for crediting his subordinates with worthy sentiments.

'How long would the change-over take?' Schellenberg asked.

'It should be possible to complete it in six months.'

Schellenberg knew that Schwarz was right. He also knew that the Obersturmführer was fighting tooth and nail to save his job. This was humanly understandable, especially in one who had listened to some of the disks cut in recent weeks, with their references to German troops in Russia dying for want of adequate winter clothing, to frost-bite and other disagreeable concomitants of the Russian counter-offensive. Schellenberg made his mind up quickly.

'All right, Obersturmführer, get cracking. Set up the necessary training courses at once. I shall hold you responsible for the selection of reliable personnel, is that clear?'

It was. Schwarz could breathe again. Six months was a long time. In company with millions of his fellow-countrymen, he longed for the coming of spring and the launching of a new offensive which would finally bring the Russians to their knees.

But the war produced some more surprises even before Christmas had come and gone. On 7 December 1941, a strong force of Japanese naval aircraft descended without warning on the US

Pacific Fleet at anchor in Pearl Harbor and sunk or severely damaged nineteen vessels.

On 8 December, the United States of America and Britain declared war on Japan.

On 11 December, Germany and Italy declared war on the United States.

The conflagration had spread from Europe to America and Asia.

The world was in flames.

Kitty Schmidt had recently been taking a keen interest in current affairs.

Her fear of Schellenberg decreased with every visit he paid to her establishment in quest of relaxation from his arduous official duties—in fact she sometimes had a vague feeling that he itched to confide in her. Early in 1942 a sort of intimacy grew up between them. Schellenberg talked far into the night, describing his life as he saw it and peppering his reminiscences with spiteful allusions to his boss, Reinhard Heydrich—remarks which he could afford to make because he had taken the precaution of switching off the monitoring equipment in advance.

Kitty listened to him with growing astonishment. So even as powerful a man as Schellenberg had his problems and pressures. She almost felt sorry for him, but the impulse waned when she recalled her taste of imprisonment in 1939. Although she was cordial to him, as to any guest of her establishment, she never granted him access to her private thoughts.

'Herr Heydrich hasn't been here for months,' she said.

'Heydrich?' mused Schellenberg. 'Heydrich has made it at last. Last September the Führer promoted him Obergruppenführer and transferred him to Prague. Now he's working off his perversions on the Czechs.'

Kitty cocked an eyebrow. 'You sound jealous, Walter. That's something new.'

'I'm not jealous, just worried about the future. I'm inundated with work and all my best men have been sent to the front. I'm surrounded by numbskulls who slept their way through school.'

His speech was noticeably slurred. Kitty felt a glimmer of triumph. Even Schellenberg had his weaknesses and she was determined to exploit them. Her thoughts were still focused on

Switzerland, and the more she thought of the place the more alluring it seemed.

But she had little time to dwell on these rosy dreams. Sirens wailed over Berlin's West End, heralding the arrival of British bombers which — if official reports were to be believed — had already been shot out of the sky several times over. She took Schellenberg by the arm and pushed him into the passage.

Agitated figures emerged from the various bedrooms, adjusting their clothing as they went. They jostled and shoved their way downstairs to the comparative safety of the cellars, where they sat silently, side by side, wondering if it was their turn this time.

Only Schellenberg seemed unperturbed. He had grabbed a bottle on the way and was slowly emptying it, gulp by gulp.

'The hell with it!' he muttered when the bottle was empty, and flung it over his shoulder.

They heard the muffled roar of anti-aircraft fire followed by the impact of the first bombs. The air-raid warden put on his over-size helmet and went to look. He returned a few minutes later.

'They've clobbered Alexanderplatz this time, judging by the glare,' he said.

Schellenberg turned to Kitty. 'Not the height of comfort, your cellar.'

'One gets used to it,' Kitty said phlegmatically. Then an idea occurred to her. 'It's hell for business, of course. What customer wants to spend the night in a communal shelter and risk being recognised?'

She waited for the fish to bite, but either Schellenberg had failed to hear or he was too drunk to catch the drift of her remarks.

It was an hour before the All Clear sounded.

'Coming upstairs again?' Kitty asked.

'Of course, that's why I'm here.' Schellenberg sounded almost savage. Back in the drawing-room, he reached for the nearest bottle. 'Get me a woman,' he said, '— a young one!'

He slept late next morning.

The bomb attack on Reinhard Heydrich in Prague was carried out on 27 May 1942 by a group of specially trained SOE agents. Heydrich succumbed to his injuries on 4 June. Despite the reprisals that followed, the Czechs felt as if a curse had been lifted from them, and even the dead man's brother-officers in the SS displayed little regret. When Sepp Dietrich, commanding general of the SS-Leibstandarte Adolf Hitler, expressed satisfaction that 'the swine' was dead at last, he was only voicing what many felt.

Heydrich's death not only had sanguinary repercussions on the Czechs—the village of Lidice was razed to the ground and the assassins committed suicide a month later when cornered in a Prague church—but wrought important changes in the Central Security Office.

Schellenberg, never one to miss a golden opportunity, sought to make the SD foreign intelligence service independent before a successor to Heydrich could be appointed. He duly produced a study in which he set out, logically and in depth, the reasons why the SD foreign intelligence service should be directly subordinated to Himmler, Reichsführer-SS and head of the German police.

Himmler, who could not fail to deduce from this study that Heydrich had kept him in the dark about certain important aspects of the Central Security Office, summoned Schellenberg and asked him to elaborate on what he had written.

Much warmer in manner than Heydrich and endowed with considerable personal charm, Schellenberg realised that his big moment had come. He tailored himself so perfectly to Himmler's requirements that the latter took the Central Security Office under his personal aegis.

From then on, Himmler never reached a major decision without first consulting Schellenberg. Apart from Kersten, Himmler's personal masseur and medical adviser, Schellenberg became the most important man in the Reichsführer's entourage and remained so until January 1943, when Dr Ernst Kaltenbrunner was appointed to head the Central Security Office.

As in Yugoslavia, the German High Command in Russia became involuntarily acquainted with a new form of fighting: partisan warfare.

Acts of sabotage against German ammunition and supply dumps multiplied, attacks on German troops became more frequent, and field post office letters addressed to wives and parents contained a growing flood of complaints which aroused fierce discontent on the home front.

The German summer offensive of 1942, aimed at capturing the oil centres of the Caucasus and cutting the Volga, nonetheless brought fresh successes with which Goebbels's propaganda machine managed to stem the rising tide of unrest.

German troops penetrated to the Don and crossed it, and the hitherto almost unknown commander of the 6th Army, General Paulus, reached the Volga north of Stalingrad. The Russian defenders of Stalingrad resisted the 6th Army so fiercely that they brought the German offensive to a standstill.

It was only natural that these events should form the chief topic of conversation at the Salon Kitty. Heydrich's assassination and the reprisals in Czechoslovakia, the Afrika Korps' withdrawal from Cyrenaica under Rommel, Japanese attacks on the Philippines, the Dutch East Indies, Thailand and Malaya, and the capture of Hongkong and Singapore—all these things were mentioned but did not call forth deep emotion. Russia was, and remained, topic No 1.

Other reverses seemed positively trivial by comparison. Obersturmführer Schwarz was finding it hard to train new personnel and his programme was behind schedule. Meanwhile, his existing SD monitoring teams were on the verge of physical exhaustion. Sickness due to malnutrition, an increasingly frequent phenomenon, compelled Schwarz to recruit extra watches from teams which had already stood duty. This did little to raise the general level of morale. Once upon a time, his men had derived occasional amusement when particularly intriguing noises issued from their headphones. Now, they were blasé. Instead of laughing, they watched the clock rather than their equipment.

More than once, exceptionally courageous voices were heard to wish that a British bomb would blow the Salon Kitty to smithereens. Although tantamount to defeatism, remarks like these were magnanimously overlooked because their authors belonged to an élite unit.

London seemed to have heard their prayers, however. On 17 July 1942 a bomb landed on 11 Giesebrechtstrasse, penetrated as far as the first floor, and temporarily put the Salon Kitty out of commission.

Down in the cellars at Prinz Albrechtstrasse, headquarters of the Security Office and site of the monitoring centre, the SD technicians heard a sharp click in their headphones, then silence.

Being soldiers, they knew where their duty lay. A messenger

was promptly dispatched to Obersturmführer Schwarz, who arrived at Giesebrechtstrasse an hour later.

What he saw was enough to dispel his hopes and dreams. The upper floors were still smouldering, and only the fact that Gruppenführer Kaltenbrunner lived next door had prompted the overworked Berlin Fire Brigade to hurry to the assistance of the voluntary fire-fighters.

Schwarz at once perceived the dangers of the situation. He raced to Prinz Albrechtstrasse by car, quickly assembled a squad of denim-clad SS men, and transported them to Giesebrechtstrasse in the duty truck, which he commandeered for the occasion.

Back at the scene once more, he gave orders that all undamaged articles of furniture on the third floor were to be retrieved at once and taken to the cellar.

War had come to the Salon Kitty at last. Schwarz surpassed himself, instantly transformed into a warrior fighting to preserve all that he held most dear. He summoned two technicians whom he had taken the precaution of bringing with him from the listening post.

'Get up to the third floor and don't let anyone into the Pension Schmidt,' he told them. 'Detain anyone who tries to enter or remove anything.'

But Schwarz's order came too late. Kitty Schmidt, her girls and such customers as happened to be on the premises had already joined forces in a salvage operation. With soot- and tear-stained faces, the women had defied the flames to save what could still be saved.

By the time the fire chief ordered 'Water on!' the courtyard and street were piled with oil paintings and chandeliers, chairs and beds, crockery and linen, and enthroned in their midst sat Kitty Schmidt, keeping an eagle eye on her goods and chattels. Looting was punishable by death, but it paid to be careful. Kitty was feeling more relieved than distressed. It grieved her to have lost a place of which she had grown fond, but she did not weep. She had struck camp too often in her life to be over-attached to material possessions. Everything was impermanent, even life itself. No one had been killed or injured, so she really had grounds for rejoicing. It didn't even dampen her spirits when she spotted Obersturmführer Schwarz deploying his squad of muscular young soldiers like a victorious general.

'Ah, there you are, Frau Schmidt!' Schwarz exclaimed, and she got the impression that he was glad to find her alive. For all that, his tone irritated her.

'Where else should I be?' she demanded.

Schwarz forbore to point out that she might have seized the opportunity to vanish. Many people did, nowadays.

'We'll have to find you some new quarters at once,' he said.

'Let me worry about that,' she replied tartly.

Schwarz registered Kitty's tone with surprise and secret fury. She was wrong if she thought a little air-raid would get her off the hook, but this was not the moment to disabuse her. He decided to banish her misconception at a more suitable time.

'Where do you propose to store your things?' he asked.

'I thought of putting them in the cellar.'

He shrugged. 'Very well, but please report to me before you leave.'

Kitty could hardly believe her ears. Had the Obersturmführer actually said 'please'? Well, what if he had? She remained un-mollified.

'As you wish,' she replied.

Schwarz dispatched a messenger to Schellenberg. Then he took his men aside and addressed them in a low voice. 'Frau Schmidt's apartment on the third floor of this building contains various installations with a maximum security rating. They've got to be dismantled and removed before morning.'

He divided his squad into small parties which at once began to tear the cables and microphones out of the walls and damage the remaining surfaces so severely that no suspicions would be aroused.

Another party was detailed to dig up the multi-core cable which led to the Post Office junction box, seal it off, remove it and fill in the trench again.

The occupants of the building—or those whose apartments were still habitable—did not receive permission to re-enter it until work was completed. Meanwhile, Kitty and her friends and customers had begun to store her possessions in the cellar.

Kitty and Schwarz completed their labours at roughly the same time. They bumped into each other in the main entrance.

'Report to me at midday sharp, Frau Schmidt,' Schwarz commanded. He seemed to have recovered his composure.

An NCO marched up to him. 'All finished, Obersturmführer!' he reported smartly.

Schwarz nodded. 'Very well, tell the men to fall in.'

He satisfied himself that all the salvaged equipment had been safely loaded. Then, taking two junior NCOs with him, he paid a final visit to the third floor, where he inspected every room in the Pension Schmidt and made sure that all traces of his men's handiwork had been thoroughly obliterated. The place looked as if it had been ravaged by vandals. Even the rooms that had escaped bomb-damage were unrecognisable.

'Good work.' Schwarz gave an approving nod. 'Just the same, we'll post a guard outside for the rest of the night and give the place another going-over in daylight.' He posted sentries with strict orders to keep everyone out. Finally, he distributed largesse in the form of cigarettes which he always carried with such eventualities in mind.

Schellenberg drove up as the Obersturmführer re-emerged into the street. Schwarz saluted and briefed him on the measures he had taken. The Standartenführer merely nodded. The Salon Kitty had been a dwindling asset recently, but it was an undeniable loss. 'Anyone hurt?' he inquired, more as a matter of form than with genuine concern.

Schwarz replied in the negative. 'Frau Schmidt has announced her intention of spending the night in the cellar.'

'I see,' was Schellenberg's sole comment. 'Later today I shall expect some suggestions on where we go from here, also what measures must be taken to maintain security.'

'Certainly, Standartenführer!' Schwarz snapped to attention and raised his arm in the Nazi salute. 'Heil Hitler!'

Schellenberg did not respond in kind. He said 'Good night' and told his driver to head for home. Mentally, he had already written the Salon Kitty off.

But Schellenberg was reckoning without Schwarz. The Obersturmführer plunged into the fray when morning came as though bent on rebuilding Berlin in a single day.

His first step was to contact the estate office which managed 11 Giesebrechtstrasse. The ground floor of the building was occupied by the consulate of a friendly nation. Schwarz had little difficulty in persuading the consular officials to move out. He was determined that the Salon Kitty should remain at its present address. Many customers might actually prefer the ground floor to the third because it would enable them to come and go more inconspicuously and with less chance of detection.

A much bigger problem was whether and how to instal microphones for the monitoring system, a time-consuming operation with which Schwarz was only too familiar. Procurement of materials was yet another problem. The Salon Kitty must not remain closed for too long or its clientèle would drift away. Overwhelmed by the magnitude of his difficulties, Schwarz decided to talk them over with Schellenberg.

'You're mad,' Schellenberg said soberly, when he had listened to Schwarz's ambitious proposals for a complete re-establishment of the old system. 'Here's what we'll do. The monitoring installation will be closed down and its recording apparatus used for other purposes. The disks will retain their top secret rating. They'll be carefully listed and kept under lock and key. The Salon Kitty will continue to operate as usual, but on the ground floor. Our women agents must be instructed to make their written reports even more comprehensive than before. The power and telephone lines to 11 Giesebrechtstrasse must be given top priority and repaired at once. Get hold of some builders and decorators—put them at Frau Schmidt's disposal and see to it that they get the place ready for reopening in two days' time. Apart from a few first-class men, all monitoring and Record Section personnel who can't be absorbed elsewhere will be posted to the Central Security Office. Before leaving, they're to be placed under oath and reminded of their unconditional pledge of secrecy.

'I want regular reports on all ex-members of the monitoring teams, stating which unit they're currently serving with. Their unit-commanders must be instructed to watch them for breaches of security. Confidential reports on them are to be submitted monthly, is that clear?'

It was a typical Schellenberg performance—no indecision, no acceptance that some problems might be insoluble.

Everything went according to plan. Two days later, on 19 July 1942, the Salon Kitty reopened for business. Obersturmführer Schwarz had achieved the impossible, scenting that he still had a chance to salvage his job and evade the transfer to a combat unit which might otherwise have threatened him.

All the Salon Kitty lacked from now on was its old inexhaustible supply of alcoholic refreshment.

The night the bomb fell on 11 Giesebrechtstrasse, the SS wines and spirits warehouse went up in flames too.

Chapter 17

The tide of war was turning against Germany. The Red Army had recovered from the shock of Hitler's lightning victories and marshalled itself for a massive counter-attack. The invaders were thrown back along a wide front, the soldiers of the German 6th Army encircled at Stalingrad and abandoned to destruction by the Führer's order to die where they stood.

Allied troops under the command of General Eisenhower landed in Morocco and Algeria, compelling Rommel and the Afrika Korps to fight a war on two fronts.

In Yugoslavia, Bulgaria, Greece, Albania, Hungary and Czechoslovakia, relatively small groups of partisans held down strong units of the German occupying forces, which often sustained considerable losses at their hands.

All this happened in the closing months of 1942.

The tide of war had turned still more decisively against Italy. Ribbentrop and Alfieri, the new Italian ambassador in Berlin, conferred unceasingly on the question of how German troops could best safeguard Italy. For their part, the Italians deliberately assumed responsibility for the defence of the French Mediterranean coast against an anticipated Allied invasion. At Toulon, the remaining French naval units scuttled their ships to prevent them from falling into Axis hands.

The morale of the German people was also declining. The worse the war went, the greater the speed with which rumours and conjectures spread.

The Salon Kitty did not share in this general decline—not for the moment and not where Kitty herself was concerned. Although she could no longer dispense unlimited quantities of food and drink as she had done in the early years of the war, there was no purely numerical decrease in her clientèle. On the contrary, never had the urge for fleeting contact with soft and compliant femininity seemed as strong as it did in those dark days.

Kitty's circle of customers had undergone a radical change since 1940 and 1941. Her Berlin 'regulars' were a vanishing breed, and most of those who sought sexual consolation from her girls were soldiers home on leave from the front. The atmosphere became less sophisticated but no less welcoming.

Diplomats and senior officers seldom came now. Ribbentrop and Canaris had heard rumours that the Gestapo used the brothel as a clearing-house for information and saw to it that their subordinates shunned the place.

This was all right with Kitty but not with Schwarz. Items of intelligence, which now came exclusively from his women agents, grew steadily sparser and less important. Schellenberg now derived better and quicker information from his European network of SD agents and used it to consolidate his privileged status, not only in the Central Security Office but with Himmler personally.

What worried Schwarz most of all, however, was that control over the Salon Kitty had progressively weakened since the monitoring centre ceased to operate. His mistrust of his own agents became obsessive, and the least slip on their part sent him into a paroxysm of rage.

Schellenberg saw more and more clearly that Schwarz was becoming a threat to his own organisation. He would happily have relieved him of his post but could not find a suitable successor. In view of the waning importance he attached to the Salon Kitty, he toyed with the idea of severing his last remaining links with the establishment. All that still eluded him was the best way of doing so.

The girl agents also noticed that supervision was not as strict as it had been before the third floor was bombed. Being human, they began to exploit the situation. Most of them had come to enjoy their 'sheltered' existence at the Salon Kitty, and they seized the opportunity to supplement their relatively low pay with pin-money. Their relations with Kitty became less formal. In direct contravention of Schwarz's orders, they turned up en masse for all-night parties.

It was inevitable that Kitty's sixtieth birthday should be marked by a major celebration. For the last time, Kitty held court in style. She invited all her girls and the few friends who had loyally

203

stood by her in recent years. Kitchen and cellar produced the best that was still available, and any stranger privileged to catch a glimpse of Kitty's birthday party would have taken it for an end-of-term celebration at some boarding-school for refined young ladies. Kitty insisted that the proprieties were strictly observed, in language as in behaviour. No ordinary customers were admitted, and a sign on the front door informed would-be patrons that the establishment was closed 'for family reasons'.

None of which enhanced the Salon Kitty's diminishing importance to the SD's foreign intelligence service.

New Year's Day 1943. The proclamations issued by Hitler, the Party and the High Command had a studiously optimistic ring, but German eyes continued to gaze spellbound in the direction of Stalingrad, where disaster was brewing for the 6th Army and the entire Russian front.

News of the disaster, which signalled a turning-point in the war, was conveyed to the Germans in undramatic communiqués from the Führer's headquarters and the Supreme Command of the Armed Forces. What they omitted to mention was the extent of the losses which the German army had sustained at Stalingrad. According to Soviet figures, the 6th Army lost 146,300 dead, and 90,000 men trod the uncertain road into Russian captivity.

In Berlin, overshadowed by events at Stalingrad, a virtually unpublicised take-over occurred at the Central Security Office. Himmler appointed Ernst Kaltenbrunner to fill Heydrich's vacant post and simultaneously promoted him SS-Obergruppenführer, a rank equivalent to lieutenant-general. Kaltenbrunner moved into Prinz Albrechtstrasse on 29 January 1943 and immediately set to work.

From then on, this technocratic manipulator of power became Himmler's evil genius and, thus, ultimately responsible for the crimes committed by the SD in Germany and the occupied territories. He also sought to consolidate the status of the Central Security Office and extend its sphere of authority.

Kaltenbrunner devoted particular attention to the intelligence services, including that of the Foreign Office, Military Intelligence (Canaris), and his own SD foreign intelligence network.

Schellenberg, who headed the SD foreign intelligence service

(Department VI) at the Central Security Office, had foreseen this development and insured himself with Himmler in advance. This did not, however, prevent him from clashing with Kaltenbrunner because the latter soon realised that Schellenberg's immense fund of confidential information had earned him a dangerously important niche in the Nazi hierarchy. Schellenberg had also managed to eclipse the Foreign Office intelligence service to an increasing extent.

Although this made Schellenberg Kaltenbrunner's chief rival, they were both SS officers and members of the Black Order, so Kaltenbrunner concentrated his initial fire on Admiral Canaris and Military Intelligence. This temporarily took the heat off Schellenberg, who used the respite to his own advantage. The Salon Kitty no longer enjoyed his favour or patronage.

Johannes Heesters, a Dutch star of stage and screen, was vastly popular with Berlin audiences. His name on a bill-board was enough to guarantee any show a succession of packed houses, and his latest show—Hentschke's *Wedding-Night in Paradise*—was no exception. Heesters enjoyed playing in Berlin and always stayed at the same private hotel for actors, where the proprietress cosseted him and winked at his notorious weakness for the fair sex.

When the rehearsals for *Wedding-Night* were over and the first few performances had met with a predictably enthusiastic reception, the Dutchman's hotel was destroyed in an air-raid.

Heesters found himself out on the street. He asked some friends if they could recommend alternative accommodation. One of them suggested in a confidential whisper that the 'Pension Schmidt' might suit him. Having packed what was left of his personal effects, he climbed into the car which the theatre had put at his disposal and told the driver to take him to 11 Giesebrechtstrasse.

Kitty had managed to salvage her 'house sign' from the air-raid, so the actor unsuspectingly pressed the bell and asked the maid-servant if there were any vacancies.

Elvira ushered him inside and asked: 'Rothenburg?'

Heesters, who spoke German better than he understood it and had no knowledge of local conventions, nodded and said yes.

He was shown into the drawing-room, which happened to be empty, and offered a chair. Entranced by his comfortable surroundings, which were just what he had hoped for, he sat down and congratulated himself on his good fortune. Then Kitty entered with her albums. She recognised her distinguished visitor at once.

'This is a great honour, Herr Heesters.'

'The privilege is mine,' Heesters replied. He regarded Kitty amiably and without guile.

'I hope you'll enjoy your visit.'

'I'm sure I shall,' Heesters said. 'But first, perhaps I'd better fetch my things—then I can send the car back to the theatre. I'm afraid they'll be waiting for it.'

Kitty agreed, thinking that he had brought his overnight bag in case of an air-raid. Politely, she held the door for him.

Heesters was back in two minutes. He tottered into the drawing-room burdened with two heavy suitcases which might have contained enough overnight things for a regiment. Kitty's misgivings were aroused.

'You plan to stay the night?' she inquired tentatively.

Heesters produced one of the charming smiles for which he was famed. 'Tonight and every night for the next six weeks, maybe even longer. I'll provide my own breakfast eggs.'

'Six weeks?' Kitty's tone was diplomatic. 'I'm not sure if I can spare a room for as long as that. Do you mind if I check?'

'Not at all. Meanwhile, may I have some coffee?'

'But of course, Herr Heesters.'

Kitty ordered coffee and hurried to her snuggery. She telephoned Obersturmführer Schwarz and informed him of the actor's request. Schwarz was furious. 'You're crazy!' he bellowed. 'It's out of the question!'

'I can hardly show him the door at this hour,' Kitty said firmly. She already sensed that the Obersturmführer's authority was waning. 'May I ask you to raise the matter with Standartenführer Schellenberg at once—or shall I ring him myself?'

Schwarz realised that she had him over a barrel. He was not blind to the fact that his chief's interest in the Salon Kitty had evaporated in the last few months.

'I'll consult him right away,' he said. 'Give Herr Heesters a room for the night. You'll be hearing from me.'

Kitty smiled thinly to herself. Politeness to one's enemies paid off, and she found it hard to believe that Schellenberg would make difficulties for so popular an artist. From her own point of view, she resolved to be as friendly and welcoming to Heesters as possible.

She made it her personal concern to see that he was given the best room in the Pension Schmidt, checked that the bed-linen and towels were fresh, helped him to unpack his bags, admired the quality of his wardrobe, and asked if he had any special requirements. Her manner was so natural that Heesters felt at home from the outset. Before withdrawing to give the new arrival a chance to freshen up, she paused in the doorway.

'I've tried to contact the guest who provisionally booked your room from tomorrow. I hope to hear in the next ten minutes whether you can keep it.'

Kitty realised that this was a unique opportunity to get the Central Security Office off her back and cursed her stupidity for not having thought of the idea earlier.

Elvira called her to the phone. It was Schellenberg.

'Did you dream this up, Kitty, or is it a coincidence?'

'Oh come, Walter! Haven't I always played the game with you?'

Schellenberg laughed. 'Yes, you have. I misjudged you at first, but that was before I got to know you. Of course Heesters can stay, and as far as I'm concerned you can let the rest of your rooms as well. We're closing down. You realise, of course, that you must never talk to anyone about our—well, relationship, let's say. I'm afraid I must ask you to come to my office and sign another undertaking to that effect. After that, I shall regard the matter as closed. We'll hand your establishment back to the brothel surveillance squad. How you make out with them will be your business —all right?'

'I understand, Walter.' Kitty's heart leapt. She longed for a coffee and schnapps. Fortune had smiled on her at last, and the mental tensions of the last few years yielded to a sense of deliverance. She had an urge to rush to her new guest and fling her arms round his neck, but how could she ever convey the extent of what she owed him? She would never breathe a word—Kitty was adamant on that point—not now and not when it was all over.

She drank her coffee and sipped her schnapps, feeling better than she had felt in ages and greeting her customers with a carefree gaiety which suggested that the war had just ended. It had, too, for her. All that remained was to survive.

The change-over from monitoring system to brothel surveillance was simpler for Kitty than for Schellenberg and the Central Security Office. Schellenberg realised that Schwarz represented more of a danger than ever because he felt sure Kaltenbrunner would try to grab the man for the sake of his inside information.

It followed that he must do his utmost to keep Schwarz under his personal supervision in Department VI. Equally, Kaltenbrunner and the other Central Security Office departments must as far as possible be kept in ignorance of the Salon Kitty and its links with the SD foreign intelligence service.

He summoned Schwarz.

'You did a magnificent job on the Salon Kitty,' he began. 'I shall be recommending you for promotion.'

Schellenberg was gratified to see his subordinate's eyes light up. 'That's why I'm determined to hang on to you, Schwarz—hold you in reserve for even bigger assignments. However, before we consider the best way of using your talents in future, all traces of the Salon Kitty must be obliterated. After all, it's still top secret. Any suggestions?'

The bureaucrat in Schwarz had come prepared for this interview. 'The installations at 11 Giesebrechtstrasse have been completely dismantled and the cables taken up as far as the Post Office junction box. Obergruppenführer Kaltenbrunner lives next door —we could put the lines at his disposal. . . .'

'Better not,' Schellenberg cut in, 'not until the whole operation has been wound up.'

'Very good, sir,' Schwarz said crisply. 'Of course, the girls are a problem.'

'Can't we simply release them?'

Schwarz had never contemplated such an easy way out. 'That's one alternative,' he mused. 'There's the question of security, though—we'd have to settle that first.'

'Quite so,' said Schellenberg. 'The trouble is, our girls are well known at the Salon Kitty. If we suddenly take them out of service, their regular customers will notice and draw their own conclusions. It might be more advisable for them to carry on. They can still supply us with information, but not at our expense—there's no room for such an item in my departmental budget. The best plan would be to tell Frau Schmidt to take them on her pay-roll —she's made enough out of us, God knows.'

'Good idea, sir.' Schwarz, who had been following Schellenberg's train of thought intently, warmed to him more and more. 'We'll have to ensure that they remain under surveillance, even after their release, otherwise they'll be a security risk.'

'Quite right, but that's your pigeon. You can handle it any way you like. What about the monitoring centre at Prinze Albrechtstrasse—has it been dismantled?'

'Most of it, sir. The Central Security Office has retained possession of the individual items of equipment. Gruppenführer Ohlendorf is distributing them throughout the country.'

'Which leaves the disks. What's happened to them?'

'I've had them stored in a cellar at Prinz Albrechtstrasse, a bomb-proof chamber with double doors. The remaining Records Section personnel are in the process of checking and listing them. There's an immense backlog of material still to be dealt with—enough to keep them going for several months. With your permission, I propose to do the same with the transcripts.'

'Agreed,' said Schellenberg. 'In addition, I'd like you to draw up lists for 1941 and 1942, on the same lines as the one for 1940. They could be vitally important, so please make a thorough job of them.'

Schellenberg felt assured that he had given Schwarz a chore which would keep him chained to his desk for at least a year.

'Also, I'd like you to move your office back here, as of now. I want you on call at all times.' Schellenberg knew that the offices and departments at Prinz Albrechtstrasse were in close contact, and he couldn't afford to expose Schwarz to hostile influence. 'What about that training course of yours?'

'We're in luck there too,' Schwarz reported. 'I've managed to off-load the women trainees, partly on to Obergruppenführer Berger's department. Some of them will be posted as SS women auxiliaries and the rest employed on secretarial work at SS operational headquarters.'

'Excellent. One last point : those recording machines and tapes we ordered—what'll happen to them when they're delivered at the end of the year?'

Schwarz stiffened as though resentful that Schellenberg could even vaguely suspect him of an oversight. 'I thought we might find a use for them in our own department.'

'Very well, I agree.'

'There's still the question of what to do with Frau Schmidt.' Schwarz's personal solution would have been to clap her behind bars, but this time the vote went against him.

'The Salon Kitty must continue to function as if nothing had changed. Frau Schmidt will be calling here today. Draw up a document reminding her that she's pledged to absolute secrecy in respect of all she's seen and heard—and put the fear of God into her.' Schellenberg smiled grimly. 'Another of your specialities, eh, Schwarz?'

Obersturmführer Schwarz was grateful to the Standarten-führer for allowing him to bow out on a punch-line.

Kitty called at Meineckestrasse the same day and asked to see Schellenberg. The duty NCO tried to contact him but was informed that Obersturmführer Schwarz would see her instead. Kitty felt uneasy.

She was feeling even more uneasy by the time Schwarz had her shown into his office a full half-hour later.

It was a bare, unwelcoming room. Schwarz had only moved in a few hours earlier and was without his filing cabinets, but he had sent for Kitty's dossier from Prinz Albrechtstrasse.

'Sit down,' he snapped, pacing slowly up and down behind his desk. He waited until she had settled herself rather uncomfortably on the hard wooden chair.

Behind the desk hung two framed photographs, one of Hitler and the other of Himmler. Kitty, waiting for Schwarz to speak, gazed at them with a semblance of patriotic devotion.

'Frau Schmidt,' Schwarz said at last, 'I suppose you know why you're here?' The martial undertone in his voice made the question a threat.

'I was asked to come,' said Kitty. 'Standartenführer Schellen-berg invited me here to sign another pledge of secrecy.' She assumed her most guileless expression.

'Nobody invited you here. You were ordered to report here so that I can decide what's to become of you, is that clear?'

Kitty realised that she had made a blunder, lulled into a false sense of security by the delusion that she was free of her obligations at last. This SS man, with whom she had never established much contact, could still be a threat to her. 'Forgive me,' she said, 'I didn't express myself correctly. Of course I was ordered here.'

210

Schwarz sat back, conscious that he had regained the upper hand. 'I've half a mind to consign you to a concentration camp—now, today. You realise that I have the power to do so?'

Kitty recoiled. Schellenberg had struck quite a different note the day before but there was no point in provoking Schwarz by mentioning the fact.

'I know,' she said, slumping in her chair, and added : 'I'm sixty years old, Obersturmführer.'

Schwarz did not pursue the implication. He reached for a typewritten sheet to which he had devoted long and careful thought.

'You're going to sign this undertaking, and God help you if you don't observe it to the letter.'

He pushed it across to her, together with a bound list of regulations. The top sheet stated that the least infringement of the rules laid down by the Central Security Office was summarily punishable, depending on the gravity of the breach of security, by graduated penalties including death. Appended were several sheets bearing regulations which seemed to have been specially framed for Kitty's benefit.

'May I take them home and study them carefully?' she asked.

'Certainly not. Read them here. If you need more time I'll be glad to put a cell at your disposal.' Schwarz relished his triumph.

'Very well,' said Kitty, 'I'll read them here.' Threading her way through the forest of paragraphs, she gathered that she had to report to the police once a month from now on, that she was forbidden to speak to anyone about what she had heard and seen, that she must observe strict secrecy, both as regards the 'redecoration' of her establishment and the names of employees and customers, that she could no longer count on the backing of the Central Security Office—indeed, that she had never in any way been associated with the institution. She further gathered that her licence would in future be issued by the appropriate police department.

Her eyes began to water and the typescript went blurred, but she tried to convey that she was reading the document carefully, word for word.

A hush had descended on Schwarz's office. The Obersturmführer sat hunched behind his desk, watching his prey with sadistic glee. He could tell from Kitty's demeanour that she was afraid, just as he had hoped.

211

'How much longer?' he demanded savagely.

Kitty dabbed her eyes with a handkerchief. 'Just coming,' she said. She tried to focus on the lines, but it was no use. She replaced the sheaf of paper on Schwarz's bare desk. He produced a pen.

'Are you going to sign?'

'Yes,' she said, 'I suppose I must. . . .'

'There's no must about it. The choice is yours. Either sign or —well, I don't have to tell you the alternative.' Schwarz lusted to arrest her, but Schellenberg's orders were clear. Impotent rage assailed him. 'Sign, blast you!'

Kitty took the pen and signed. She didn't know whether she was acting for the best or the worst. She only knew that she wanted to get out of there as fast as she could, take a deep breath of fresh air and pretend that it had all been a dream.

She made a move to rise, but Schwarz was determined to drain his cup of pleasure to the dregs. 'Sit down!'

Kitty wondered what more he wanted. Hadn't he tormented her enough?

'As of now, all the girls in your establishment will be paid by you, including those who haven't so far received any money from you. You will not be entitled to refuse them access or eject them. We shall expect you to report to us at once if any girl fails to put in an appearance for a period exceeding two weeks, is that clear?'

It wasn't, but Kitty's desire to escape from the room had become overwhelming, so she said yes.

Schwarz dismissed her with a brusque gesture.

Once outside in the street, she did not linger but stumbled the few steps to the Kurfürstendamm like a blind woman. Then she slackened her pace and made her way back to Giesebrechtstrasse past heaps of rubble and ruined buildings, shattered pavements and fenced-off bomb craters.

The air did her good and fortified her sufficiently to reflect on what had just happened. The more she thought about it, the more certain she felt that it was a final act of impotence on the part of Obersturmführer Schwarz. Kitty had heard a great deal in recent weeks. She knew that the war would end one day and that, whoever won, it would not be the SS.

She had always avoided political discussions, but she had always been a good listener. She resolved to remain so in future. The SS

212

men of the Security Service had not only taught her the meaning of fear; they had taught her that silence was golden. Kitty Schmidt obeyed that precept to the end of her life.

The first thing she did on reaching home was to brew herself a strong cup of the coffee which, war-time shortages notwithstanding, she still managed to obtain by dark and devious means. She wasn't short of her favourite schnapps either, even though she had to hide the bottles from prying eyes.

'What's up?' asked Elvira.

'Nothing special,' Kitty replied casually. 'We'll be getting our licence from the police again in future.'

As far as she was concerned, that ended the matter.

Also at an end was the pressure exterted on her by Schellenberg, Schwarz and the SD. Kitty reported regularly in the years that followed without being subjected to any further inquisitions, but the war went on.

In August 1943, Himmler achieved his ambition. He was appointed Minister of the Interior and retained the post for another eighteen months. He assigned Schellenberg to conduct clandestine negotiations with all the powers ranged against Germany. The aim : an early end to hostilities. The price : Hitler's head.

There was a steady intensification of day and night raids by the British and, to an increasing extent, by the Americans. Architectural treasures of inestimable value were reduced to rubble and ashes, the worst affected cities being Cologne, Wuppertal, Hamburg, Berlin and Dresden.

On 20 July 1944, Colonel Count Schenk von Stauffenberg tried to eliminate Hitler by planting a bomb at his headquarters in East Prussia, otherwise known as the Wolf's Lair. The attempt failed, and Hitler exacted terrible vengeance. Goerdeler, Leuschner, von Witzleben, von Hassel and many other men of courage and integrity were summarily hauled before the People's Court, sentenced to death by Roland Freisler, Germany's 'hanging judge', and executed. A number of senior military commanders such as Rommel, Beck and von Kluge committed suicide.

Germany surrendered unconditionally on 7 May 1945 and was split into four occupied zones. Berlin underwent the same dismemberment. When the war ended, Kitty Schmidt was sixty-three years old and could reasonably hope to have wiped her slate clean.

But no one who has once become entangled in the toils of an intelligence network can readily escape. The Russian conquerors of Berlin soon heard about the Salon Kitty and tried to exploit the system for their own ends, as did the British and Americans when they took over their sectors of the city. All essays in this direction failed, however, perhaps because it needed the perfidious organising skill of the SS to put such a plan into effect.

An additional factor was Kitty's silence. Aided by Ronge, her celebrated Berlin defence counsel, she did her best to scotch all the rumours and legends that grew up round the Salon Kitty after the war. In most cases, her efforts succeeded.

Vast crowds attended Kitty's funeral in 1954. Whatever the reason for their keen interest in the woman and her career, it demonstrated that she had been compelled at the unpredictable behest of chance, providence or destiny, to play the part of a small and ephemeral cog in the workings of contemporary history.

Postscript

The top secret project known as the Salon Kitty was researched and investigated by the author and his associates from 1949 onwards. Nearly a score of researchers have contributed to this work, and I should like at this point to express my appreciation of their help.

Thanks are also due to the directors of the Document Centre in West Berlin and Washington, to members of the Institute of Contemporary History, to historians and archivists, newspaper editors and publishers, all of whom were kind enough to further my work on this book.

It was a difficult task, for the surviving witnesses—and there are hundreds of them—tended to be contradictory and unreliable in their testimony. This is not, of course, to imply that surviving witnesses were unimportant to me. It was they who supplied the innumerable little mosaic-stones without which the foregoing picture could never have been built up.

Just as numerous legal hearings demonstrate, however, so I found renewed confirmation that the human memory fades rapidly in this hectic age of ours. Where the Salon Kitty was concerned, an additional problem arose. In its original form, the Salon Kitty was a high-class Berlin brothel patronised until 1939 by members of the capital's 'upper crust'.

As soon as Heydrich and Schellenberg decided to enlist the establishment on behalf of the SD foreign intelligence service, there was a blurring of boundaries. The Salon Kitty's clientèle became more varied. Regular patrons apart, senior representatives of the Party, administration, armed forces and diplomatic corps were piped into the brothel via prearranged channels.

The disciplinary organs of the Third Reich—police, Gestapo and Security Service (SD)—were suddenly granted new powers in this matter. Like the trained women agents, their knowledge of

215

the full picture was only fragmentary. What was more, they were bound by the Nazi régime's maximum security rating.

Anachronistic as it may seem, some officials who served under the Third Reich still feel so inhibited by this oath that they quoted it to the author and his collaborators as a reason for declining to supply information, some of it important.

The Salon Kitty's heyday embraced the years 1940 and 1941, a period marked by spectacular military successes and public festivities on a heroic scale. This may explain why prominent figures of the period should now wish to dissociate themselves from the Salon Kitty.

It should at the same time be mentioned that even those who held junior rank during the relevant period show considerable reluctance to give a precise account of their minor function in the Central Security Office's large intelligence network. Many of them regard the disclosure of such facts as a potential threat to their post-war careers. This applies in particular to the monitoring personnel employed at the listening-posts in Giesebrechtstrasse, Meineckestrasse and Prinz Albrechtstrasse. It applies even more to the women agents whose job it was, as SD decoys, to loosen the tongues of those who had secrets to divulge.

Although the identity of all the women agents assigned to the Salon Kitty has been disguised, their correct names and addresses are known to the author and publisher and have been deposited with a notary.

The author was obliged to give an undertaking that these particulars would not be disclosed before 1990, by which time all 'girl graduates' of the Salon Kitty should— actuarially speaking—be dead.

Verbal exchanges between agents and patrons of the Salon Kitty were recorded by the SD on wax disks and were intended from 1943 onwards to be recorded on tape. Thereafter, these recordings were assembled in the Central Security Office archives at Prinz Albrechtstrasse.

A large part of this unique historical library in sound was destroyed or reduced to a molten state by the air-raids which Berlin sustained in the final years of war. Miraculously, several thousand disks survived the war and were seized by the Russians in 1945. These disks are still strictly guarded and supervised by the East German State Security Service (SSD).

216

I and my associates were twice granted an opportunity to listen to several dozen records, once in 1959 and again in 1963.

My request to be sent one such disk or tape from the Salon Kitty for documentary purposes could not be granted for a number of reasons, the chief one being that some of those familiar with this unique record library under the Third Reich and during the post-war period are once more engaged in Intelligence work.

The same difficulty attended our inquiries in Britain among members of the Secret Service. It is incompatible with the centuries-old tradition of the Secret Service to divulge anything, however long after the event, which may have helped the British government to form a picture of its enemies. It was therefore necessary, here as elsewhere, to fall back on laboriously compiled items of information. Foremost among these were statements and stenographic records made during the interrogation of captured agents by the police, Gestapo and courts; conversations recalled after the war by fellow-prisoners, either in publications or in personal discourse with the author; and finally, historical sources readily made available by the scientific institutes mentioned above.

One further difficulty of special note arose from the fact that even the originators of the Salon Kitty proved an unreliable source. Of the relevant correspondence between Reinhard Heydrich, the all-powerful head of the Central Security Office, and Walter Schellenberg, his shrewd and ambitious subordinate, only three items are preserved in the records of the Nuremberg major war crimes trials.

Even Schellenberg, who was the chief initiator and beneficiary of the Salon Kitty apart from Heydrich and Schwarz, errs in his detailed description of the establishment. His memoirs state, for instance, that he not only coerced Kitty Schmidt into co-operating but sent all her girls on special courses of instruction and ensured that the Salon Kitty's male staff were specially trained by the SS or SD. Schellenberg—one of the only three men with a comprehensive knowledge of the Salon Kitty—is at fault here : there never were any male staff.

It is understandable, under these circumstances, that I and my collaborators were more than once tempted to shelve or abandon the whole project. Hard facts—or what appeared to be such—repeatedly dissolved in the face of new documentary evidence, a feature which hardly contributed to our enjoyment and may also explain why Heinz Höhne's comprehensive account of the SS (*The Order of the Death's Head*) omits to describe this perfidious episode in the history of the SD and its foreign intelligence service.

How did Walter Schellenberg and his department succeed for three years in restricting the circle of initiates to a minimum? Although two hundred people were employed in and around the Salon Kitty, none of them had a complete picture of the operation. No one in any way connected with this sophisticated surveillance system was acquainted with more than his, or her, limited function. Kitty Schmidt herself, whom the Central Security Office held constantly in thrall by threatening her life and liberty, never knew what was really happening on her premises. For Heydrich and Schellenberg, her past career made her simply an instrument, a means to an end.

Her relations with the prostitutes introduced by the SD were friendly in a superficial way. The fact remains, however, that Schellenberg's picked women agents—sixteen in all—were forbidden on pain of death to give her even the slightest indication of their real duties or the form their activities took.

As for the agents themselves, they believed to the bitter end that Schellenberg's foreign intelligence service depended solely on their written reports. They were quite unaware that every word they said was overheard, via skilfully concealed microphones, by a large monitoring centre.

In this system, which they controlled and administered with the conscientious efficiency of Prussian civil servants, Schellenberg and Schwarz possessed a means of surveillance which not only gave them access to confidential information and views but simultaneously enabled them to check on their own personnel and subject them to unremitting pressure. The monitoring teams consisted entirely of Waffen-SS signallers commanded by an SD man from the Central Security Office. From July 1940 onwards, they were replaced every six months and in most cases posted to combat units popularly referred to as 'suicide squads'. Despite this, my research indicates that over thirty former members of these monitoring teams survived the war.

Tightly organised as the SS and SD were, the Salon Kitty project became the tightest security organisation of all. This accounts for the abundance of myths and rumours that surrounded it after the war.

218

From the war's end until her death in 1954, Kitty Schmidt persistently denied that any form of monitoring apparatus had been installed in her establishment. Her surviving relatives, all of whom pursue careers of the utmost respectability, have done their best to thwart or misdirect research by serious writers and sensationalists alike. What has aided their endeavours is that, curiously enough, the Gestapo maintained yet another 'Salon Kitty' in Vienna run by a woman who styled herself Kitty Schmidt. This brothel was not, however, an official institution of the SS, SD or German police. The Gestapo used the Viennese 'Salon Kitty' as a meeting-place for picked agents, male and female, because it was patronised, like its Berlin namesake, by prominent figures drawn mainly from Viennese society and friendly Balkan countries.

Many illustrated magazines have published features on the Salon Kitty, thereby contributing still further to the chaos of misinformation. I and my collaborators were obliged to thread our way through this jungle of erroneous accounts and misinterpretations. Every lead was followed up—often a time-consuming process. Most of our inquiries led ultimately to rumours which had grown up in the locality of the Salon Kitty. They did so because some things were hard to conceal—e.g. the frequent arrival of large saloon cars despite war-time restrictions on private travel, or the often boisterous parties held at 11 Giesebrechtstrasse, or—naturally enough—the exceptional amount of building work carried out there and at No 12.

Not the least important of Schellenberg's motives in choosing Kitty Schmidt's establishment was that she happened to be a next-door neighbour of SS-Obergruppenführer Dr Ernst Kaltenbrunner, who became head of the Central Security Office after Heydrich's death. This made it possible to instal technical apparatus in the Salon Kitty without attracting undue attention.

As presented in this book, the Salon Kitty was a product of perverse minds which won surprise and admiration even from the British Secret Service. No government in the world was as well informed about the mood prevailing among its own senior representatives as the German government or the leaders of the 'State within a State', Himmler and Heydrich.

Only in a very few proven instances did indiscretions uttered at the Salon Kitty lead directly to legal proceedings. It has, however, been demonstrated beyond doubt that information derived from the Salon Kitty was added to the personal files of those involved and became a threat to their survival after 1943.

Kitty Schmidt, who gave the establishment its name and outward tone, often preened herself after the war on her good relations with Walter Schellenberg, who was a frequent visitor from summer 1940 onwards. On the other hand, she knew that she was utterly at the SD's mercy.

If an attempt has here been made to clarify the circumstances surrounding this controversial venture on the part of the Central Security Office, its aim is to shed further light on the perfection of criminal methods which underlay the conduct of government in the Third Reich.

REINHARD HEYDRICH

To illustrate the forces at work in and around the Salon Kitty, it is necessary to grasp how the rival intelligence services were organised during the years 1939-43.

Reinhard Heydrich, the initiator of the entire scheme, was born on 7 March 1904 at Halle, near Leipzig, and attended the high school there. He was a member of the German National Youth League from 1918 to 1919 and later of the German National Protection League and Free Corps. In 1922, at the age of eighteen, he joined the navy. After serving as a naval cadet at Kiel, he was promoted sub-lieutenant in 1926 and lieutenant in 1928. 1931 saw him dismissed the service for personal impropriety, and in the same year he joined the Nazi Party and SS, to which he was appointed that autumn. His career was meteoric. In 1932 he was promoted Standartenführer (colonel), in March 1933 Oberführer (senior colonel) and head of the political section of the Munich police department, and shortly afterwards 'Political Police Commander, Bavaria' at the Bavarian Ministry of the Interior. On 22 April 1934 he became head of the Gestapo office in Berlin and a Prussian councillor of state. By this time he already held the rank of Brigadeführer (brigadier). On 30 June 1934 he was promoted Gruppenführer (major-general) and on 29 September 1941 Obergruppenführer (lieutenant-general).

In order to assure the Party of permanent control over the police and security system of the Third Reich, Heydrich planned the establishment of the Reichssicherheitshauptamt (Reich Central

Security Office), a scheme which was largely devised by Walter Schellenberg. The RSHA came into being on 27 September 1939, the day Warsaw surrendered, and Heydrich instructed Schellenberg to start work on the Salon Kitty. As head of the RSHA, Heydrich soon tangled with Admiral Canaris of Military Intelligence and, thus, with the High Command. Historians surmise that no outright clash occurred between the RSHA and Canaris only because Heydrich suspected that Canaris possessed documentary evidence of his not entirely Aryan origins and earlier military career.

Heydrich reported for combat duty as a fighter pilot at the beginning of the war and flew numerous sorties over Norway, Holland and the British Isles. He was shot down on the Russian front in 1941 but rescued by German troops. When the situation in occupied Czech territory deteriorated, Hitler relieved von Neurath of his governor's duties and on 27 September 1941 appointed Heydrich acting Reich Protector of Bohemia and Moravia. On 27 May 1942 he was attacked in a Prague suburb by two British-trained Czech agents. He died on 4 June, despite every effort by Hitler and Himmler to save his life.

ERNST KALTENBRUNNER

Heydrich's successor at the RSHA was SS-Obergruppenführer Dr Ernst Kaltenbrunner. Kaltenbrunner came from a family of Austrian lawyers and joined the National Socialist movement at an early stage. In autumn 1932 he entered the SS, was sentenced to several months' imprisonment in 1935 for anti-government activities, and in January 1937, after his release, became head of the Austrian SS. He was closely involved in the downfall of the Schuschnigg government. When the Germans marched into Austria, the then Reich Governor, Arthur Seyss-Inquart, appointed him head of the entire Austrian security system. From 1938 onwards he was a member of the German Reichstag and resided in that capacity at 12 Giesebrechtstrasse in the Charlottenburg quarter of Berlin.

Kaltenbrunner not only headed the RSHA after Heydrich's death but became chief of the Security Police on 29 January 1943. It was he who ordered the arrest of Admiral Canaris on 20 July 1944. Canaris was later tried at Hitler's behest by a makeshift court martial and executed on 9 April 1945.

Kaltenbrunner himself was sentenced to death by the International Military Tribunal at Nuremberg and hanged on 30 September 1946.

WALTER SCHELLENBERG
Walter Schellenberg, ultimately head of the SD's intelligence service and SS-Brigadeführer, was a professional associate both of Heydrich and, later, Kaltenbrunner. He was born at Saarbrücken on 16 January 1910 and died at Turin on 31 March 1952.

A man of keen and nimble intellect, he was one of those young men who seized on Nazism as the key to a swift and successful career. He joined the SS as a lawyer on 1 April 1933 and first came into contact with the SD in 1934. In 1936, at the age of twenty-six, he passed his second State Examination and was posted to the Ministry of the Interior. In April 1937 he became an SS-Untersturmführer (2nd lieutenant) and, after a brief spell at Dortmund police headquarters, joined the SS-Hauptamt as head of the Intelligence Section. On 15 November 1939 he was appointed to command Group IVE at the RSHA as a reward for his active part in planning that institution, and from June 1941 he was head of Department VI (foreign intelligence service) of the RSHA.

On 14 April 1949 he was sentenced to six years' imprisonment at the Wilhelmstrasse hearing held before the Nuremberg Tribunal, but released on account of ill health.

Schellenberg not only evolved fantastic plans but could put them into effect, which made him a man to Heydrich's taste. In 1938 he worked as an agent in Dakar (Senegal), in 1939 he engineered the Venlo Incident, in 1940 he planned the abduction of the Duke and Duchess of Windsor from Portugal. His chief preoccupation was the development of the SS foreign counter-espionage service. This put him at loggerheads with Admiral Canaris, especially after he was promoted SS-Standartenführer (colonel) in 1941 and appointed head of Department VI of the RSHA. The latter department increasingly developed into a competitor of the military intelligence service. Schellenberg devoted particular attention to the departments activities in Norway and Sweden. In 1942 he directed operations against the resistance group known as the 'Red Orchestra'.

Throughout the war, Schellenberg managed to persuade Himmler that, whatever the state of hostilities, a continuous dialogue with the British was essential to the negotiation of a separate peace with Great Britain if the worst came to the worst. As early as 1942, after Heydrich's assassination, Schellenberg and his intelligence service were directly subordinated to Himmler, Reichsführer-SS and head of the German police. On the latter's instructions, he not only put out feelers towards Britain but planned a compromise peace with all the countries at war with Germany. He even negotiated fruitlessly with Soviet intermediaries in Stockholm.

Schellenberg's status did not prevent his large accumulation of intelligence material from giving him a dangerous hold over senior members of the Nazi hierarchy, and he automatically embarked on a collision course with Kaltenbrunner, the new head of the RSHA, whom he described as Himmler's evil genius. His once good relations with Ribbentrop and the Foreign Office also suffered rapid deterioration as the SS intelligence service steadily eclipsed that of the Foreign Office. Schellenberg played an important part in directing espionage activity in Turkey (Cicero).

In February 1944, the Vermehren affair brought about the final downfall of Canaris. Hitler thereupon absorbed Military Intelligence into the foreign intelligence service of the RSHA, thus making Schellenberg the *de facto* head of the German secret service.

In 1944 and 1945, Schellenberg again put out peace-feelers to the Western powers and even offered to eliminate Hitler on condition that they joined forces with Germany against the Soviet Union.

After the collapse, Schellenberg sought refuge in the Swedish village of Trosa, where he drafted the so-called Trosa Memorandum. He was handed over to the Allies in June 1945 and gave evidence at the war crimes trial which began the same year. He himself was sentenced, as we have already said, to six years' imprisonment for his membership of the SD and his part in Operation Zeppelin (liquidation of prisoners of war). Released on grounds of ill health, he at first settled in Switzerland and started work on his memoirs for the Scherz-Verlag. Later, after being expelled from Switzerland, he moved to Pallanza in Italy, where he completed his memoirs. He died at Turin, prior to their publication.

Peter Norden